The Voice of America
and the Domestic Propaganda Battles, 1945–1953

DAVID F. KRUGLER

University of Missouri Press
Columbia and London

Copyright © 2000 by
The Curators of the University of Missouri
University of Missouri Press, Columbia, Missouri 65201
Printed and bound in the United States of America
All rights reserved
5 4 3 2 1   04 03 02 01 00

Library of Congress Cataloging-in-Publicaton Data

Krugler, David F., 1969–
    The Voice of America and the domestic propaganda battles, 1945–1953 /
    David F. Krugler.
        p. cm.
    Includes bibliographical references and index.
    ISBN 0-8262-1302-2 (alk. paper)
    1. Voice of America (Organization)—History. 2. International broadcast
    ing—United States—History.

    HE8697.45.U6 K78 2000
    327.1'4'097309044—dc21   00–055195

☺™ This paper meets the requirements of the
American National Standard for Permanence of Paper
for Printed Library Materials, Z39.48, 1984.

Design and composition: Vickie Kersey DuBois
Printer and binder: Edwards Brothers, Inc.
Typefaces: ITC Kabel, Palatino

TO DEE AND JOHN KRUGLER

CONTENTS

Acknowledgments

I hope my gratitude exceeds my debts, which are many.

For financial support for research, I thank the Dirksen Congressional Center, the Caterpillar Foundation, the Hoover Presidential Library Association, the Harry S. Truman Library Institute, and the Graduate College and Department of History of the University of Illinois at Urbana-Champaign. For guidance and aid in sorting through a variety of manuscript collections, I thank the archivists and staff of the following institutions: the Nebraska State Historical Society in Lincoln; the Karl E. Mundt Library in Madison, South Dakota; the Department of Special Collections, University of Chicago; the National Archives in College Park, Maryland, and Washington, D.C.; the Hoover Presidential Library in West Branch, Iowa; and the Harry S. Truman Presidential Library in Independence, Missouri. Martin Manning of the United States Information Agency Historical Collection in Washington, D.C., was particularly helpful, and I owe him special thanks.

Portions of chapter 5 originally appeared as "Radio's Cold War Sleight of Hand: The Voice of America and Republican Dissent, 1950–51," *Historical Journal of Film, Radio and Television* 19, no. 1 (March 1999): 27–38. I am grateful to Carfax Publishing Ltd., P.O. Box 25, Abingdon, Oxfordshire OX14 3UE, United Kingdom, for granting permission to use this material. In April 1998 part of chapter 7 was read at the annual convention of the Organization of American Historians in Indianapolis, and I would like to thank Walter Hixson, Holly Cowan Shulman, and Nick Cull for their helpful comments and criticism.

Former State Department employees Robert Bauer, Wilson Dizard, Roger Lyons, Hans Tuch, and Barry Zorthian agreed to meet for interviews, as did Robert McCaughey, a former administrative assistant to Senator Karl E. Mundt. I want to thank each of them for so generously sharing their time with me. Essie and Jamey Wagner graciously opened their home to me during a 1998 research visit to Washington, D.C.; their hospitality was greatly appreciated.

This study began as a paper written in a seminar at the University of Illinois at Urbana-Champaign, and its transformation into a book was not possible without the erudite guidance of Professor William C. Widenor, the director of that seminar and my dissertation adviser. I also benefited from the insight and encouragement of dissertation committee members Mark H. Leff and Paul W. Schroeder. For companionship and conversation, I must thank J. Dwyer, Dawn Flood, Jon Huener, Don Litteau, Eric Pullin, and Frank Valadez. Professor Juliet E. K. Walker of the University of Illinois at Urbana-Champaign and Professor Paula M. Nelson, my colleague at the University of Wisconsin–Platteville, each provided invaluable advice on the intricacies of the publishing process. Completion of this manuscript took place at the University of Wisconsin–Platteville, and I am grateful to both Paula and Associate Professor Tom Waters, the chair of the Social Sciences Department, for helping provide a genial writing environment.

Amy M. Lewis: a steadfast witness to the research and writing of this book, she has provided support and encouragement at every step. She deserves special praise. Finally, my mother and father, Dee and John Krugler, have given love and support without which I could not have completed this project. I cannot thank them enough, and it is to them that I dedicate this book.

Abbreviations

ASNE	American Society of Newspaper Editors
ASPA	Assistant Secretary of State for Public Affairs
CEEC	Committee on European Economic Cooperation
CIAA	Office of the Coordinator of Inter-American Affairs
COI	Office of the Coordinator of Information
CPI	Committee on Public Information
DCR	Division of Cultural Relations
ECA	Economic Cooperation Administration
ERP	European Recovery Program (Marshall Plan)
FCC	Federal Communications Commission
GOP	Republican Party
HUAC	House Un-American Activities Committee
IAC	Intelligence Advisory Committee
IBF	International Broadcasting Foundation
IIA	International Information Administration
IIIS	Interim International Information Service
JCS	Joint Chiefs of Staff
MSA	Mutual Security Agency
NCFE	National Committee for a Free Europe
NSC	National Security Council
OIC	Office of International Information and Cultural Affairs
OIE	Office of International Information and Educational Exchange
OII	Office of International Information
OPC	Office of Policy Coordination
OPA	Office of Public Affairs
OSP	Office of Special Projects
OSS	Office of Strategic Services
OWI	Office of War Information

PSB   Psychological Strategy Board
RCA   Radio Corporation of America
RFE   Radio Free Europe
RL   Radio Liberation/Liberty
RNC   Republican National Committee
SANACC   State-Army-Navy-Air Force Coordinating Committee
USIA   United States Information Agency
USIS   United States Information Service
WPA   Works Progress Administration
WWBF   World-Wide Broadcasting Foundation

The Voice of America
and the Domestic Propaganda Battles, 1945–1953

Introduction

The Voice of America (VOA) is the U.S. government's international radio agency, broadcasting on shortwave frequencies throughout the world, excluding the United States.[1] The VOA debuted in February 1942, shortly after the United States entered World War II. As part of the Office of War Information, the VOA transmitted abroad programming that explained American war aims and postwar plans. As the war was ending, VOA administrators and supporters in Congress advocated keeping the radio agency on the air, arguing that the world needed to know about U.S. policies during times of peace as well as war. Democratic President Harry S. Truman agreed; in late August 1945 he signed an executive order that liquidated the Office of War Information but moved the VOA to the State Department. As tensions between the United States and the Soviet Union cohered into the Cold War, the VOA quickly became the nation's ideological arm of anticommunism, seeking to win allies at the same time that it tried to discredit the Soviet Union and other communist nations.[2] For the duration of the Cold War, these remained the VOA's essential goals.

Given the bipartisan political consensus that underwrote the United States' anticommunism, and the fear of communism that pervaded the

1. Via the World Wide Web, Americans can now tune into the VOA at http://www.voa.gov.
2. Because the VOA was the most prominent of five media or cultural programs operated by the State Department between 1945 and 1953, the focus of the book is limited to the VOA. The other four programs were press and publications, motion pictures, exchange of persons, and overseas libraries. With its ability to reach audiences behind the so-called "Iron Curtain," the VOA served as the vanguard of American propaganda abroad. The radio agency also had the largest and fastest-growing budget. For example, for the 1948 fiscal year the VOA's budget represented

1

general populace, it seems reasonable to expect that the VOA would have carried out its operations with little domestic disruption or criticism. But this was not the case. During the years 1945 to 1953, the VOA led a beleaguered existence. In January 1946 two major wire services, the Associated Press and United Press, stopped providing the VOA with news material because they worried that a relationship with a government media service impugned their objectivity. In Congress hostility to the VOA mounted during 1945 and 1946, especially among Republicans and conservative Southern Democrats, who believed that the federal government had no business working in broadcasting. In early 1947 the Republican-controlled Congress slashed the VOA's budget and rejected legislation seeking to provide the agency with permanent standing. That September a former FBI agent employed by a congressional subcommittee began sifting through State Department and VOA files and identified 108 individuals whom he considered subversive—this list later served as Senator Joe McCarthy's (R–Wisc.) evidence that communists had infiltrated the State Department. In early 1950 a VOA broadcast sparked heated debate between congressional Republicans and the Truman administration over U.S. policy in the Far East. And in 1953 the VOA withered under the glare of an investigation led by McCarthy that purported to find employees engaged in sabotage and sexual misconduct.

Since the VOA was part of a broad-based, bipartisan offensive to stop the spread of communism abroad and to win economic and military allies for the United States, why then did it experience so many troubles? Providing an answer to this question is the basic purpose of this book. Between 1945 and 1953 the VOA was embroiled in what I have designated as domestic propaganda battles: first, the conservative-led drive to roll back the New Deal and discredit its precept of activist government; second, struggles between the legislative and executive branches over the proper prerogative

---

43 percent of the total amount requested to operate all of the media and cultural units. Furthermore, the VOA had more employees than any one of the other four units. By the fall of 1951 the VOA had nearly 2,000 employees, while the number of employees for the four other programs totaled only 1,346. House Subcommittee of the Committee on Appropriations, *Department of State Appropriation Bill for 1948, Hearings before the Subcommittee of the Committee on Appropriations*, 80th Cong., 1st sess., 1947, 494; Senate, Subcommittee of the Committee on Appropriations, *Departments of State, Justice, Commerce, and the Judiciary, Hearings before the Subcommittee of the Committee on Appropriations for 1953*, 82d Cong., 2d sess., 1952, 1010–11.

of each in foreign affairs; third, the use of foreign affairs and policies to serve partisan, even personal, aims; and fourth, intra-executive branch disagreement over the purposes of propaganda. It should be pointed out that the term "domestic propaganda battles" refers not to the use of the VOA to disseminate propaganda at home, but rather to the frequent use of the agency to symbolize or to serve political goals not directly related to its basic mission. This use took many forms: criticism of VOA broadcasts, manipulation of broadcast content, congressional committee investigations into the agency's operations, background checks on personnel, budget cuts (or the threat of cuts), and executive branch campaigns to improve or expand the VOA. Accordingly, a systematic analysis of VOA broadcasts and their effectiveness abroad is not undertaken here. Instead, this book concentrates on what members of Congress, executive branch officials, VOA employees, Presidents Truman and Eisenhower, and the domestic press, among others, said about the agency's broadcasts, and what motives lay behind these various parties' interest in and involvement with the VOA. This basic purpose thus creates a double meaning for propaganda as used in the following chapters. The VOA's broadcasts themselves were propaganda—efforts to convince listeners that the presentation offered was the truth, and that listeners' beliefs and actions should correspond to this truth.[3] At the same time, the attention directed toward the agency and its broadcasts was itself a form of propaganda, because it too sought to influence people's beliefs and actions.

Most of the VOA's troubles resulted from friction between liberal internationalists in the executive branch, particularly the State Department, and congressional conservatives who shared a "parochial" mind-set, that is, the evaluation of foreign policy issues according to the perceived consequences for a domestic political agenda.[4] This included: curtailment of government size and responsibilities, which meant strong opposition to

3. Definitions of propaganda abound. For a recent bibliography, see "Propaganda: The Concept," in Robert Cole, *Propaganda in Twentieth Century War and Politics: An Annotated Bibliography*, 13–87. The definition offered here is adapted from several sources, including Alfred McLung Lee and Elizabeth Briant Lee, *The Fine Art of Propaganda, Prepared for the Institute of Propaganda Analysis*, 15; Garth S. Jowett and Victoria O'Donnell, *Propaganda and Persuasion*, 16.

4. A path-breaking study of the partisan uses of foreign policy is Athan G. Theoharis, *The Yalta Myths: An Issue in U.S. Politics, 1945–1955*. Theoharis argues that in an attempt to restrict executive authority and dismantle the New Deal, congressional Republicans characterized the February 1945 Yalta Conference as a deliberate

the New Deal and its continuation; reduction of government expenditures; strengthened domestic antisubversive programs; efforts to prevent liberals from using government media to serve partisan aims; and legislative control of foreign policy. At first glance, this mind-set might appear to be isolationist; however, parochialism is a more precise and accurate concept to use, given these legislators' seemingly contradictory actions.[5] They voted for anticommunist foreign aid programs but cut the budgets needed to pay for them; they slowly accepted the VOA as the ideological arm of U.S. anticommunism yet constantly denounced its programs and personnel; they supported the U.S.-led United Nations defense of the Republic of Korea at the same time they blamed the Roosevelt and Truman administrations for the war in Korea. Accordingly, attention in this study is focused on the preponderance of influence on the decision-making process rather than politicians' choices to simply vote for or against long-term international commitments.

While the parochial mind-set exemplified itself in the actions and attitudes of hundreds of members of Congress between 1945 and 1953, attention in this study is focused primarily on the approximately forty legislators who took a sustained interest in the VOA. Most of them were Republicans. Examples include Karl Mundt, first a representative, then after 1948 a senator, from South Dakota. Mundt's fixation with communist activity in the United States led him to support international anticommunist policies at the same time that he harshly criticized the Truman administration for being soft on domestic communism. Mundt's ardent anticommunism would lead him to become an early and vocal supporter of the VOA, but only on terms acceptable to himself and his conservative colleagues. Representative John Taber (R–N.Y.) used his senior position on the House Appropriations Committee to slash the

---

sellout by Roosevelt to the Soviet Union that the Truman administration was trying to hide. Another valuable, and more recent, work is John E. Moser, *Twisting the Lion's Tail: American Anglophobia between the World Wars.* Moser in part analyzes the use of anglophobia by members of Congress as a way of winning election and gathering support or opposition to various domestic and foreign policies.

5. American isolationism is a difficult concept to define sharply, given the frequently conflicting aims of its proponents. See Selig Adler, *The Isolationist Impulse: Its Twentieth-Century Reaction,* 28–31; Thomas N. Guinsburg, *The Pursuit of Isolationism in the United States Senate from Versailles to Pearl Harbor,* 3–18; Manfred Jonas, *Isolationism in America, 1935–1941,* 32–69.

VOA's budgets as part of his larger initiative to dismantle the New Deal. Senator Kenneth Wherry (R–Nebr.) received national attention in early 1951 for his effort to prevent Truman from dispatching additional U.S. troops to Europe without Senate approval; this attempt showed Wherry's alarm that the Senate's control over foreign policy was rapidly eroding. Wherry's concern over legislative prerogative helped prompt his interest in the content of VOA broadcasts during the Korean War. Senator Joe McCarthy's search for supposed communists helped advance the Republicans' goal of regaining control of Congress and the White House, while his attacks on VOA personnel furthered continuing efforts to discredit liberals. The ranks of VOA critics were not limited to Republicans, though; a few conservative Democrats counted among them as well. Senator Pat McCarran's (D–Nev.) efforts to identify and remove suspected communists from government employment, including the VOA, kept apace with McCarthy's efforts, even outstripping them in some instances. In a similar fashion, Representative Eugene Cox's (D–Ga.) distrust of the Truman administration's domestic security measures led him to oppose keeping the VOA on the air after World War II. (A list of the legislators who recur throughout this study can be found in the Appendix.) When compared with the membership of Congress as a whole, the list of the legislators with sustained interest in the VOA is small, but the tangible and dramatic ways in which these members of Congress impacted the VOA's operations and broadcasts were much more important than their actual numbers. Mundt, for example, wrote legislation that determined hiring practices and broadcast review procedures for the VOA, while McCarthy single-handedly nearly ruined the VOA in 1953.

Moreover, these legislators found in the VOA a channel through which to advance or fulfill the various aims of a domestic political program that they shared with powerful blocs in Congress. In 1945 and 1946, for example, Republicans and Southern Democrats were eager to liquidate the VOA because it represented exactly the sort of program they wanted to excise from the federal bureaucracy: it duplicated and competed with private enterprise, it was costly, and from their perspective there was no apparent need to tell the world about the United States and its policies. Attacks on the VOA thus furthered the broader campaign being carried out by conservatives to undermine liberalism and prevent the New Deal's continuation under Truman. This campaign almost succeeded in silencing the VOA in 1947, when the House Appropriations Committee eliminated all operating funds for the agency from the State Department's 1948 budget. Only a last-ditch effort by Secretary of State George C. Marshall and Truman convinced the Senate to restore the funds.

Protection of legislative prerogative in foreign policy was another widespread concern, and the VOA involuntarily became a part of Republicans' struggle to prevent further erosion of Congress's powers. In 1947 the Republican-controlled Congress voted to provide military and economic aid to Greece and Turkey so that those two nations could combat communism within their borders. Yet at the same time they cast "yea" votes, Republicans complained that the president and the State Department had not adequately consulted the legislative branch. In the ensuing years, the belief grew among Republicans that the executive branch was circumventing Congress, especially with regard to U.S. policy in the Far East. During 1949 and 1950 congressional Republicans began requesting VOA scripts in order to evaluate coverage of the Chinese Nationalists (Kuomintang) and statements of U.S. purposes. Republicans did not believe that they could change policy simply by looking over VOA scripts, but they recognized that the scripts might reveal policy changes that they opposed. Such was the case in December 1949, when the agency announced that the United States would not defend the island of Taiwan (then called Formosa) from a Chinese Communist takeover. With this announcement, which preceded any other official word, the VOA landed in the middle of the growing conflict between congressional Republicans and the president and the State Department over control of Far East policy.

Related to the struggle over prerogative was the suspicion among Republicans that the VOA's broadcasts leaned left, that liberals within the State Department and the VOA used the radio agency to promote abroad only the policies and accomplishments of the Truman administration. Efforts to "right" broadcast content thus showed how the VOA was used to serve partisan political aims. By simply reporting an administration decision or action that conflicted with the aims of a rival political bloc, the VOA opened itself to charges of trying to "sell" that policy. Moreover, the agency became a conduit for attacking the contested policy. By charging the VOA with ignoring their views, conservatives were, in effect, charging the administration with slighting them and the constituency that they represented. The VOA's propagandistic potential was inverted; the push to revise or criticize VOA broadcast content and personnel helped construct a domestic political picture in which the Truman administration ignored the will of Congress and the American people.

As opponents, the congressional conservatives confronted internationally minded liberals within the executive branch who were responsible for the VOA. President Truman was the most prominent, of course, joined by his last two Secretaries of State, George C. Marshall (1947–1949) and Dean Acheson (1949–1953). Truman's 1945 executive order keeping the VOA on the air prompted the postwar domestic propaganda battles; the order also reflected the liberal proposition that efforts to educate the world about the United States would promote both democracy and a lasting peace. Marshall presided over the VOA's shift from the "full and fair" approach, which cast the agency as an unbiased, objective news service, to a more aggressive tactic that sought to rebut Soviet radio and print propaganda. Both Truman and Marshall regarded the VOA as an important corollary to the anticommunist foreign policies introduced in 1947. Though Acheson privately doubted the agency's usefulness and often took behind-the-scenes action to marginalize it within the State Department, his public statements and actions supported the VOA.

The task of administering the day-to-day operations of the VOA during most of Truman's time in office fell to three successive Assistant Secretaries of State for Public Affairs: William Benton, George V. Allen, and Edward Barrett. While Allen was a career Foreign Service officer, Benton and Barrett were not. Both came to government work after successful careers in advertising and publishing (Benton) and journalism (Barrett). Benton and Barrett were liberal Democrats, and they agreed with Truman that a government-sponsored information program could help spread democracy and peace. As the Cold War intensified, so too did their faith in using the VOA to promote abroad American aims and to discredit the Soviet Union and other communist nations, and they staffed the agency's offices and language desks with like-minded persons. Both Benton and Barrett were influential in transforming the VOA into a hard-hitting propaganda agency, a change that each justified on the grounds that the Soviet Union's international radio and news services were openly slandering, provoking, and lying about the United States. In an intensive effort to save the VOA from liquidation in 1947, Benton and his staff worked to convince the agency's critics in Congress that Soviet propaganda was directly harming the international reputation of the United States and thus its relations with other nations, especially in Europe. This initiative helped win passage in 1948 of the Smith-Mundt Act, legislation that provided permanent standing for the VOA. Two years later, Barrett oversaw the drafting and unveiling of the "Campaign of Truth," an ambitious program to add new languages to the agency's broadcasts and to upgrade transmission equipment in an effort to overcome Soviet jamming of the VOA. Congressional approval of the Campaign of Truth, which was hastened by the Korean War, was an important victory for the VOA and its administrators over those in Congress who still doubted the need for a propaganda program.

While the Smith-Mundt Act and the Campaign of Truth fixed the VOA as a permanent part of the nation's fight against global communism, it did not spell an end to the VOA's domestic troubles. Certainly, congressional conservatives wanted to win the Cold War too, but they wanted victory on their terms. The rapidly increasing budgets that Truman and Acheson requested for anticommunist programs, including the Campaign of Truth, spurred charges that the administration was fiscally irresponsible. While Truman and Acheson had no qualms over maintaining tight control over U.S. foreign policy, congressional conservatives wanted to guard legislative prerogative in this area; attacks on the VOA's presentation of U.S. policy helped draw attention to their concern that Congress was being marginalized. By prioritizing international communism as a greater threat than domestic communism, the Truman administration further earned conservatives' enmity. Although the president did institute a federal employee loyalty program in March 1947, efforts in this area, as stringent as they were, failed to satisfy conservatives. As a result, the VOA found itself the target of investigation and public attacks, as its critics in Congress tried to uncover "subversives" and "communists" in order to show that the administration could not be trusted to screen federal employees. Finally, the liberal internationalists became increasingly frustrated with congressional conservatives' willingness to use the VOA as a cover for other aims. For these internationalists, liberal domestic programs were separate from fighting communism abroad, and they resented attempts to use the VOA to further a partisan attack on these programs.

At the same time that the VOA found itself caught in the various struggles between liberal internationalists and parochially minded conservatives, it also contended with intra–executive branch disagreements over the uses and oversight of propaganda. Ironically, the greatest problems for the VOA lay within the State Department. In August 1945 Secretary of State James Byrnes had opposed moving the VOA into the State Department; his opposition was shared by subordinates and successors alike. From the secretariat level down to Foreign Service officers in the field, propaganda was considered by many to be ineffective, unnecessary, and an obstacle to traditional diplomacy. State Department officials who did believe that the VOA served an important purpose in international relations worked constantly to persuade their colleagues of the VOA's worth. For those who oversaw and operated the VOA, like Benton and Barrett, the struggle was especially arduous since they came to their work from advertising or journalism, fields regarded with disdain in the cloistered world of the Foreign Service. As a result, the VOA continually experienced difficulty in procuring timely and specific guidance on U.S. foreign policy, especially in crises or during unexpected events.

The VOA confronted hostility from other executive branch agencies as well, especially those that composed the national security structure. In early 1950 the CIA explained that Soviet jamming of the VOA was actually desirable because it demonstrated to Soviet citizens that their government was going to great lengths to block access to the VOA's programs. This advantage accrued whether or not any VOA broadcasts penetrated the jamming. In other words, the message itself did not matter, only the fact that Soviet authorities did not want it heard. The CIA's novel evaluation came at precisely the time that the VOA sought the agency's help in developing counter-jamming methods. During this same period Secretary of Defense Louis Johnson also brushed off the VOA's initiative, explaining that it was not the Defense Department's concern. Edward Barrett hoped that the National Security Council (NSC) would help by prioritizing counter-jamming, but the NSC merely indicated that the problem of blocked broadcasts needed further study. The formation of the Psychological Strategy Board (PSB) in April 1951 did not shore up the VOA's precarious position within the executive branch. Created by an executive order from Truman, the PSB's members included representatives from the CIA, NSC, Department of Defense, and State Department. Its purpose was to provide guidance for the propaganda activities of executive agencies. Board members never precisely defined their function, though. Some thought the PSB should simply watch over these activities, while others thought that the PSB should actually plan and coordinate them. For the VOA, the PSB was just another entity that muddled rather than clarified its purposes.

These troubles pale in comparison to the difficulties incurred by McCarthy's 1953 investigation of the VOA and the newly elected Eisenhower administration's response. Seeking to enhance his reputation as the nation's most vigilant anticommunist, McCarthy used his position as chair of both the Senate's Committee on Government Operations and its Permanent Subcommittee on Investigations to hold hearings on the

VOA. Relying on stories provided by disgruntled agency employees, McCarthy accused VOA officials of, among other wrongdoings, allowing saboteurs to disrupt construction of new transmitters and to tone down anticommunist programming. McCarthy's highly publicized investigation wrought immediate and profound damage: resignations of top officials, cancellation of transmitter projects, the firing of scores of employees, and plummeting morale among the men and women who remained in the VOA's studios. The investigation also gave the new Republican Secretary of State, John Foster Dulles, an opportunity to detach the VOA from the State Department, a move he had supported even before he took office. Dulles was motivated less out of concern at improving the agency's effectiveness than by relieving himself and the State Department of an expensive and troubled operational program. With Eisenhower's tacit approval, Dulles did nothing to shield the VOA from McCarthy's investigation during the first months of 1953, though he had opportunities to do so. That summer a reorganization plan submitted by the president to Congress set up the removal of the VOA from the State Department and its placement in a new executive branch outfit, the United States Information Agency. Once again, the VOA found itself caught up in issues not directly related to its basic mission.

The VOA's domestic troubles might seem to be of limited consequence in shaping the broad contours of the United States' Cold War propaganda; after all, despite the constant disruptions, the VOA remained on the air. Furthermore, as recent studies have demonstrated, this propaganda and the dissemination of American culture abroad brought tangible results in making the American style of democracy and capitalism desirable to foreign audiences while simultaneously minimizing the attraction of communism.[6] Certainly, the VOA contributed toward these results, but during the early years of the Cold War, it hobbled toward them. So pronounced was partisanship that at key points—the drafting and struggle to enact the Smith-Mundt bill in 1947–1948, planning for the Campaign of Truth in 1950, Eisenhower's and Dulles's reluctance to defend the VOA in 1953—narrow domestic political concerns practically

6. Walter L. Hixson, *Parting the Curtain: Propaganda, Culture, and the Cold War, 1945–1961*; Reinhold Wagnleitner, *Coca-Colonization and the Cold War: The Cultural Mission of the United States in Austria after the Second World War*; Richard Pells, *Not Like Us: How Europeans Have Loved, Hated, and Transformed American Culture since World War II*; Laura A. Belmonte, "Defending a Way of Life: American Propaganda and the Cold War, 1954–1959."

stood on equal footing with the basic aim of stopping the spread of communism abroad. Whatever the ultimate effects of American propaganda abroad, the VOA's travails between 1945 and 1953 remind us that even at the height of internationalism, many political participants could not or would not resist the temptation to deploy a supposedly nonpartisan agent in the Cold War against one another in the political battles being waged in Washington.

Chapter 1

Broadcasting without a License
The Origins of the Voice of America

At the time the VOA made its first broadcast in February 1942 the U.S. government was no neophyte to the dissemination of propaganda abroad. Most notably, the Foreign Section of the Committee on Public Information (CPI), created in April 1917 to build support for American entry into World War I, had carried out a variety of propaganda activities in fifteen nations: the production and showing of films, publication and distribution of pamphlets, organization of lecture tours, sponsorship of art exhibits, even the operation of a school to teach English in Mexico.[1] The CPI's various worldwide activities did not, however, produce a permanent spot for propaganda operations within the U.S. government. In June 1919 Congress ended the CPI's authority and dissolved the agency. During its two-year existence, the CPI had frequently run afoul of many members of Congress who strongly disliked its energetic and outspoken leader, progressive journalist and Wilson admirer George Creel. The CPI's problems had other sources, though, and they presaged the domestic political difficulties that the VOA would later experience in its relations with Congress concerning political bias, interference with private enterprise, fiscal responsibility, and legislative authority. Dormant during the interwar years, such suspicions about government propaganda revived during and after World War II as part of congressional conservatives' drive to silence the VOA and to cease the other operations of its parent agency, the Office of War Information (OWI).

Similar in purpose to the CPI, the OWI used radio, films, and publications to explain U.S. war aims to the world, as well as to nurture and sustain domestic support for American involvement. As the war drew to a

1. Gregg Wolper, "The Origins of Public Diplomacy: Woodrow Wilson, George Creel, and the Committee on Public Information," 347–50.

close, OWI officials lobbied to keep the VOA on the air, claiming that the U.S. government needed to keep the world informed about its policies during peace as well as war. Members of Congress, primarily Republicans, opposed continuation of an international information program, contending that it was unnecessary and that it encroached into the domain of private media. The VOA thus led a precarious existence right after World War II. By July 1947 the VOA seemed sure to cease broadcasting: three enabling bills had each stalled, and the Republican-controlled Eightieth Congress had struck, then restored funds for 1948. As a VOA employee from this period remarked years later, "[a]t times I never knew if I had a job to come back to—I'd read the papers each morning to find out if the Voice had been dropped."[2]

Debate over the VOA's continued existence resulted from two points of conflict between conservatives and liberals: the normative responsibilities of the federal government, and the political orientation of its employees. While few in Washington in 1945 expected a return to prewar isolationism, the parameters of American international obligations were far from clear, especially to congressional conservatives who wanted to turn their attention to domestic affairs. Believing that the war had delayed rather than ended efforts to roll back the New Deal, conservatives relished the opportunity to expunge the programs of an activist government. The results of the 1946 midterm elections, which placed both houses of Congress under Republican control, presented this chance. Democratic President Harry S. Truman intended to continue the New Deal, however, as he had made clear in a September 1945 speech that outlined a twenty-one-point legislative program proposing, among other things, national health insurance and expanded unemployment insurance. Truman also supported keeping the VOA on the air, asserting that international information activities were "an integral part of the conduct of our foreign affairs."[3] Keeping the world informed complemented the United States' incipient postwar internationalism, already evidenced by its involvement with the UN and the 1944 Bretton Woods Conference, in which the United States, along with forty-four other nations, set currency exchange rates,

2. Harold Berman, interview by Robert Pirsein, September 20, 1965, in Pirsein, "The Voice of America: An History of the International Broadcasting Activities of the United States Government, 1940–1962," 123.
3. Harry S. Truman, "Termination of O.W.I and Disposition of Certain Functions of O.I.A.A."

cut tariffs, and established the International Monetary Fund and World Bank. The VOA was also caught in a drive to purge suspected liberal partisans from the employment ranks of the federal government. During the summer of 1946 congressional Republicans and Southern Democrats expressed concern that the VOA and State Department harbored "Communists," "red sympathizers," "Marxists," and advocates of "left-wing philosophy." There were several purposes to such charges: first, to discredit the New Deal; second, to prevent the administration from staffing the bureaucracy with partisans who might carry out a liberal agenda while blocking the legislative goals of conservatives in Congress; and third, to build support for stronger internal security measures.

I. Precedents for Propaganda, 1890s–1941

Before describing the creation of the VOA in 1942, it is useful to sketch its precedents, beginning with Americans' conflicting attitudes concerning their image abroad. American forays into public diplomacy and propaganda, both governmental and private, were shaped distinctly by tensions between two deep-seated traditions, isolationism and exceptionalism. In the early years of the Republic, America's leaders sought to minimize the nation's foreign affairs, and a natural outgrowth of this conscious attempt at detachment was a general lack of concern for foreigners' opinions of Americans and their nation. The quality of American diplomats underscores this point. Until 1893, ministers rather than ambassadors represented the nation abroad; few of these men and their staffs gave their hosts reason to respect the United States. A Grant appointee tried to assassinate the British ambassador to Ecuador, while an American consul in Mexico supplemented his income through smuggling. In Europe, the American legations ignored major international developments and sent back trivial dispatches. Contradicting this breezy neglect of diplomatic propriety and competence, however, was an abiding aim to demonstrate the superiority and exceptional nature of American political, religious, and economic institutions, and to prove them worthy of emulation. The democratic ideology of the nation had easily incorporated the missionizing tradition upon which several colonies had been founded, and this missionary thread, along with confident assumptions about the racial superiority of white Americans, wove itself into the nation's foreign policy.[4]

4. Robert L. Beisner, *From the Old Diplomacy to the New, 1865–1900*, 2d ed., 28–31; Ernest Lee Tuveson, *Redeemer Nation: The Idea of America's Millennial Role*, 138–75.

The tensions between isolation and involvement, between benign exemplification and active guidance, impelled attempts to present a positive, self-assured picture of the nation to the world, as seen—literally—at the 1893 World's Columbian Exposition in Chicago. Ostensibly a fair commemorating Christopher Columbus's arrival in the New World in 1492, the Columbian Exposition afforded its organizers and host nation an open-ended opportunity to educate the world about American economic, political, and cultural progress. As U.S. Agriculture Department official Wilbur O. Atwater wrote, the exposition needed to "teach not only to our people, but to the world, what a young republic, with all the crudeness of youth, but heir to the experience of the ages, has done in its brief past, is doing in the present, and hopes to do in the greater future for its people and for mankind." Exhibits proudly displayed models of American industry and technology, while the "White City" showed off American architecture and urban planning. The name of the city pointed to another purpose of the fair: affirmation of whites' supposed racial superiority. The Midway, a mile-long swath between two parks on Chicago's south side, offered a curious combination of amusement rides, including a massive Ferris wheel, eateries, and specially constructed villages depicting a cross section of the world's people in their "natural" habitats. The physical layout of the villages revealed the prevailing social scientific belief that the white race represented the acme of humankind's evolutionary advancement, while the darker races languished behind in childlike barbarity. Behind the Teutonic and Celtic villages, for example, were Middle Eastern, West Asian, and East Asian villages, while Africans and American Indians were relegated to the back. This hierarchy not only validated white American visitors' belief in their own essential superiority but also reminded them that their nation had an important task to fulfill vis-à-vis the rest of the world: help the supposedly backward peoples of the world catch up. Exposition President Harlow N. Higinbotham indicated another use for programs like the Columbian fair when he suggested that future expositions would further world peace by lessening tensions resulting from American capitalism's expansion abroad.[5]

Ironically, the very location of the fair revealed limits to American efforts to tell the world about itself; the exposition exuberantly presented to the world the United States' self-assumed superiority, but the world was

5. Robert W. Rydell, *All the World's a Fair: Visions of Empire at American International Expositions, 1876–1916,* 7, 60–67, 70.

expected to come to Middle America to see it firsthand. Still, the fair marked an important early effort to project abroad a positive image of the United States. Harlow Higinbotham was not alone in connecting the growth of American capitalism overseas with demonstrations of national accomplishment and exceptionalism. As Emily Smith Rosenberg has explained, the 1890s witnessed the articulation and execution of "liberal developmentalism," an ideology that mixed democracy, capitalism, and diplomacy. American businessmen and government leaders began explicitly linking the worldwide free flow of information and culture to open markets and investment opportunities abroad. Furthermore, while private enterprise or initiative was expected to carry out economic and cultural exchange, American businessmen began to accept, and in some cases expect, their government's help in defending and encouraging economic activity abroad. Liberal developmentalism also blended smoothly with Americans' notions of their superiority and helped them perceive economic activity abroad as offering two different benefits: payoff for domestic investors, and improvement for the rest of world as it modeled itself after the United States. During the 1890s and 1900s modernization of the navy, revision of protectionist tariffs, and government support of American business activity in China and Latin America all showed liberal developmentalism fulfilling itself, in the process offering alternatives to laissez-faire and isolationist tenets.[6]

As the twentieth century began, however, private initiative remained the primary means of educating the world about the United States and projecting a positive image. Since capitalist enterprise abroad was supposed to establish, ipso facto, proof of America's greatness and emulative attraction, government sponsorship of cultural, educational, and informational programs seemed unnecessary. Protestant missions, especially in China, were already engaged in disseminating American culture as they proselytized, and several private and philanthropic foundations were setting up programs designed to educate foreigners about the United States, and, to a lesser extent, give Americans an opportunity to learn more about the rest of the world. In 1910 the Carnegie Endowment for International Peace commenced exchanges of books, students, and teachers, while also providing translation and educational services. Within a few years the Rockefeller Foundation and the John Simon Guggenheim Foundation set

6. Emily Smith Rosenberg, *Spreading the American Dream: American Economic and Cultural Expansion, 1890–1945*, 7–61.

up similar programs. These organizations were opposed to government involvement in such exchanges, preferring to facilitate cultural relations on their own terms.[7] For its part, the federal government, represented in these issues by the State Department, was content to allow private initiative to carry out cultural and educational missions abroad.

The election of Woodrow Wilson as president in 1912 opened the door to direct government involvement in international cultural, educational, and informational activities, collectively known as public diplomacy. (Though public diplomacy and propaganda are closely related, there is a distinction. The former refers to state-sponsored activities designed to reach and influence foreign publics, as opposed to a nation's diplomats. Such activities include display of art exhibits, administration of libraries and schools, production and showing of films, exchanges of students and scholars, publication of newspapers and pamphlets, and operation of media channels. Propaganda, as explained in the introduction, is material—whether printed, visual, or audio—aimed at convincing the audience that the presentation offered of a certain event is the truth, and that the audiences' beliefs and behavior should match this truth. In this sense, public diplomacy is frequently used to deliver propaganda, but the connection is not necessarily automatic.) Wilson was a former college professor and the author of numerous books and articles on political history and the structure of American government, and his thinking tapped currents in late-nineteenth- and early-twentieth-century Anglo-American historiography and social and political science. Specifically, Wilson centered his ideas around the Teutonic seed theory, which postulated that democratic institutions had their origins in the ancient Teutons before spreading to England and taking root there; British colonists then transplanted the democratic political tradition to North America, where it had flourished. After reading Frederick Jackson Turner's 1893 essay on the American frontier, Wilson adapted his views on the seed theory to include the special nature of the frontier as the crucible of American democracy and character. Underlying both the seed theory and Turner's thesis was the assumption that history was inherently progressive, that is, civilizations moved forward through time from an inchoate state to a well-developed, stable condition. Believing the United States to be the most politically advanced nation, Wilson reflexively accepted its role as exemplar and leader for the rest of the world. The effects of

7. Frank Ninkovich, *The Diplomacy of Ideas: U.S. Foreign Policy and Cultural Relations, 1938–1950,* 8–23.

religion and race on Wilson's thinking were also profound. Wilson was a devout Presbyterian, and he incorporated his faith's keen sense of mission and redemption into his understanding of America's international responsibilities. Wilson also assumed the natural superiority of whites over persons of color, both in the United States and around the world. Combined, these ideas shaped Wilson's liberal internationalist vision: the United States was a paragon of democratic advancement; the United States should spread democracy past its borders; democracies were inherently peaceful; an international collective security organization, properly organized and directed, could ensure world peace in the future.[8]

Wilson's liberal internationalism provided his justification for American entry into World War I, and led to the establishment in April 1917 of the federal government's first program of public diplomacy and propaganda. In order to make the world safe for democracy, Wilson recognized that the United States needed to explain its aims to the peoples of the world, not just to their leaders and diplomats, and had to unify the ethnically diverse American people in order to support an abrupt end to nearly three years of eroding but still popular neutrality. The president believed that given the magnitude and importance of this task, private initiative and media were insufficient. Accordingly, an executive order issued just two weeks after America's declaration of war on Germany authorized the creation of the Committee on Public Information. To head the agency, the president turned to George Creel, a journalist, progressive reformer, and an enthusiastic backer of Wilson. As a young man, Creel had heard Wilson speak in Kansas City before the professor had entered politics; after Wilson became president, Creel worked on his reelection campaign during 1916. Creel was strident, tireless, and smugly confident of his abilities; he also believed fervently in the efficacy of an informed citizenry and sustained an unwavering, almost messianic faith in the nobility of American war aims. With regard to the CPI's task, Creel wrote after the war that it was "to teach the motives, purposes, and ideals of America so that friend, foe, and neutral alike might come to see us as a people without selfishness and in love with justice."[9]

---

8. Lloyd E. Ambrosius, *Wilsonian Statecraft: Theory and Practice of Liberal Internationalism during World War I*, 1–33; John Milton Cooper, *The Vanity of Power: American Isolationism and the First World War, 1914–1917*, 147–52.

9. Wolper, "The Origins of Public Diplomacy," 41–42; Stephen Vaughn, *Holding Fast the Inner Lines: Democracy, Nationalism, and the Committee on Public Information*, 3–6, 17–20; George Creel, *How We Advertised America*, 5, 237.

The CPI had two sections, foreign and domestic. The foreign section's basic responsibility was to educate foreign publics about the United States' purposes in waging war against the Central Powers and to convince them that Allied victory was certain. To meet these goals the CPI, among other activities, projected movies in various European nations, showed slides in Italy, displayed art in Spain, and gave away copies of Wilson's plan for peace, the Fourteen Points, which later served as the template for the postwar peace proceedings. In administering its overseas operations the CPI clashed constantly with the State Department, which regarded the CPI as a usurper. In Switzerland, for example, CPI Commissioner Vera Whitehouse struggled to carry out such basic tasks as distributing reprinted articles from the United States; Legation officers Hugh Wilson and Allen Dulles, the twenty-five-year-old nephew of Secretary of State Robert Lansing, viewed even such benign activities as a disruption of traditional diplomacy. So fierce was the infighting that President Wilson himself was asked—twice—to delineate the CPI's domain. Because Wilson wanted to influence foreign public opinion, a task ill-suited for the State Department, he sided with the CPI.[10] (Ironically, as director of the CIA during the 1950s, Dulles would be responsible for all sorts of propaganda, including Radio Free Europe and Radio Liberty, two privately chartered international broadcasting agencies that received substantial and secret support from the CIA. See chapter 6.) However, Wilson's preference for the CPI did not substantially alter American diplomats' hostility toward public diplomacy and propaganda, which would persist for decades to come. Diplomats' animus resulted not only from a desire to guard their "turf" but also from their belief that they, and not the parvenu propagandists, best understood the nation in which they were stationed.

By the war's end the CPI had carried out operations in fifteen countries; however, the United States was not the first Allied nation to use public diplomacy and propaganda during World War I. Before American entry into the war, Britain engaged in similar activities in the United States in order to build both pro-British support and anti-German sentiment. By cutting Germany's telegraph cables to the United States early in the war, Britain was able to control the cross-Atlantic flow of information about the war. Britain also sponsored a direct mail campaign in which various Britons offered to send to prominent Americans documents proving that Germany was responsible for starting the war. Other publications empha-

10. Wolper, "Origins of Public Diplomacy," 30–42, 75–86, 350.

sized the threat that Germany posed to the United States.[11] There was an essential difference, though, between British and American propaganda. British activities extended from a basic war aim: to win, Britain needed the favor and support of the most powerful neutral nation in the world, hopefully even its entry into the war on the Allied side. In other words, British propaganda had practical, strategic purposes, while the CPI's output had far more idealistic goals. Britain was trying to win a world war; the United States was trying to change the world. In this sense, the CPI manifested American exceptionalism, the root of earlier attempts to project a positive national image abroad, and, as explained, a major source of Wilson's liberal internationalist vision.

The domestic branch of the CPI was even more ambitious than the foreign side. Initially, the domestic side of the CPI was viewed as a way of balancing freedom of the press with the government's need to withhold or censor war-sensitive information. At the same time, the CPI's domestic branch sought to diminish ethnic loyalties among hyphenate Americans, particularly German- and Irish-Americans, and to promote support for the war. Accordingly, the CPI maintained a variety of offices. The Division of Pictorial Publicity produced posters, postcards, cartoons, even massive murals publicly displayed in New York City and Washington. "Four Minute Men" delivered rapid, enthusiastic public speeches exhorting listeners to buy Liberty Bonds, while the Division of Films produced its own documentaries and worked with Hollywood to distribute patriotic films. In order to inculcate a common American identity, the Division of Civic and Educational Cooperation produced more than ninety publications that linked Americanism to democratic ideals. The pamphlets, which had a circulation of more than seventy-five million, also emphasized the special nature of the nation's culture and the need for all newcomers to the nation to assimilate: master English, jettison the culture of the old country, and learn about democracy. As revealed by these goals, the CPI was doing more than promoting the war; it was engaged in a vast educational effort aimed at constructing a common American identity. Considering the number of progressives working for the CPI, this reform impulse is understandable.[12]

11. Stewart Halsey Ross, *Propaganda for War: How the United States Was Conditioned to Fight the Great War of 1914–1918*, 27–35; Susan A. Brewer, *To Win the Peace: British Propaganda in the United States during World War II*, 13–14.

12. Vaughn, *Holding Fast the Inner Lines*, 23–60; James R. Mock and Cedric Larson, *Words That Won the War: The Story of the Committee on Public Information, 1917–1919*, 81–89, 101–8, 113–42.

Within the United States the CPI did not lack for critics, especially in Congress. As a progressive journalist, Creel had written articles critical of Senators Hiram Johnson (R–Calif.), James Reed (D–Mo.), and James Watson (R–Ind.), and each man was eager for vengeance. In search of embarrassing or damaging information, Watson even hired investigators to look into Creel's background and activities. Creel's willingness to publicly express his low opinion of the legislative branch earned him and the CPI additional retribution. While delivering a speech in New York in May 1918, Creel had coyly declined to speculate about the loyalty of members of Congress, instead saying that since he had not been "slumming," he was not in a position to judge "the hearts of Congress." The next month, Creel appeared before the House Appropriations Committee to justify the CPI's budget request for 1918–1919; not surprisingly, the hearings did not go well. For three days committee members grilled Creel about his public statements, the CPI's use of funds, the political affiliation of the CPI's staff, and alleged lies to the American public about German submarine attacks. After the hearings, the House cut the CPI's budget almost in half, to $1.25 million.[13]

However, Creel's flippancy does not alone explain Congress's efforts to disrupt or even dismantle the CPI. During the war Representative Harold Knutson (R–Minn.) charged the CPI with distributing pamphlets promoting the platform of the Democratic party, a charge made by another representative, who mistook the censorship sticker placed on an independently written and distributed pamphlet as evidence that the CPI was its sponsor. In order to dispel such suspicions, in May 1918 Creel wrote a letter to the chair of the House's Committee on Rules in which he defended the objectivity of the CPI's personnel and his own loyalty. Creel even attached a list describing the political affiliations of all division heads within the CPI. In the Senate Lawrence Sherman (R–Ill.) accused the CPI of granting a monopoly to the company distributing CPI films, while Senator Henry Cabot Lodge (R–Mass.) criticized Creel and the CPI for wasting money and operating without proper congressional authority. Referring to supposed inaccuracies in CPI material, Lodge's colleague James Wadsworth (R–N.Y.) said on the Senate floor: "I do not know what the Senate can do about such things. We have no direct jurisdiction over the Committee on Public Information."[14]

13. Creel, *How We Advertised America*, 57–58, 63–69; Mock and Larson, *Words That Won the War*, 61–62.

14. Creel, *How We Advertised America*, 54–59; *Congressional Record*, 65th Cong., 2d sess., March 29 and July 13, 1918, vol. 56, 4255, 9061.

In his postwar memoir Creel interpreted these criticisms as evidence of Congress's obdurate short-sightedness, its crippling partisanship, and its inexcusable failure to support efforts necessary to win the war. Now safely removed from the reach of Capitol Hill, Creel remarked acidly, "[o]f all the war-work executives in Washington, Republicans and Democrats alike, it is safe to say that there was not one who did not go to bed at night with the prayer that he might wake in the morning to find Congress only the horrible imagining of uneasy slumber."[15] Harsh words indeed, especially from a progressive. What Creel failed to realize, though, was that much of Congress's antipathy toward the CPI and other wartime agencies resulted from the sudden growth of the executive branch's powers and responsibilities. Created by executive order, the CPI operated without legislative standing; that is, Congress had not formally approved of either the CPI's existence or its responsibilities, as Lodge had pointed out. Although in Creel's opinion the 1918 appropriations hearings were merely a veil for an ad hominem attack, in fact the hearings served two purposes: to upbraid Creel and to reassert legislative jurisdiction. Creel was also half-right in his view that Knutson's and others' concerns about Democratic bias in CPI output was nothing more than reverse partisanship. It was, but their criticisms also raised legitimate questions about the CPI's activities. If the CPI intended to carry out international and domestic campaigns to teach and preach Americanism and democracy, which it did, and if Wilsonians, Democrats, progressives, and even some socialists dominated the ranks of the CPI, which was the case, then was it not legitimate to wonder whether hidden political agendas lurked beneath the starkly red, white, and blue colors of the CPI? The words of Congressman Frederick Huntington Gillett (R–Mass.), a member of the House Appropriations Committee, revealed this worry: "it [the CPI] is a very dangerous thing in a Republic; because, if used in a partisan spirit or for the partisan advantage of the administration, it has tremendous power, and in ordinary peace times I do not think any party or any administration would justify it or approve it."[16]

The CPI thus revealed the tension between the growing expectation that the United States needed to explain itself to the world and persistent isolationism, which combined abiding doubts about the nation's need for self-projection abroad with the domestic political concerns explained above. The CPI marked an important turning point in the development of public

15. Creel, *How We Advertised America*, 51.
16. *Congressional Record*, 65th Cong., 2d sess., June 17, 1918, vol. 56, 7915.

diplomacy and propaganda, but it also marked a turning back. In June 1919 Congress abruptly terminated all appropriations for the CPI, and it was disbanded. The State Department did not assume responsibility for any of the CPI's overseas activities, and the task of telling the world about the United States returned to the private sector. Nevertheless, the 1920s brought important developments in public diplomacy, particularly in Europe and Latin America, and during the 1930s the U.S. government reentered the field of public diplomacy, with the resulting agencies providing, in large part, the base for the World War II–era propaganda operations.

The end of World War I helped increase the number of private U.S. foundations and organizations carrying out international cultural relations. The American Council of Learned Societies (ACLS) was formed in late 1919 with the aim of using the worldwide exchange of knowledge and facts to promote peace. Beginning in the early 1920s the American Library Association (ALA) administered book and scholar exchanges as well as library training. Both the ACLS and the ALA became part of a privately maintained network carrying out international cultural relations during the 1920s. Through other, less formal channels, private American citizens also served as carriers of culture, particularly to Europe. Travel overseas, a luxury previously limited to America's wealthy and privileged, now became an option for more and more Americans, due to the general economic prosperity of the decade. (American tourists would spend between $500 million and $1 billion overseas during the 1920s.) Whether they realized it or not, these tourists shaped Europeans' impressions of the United States, usually in negative ways: "From the European perspective, American tourists were loud, arrogant, materialistic, and provincial."[17]

The continuing fulfillment of liberal developmentalism also served to project America's image abroad. The 1920s marked a sustained expansion of American capitalism abroad; in Europe alone U.S. corporations such as Ford, Du Pont, General Electric, and General Motors, among many others, constructed factories and formed subsidiaries. Latin America, the Near East, and Asia also hosted new or growing U.S. business activity. All told, some twelve billion American dollars went overseas between 1919 and 1929 (this figure includes loans). To set up and administer their operations, U.S. corporations relocated experienced

17. Ninkovich, *Diplomacy of Ideas,* 16–23; Warren I. Cohen, *Empire without Tears: America's Foreign Relations, 1921–1933,* 42; Richard Pells, *Not Like Us: How Europeans Have Loved, Hated, and Transformed American Culture since World War II,* 11.

managers and executives; these business professionals and their families became important definers of the nation's international image. Not surprisingly, Europeans perceived of the United States as a society fixated on technology, efficiency, and wealth. Hollywood movies, many of which relied on stories about rich and fashionable American characters, filled out this image of the United States as materialistic—during the 1920s, 60 percent or more of the films shown in major European countries were U.S.-produced.[18]

To nurture awareness of America's involvement with the rest of the world, elite government and business leaders founded the Council on Foreign Relations in 1921. The Foreign Policy Association and the Williamstown Institute of Politics were also formed during the 1920s. Each of these organizations used advertising and publicity to promote to the American public the importance of U.S. trade with Europe. A related goal was to promote cultural and business ties between Europe and the United States. At the same time, increasing American domination of the international communications industry provided control of the channels needed to reach foreign publics. Prior to World War I British companies enjoyed a near monopoly on global telegraph lines, but during the 1920s various U.S. companies launched campaigns to secure a share of cable construction contracts in Latin America and the Far East. In the new field of broadcasting, the Radio Corporation of America (RCA) aggressively established control of major European, Latin American, and Far Eastern radio markets. RCA was formed in 1919 by four powerful U.S. companies that already had substantial international business interests: General Electric, AT&T, Western Electric, and United Fruit. Yet the impetus for RCA did not come solely from these corporations; the Wilson administration had actually pitched to General Electric the idea of an American-controlled radio monopoly that would sell GE products and provide the U.S. government with a reliable outlet to reach the rest of the world.[19]

As demonstrated by these examples—private foundations, tourists, movies, and multinational corporations—American projections abroad of the nation, its people, and its purposes sprang from mixed sources during the 1920s. Nevertheless, a roughly similar picture of the United

18. Pells, *Not Like Us;* 10–16; Cohen, *Empire without Tears,* 18–45; Frank Costigliola, *Awkward Dominion: American Political, Economic, and Cultural Relations with Europe, 1919–1933,* 167–69.
19. Rosenberg, *Spreading the American Dream,* 87–97.

States and its citizens emerged from these efforts: as a democratic and capitalist nation, the United States wanted open markets and unrestricted access to communications channels; while private endeavor was responsible for fulfilling the nation's economic interests, government support was growing; Americans tended to measure success in material terms; and American culture manifested itself in materialistic ways such as radios, cars, and other consumer goods. Furthermore, as evidenced by the Wilson administration's encouragement of U.S. domination of international radio broadcasting, the U.S. government still recognized the importance of maintaining lines of communications with foreign publics. The three Republican presidents who followed Wilson—Harding, Coolidge, and Hoover—had no intention, however, of reviving the CPI or providing government sponsorship of public diplomacy.

Franklin Roosevelt, the first Democratic president since Wilson, was much more receptive to government information programs than his Republican predecessors. Indeed, Roosevelt was an admirer of both Wilson and George Creel, and like them he believed that the federal government needed to directly inform and educate the public rather than rely solely on the press to fulfill these two tasks. During his first seven years in office, the president directed at the American public several government information programs that sought to explain and justify the New Deal, his multifaceted, elastic program of recovery from the Great Depression. The Civilian Conservation Corps, the Works Progress Administration, and the Social Security Administration, along with many other New Deal agencies, undertook their own public relations initiatives; much of the output described the local effects and benefits of these nationwide programs. Stephen Early, Roosevelt's first press secretary, even provided small-town newspapers with print-ready articles written by government officials. The Roosevelt administration also made extensive use of radio, a medium that appealed to the president because it provided a direct channel through which to reach the public, without having to filter the message through reporters and editors. Roosevelt's occasional Fireside Chats were, of course, the most prominent examples of the president's use of radio, but other administration officials were also broadcast regularly, and in 1938 and 1939 the Office of Education within the Department of the Interior sponsored a radio series entitled "Americans All, Immigrants, All," which sought to emphasize the shared experiences and accomplishments of the ethnically and racially diverse nation. Roosevelt also was not reluctant to use federal oversight of the airwaves to cause trouble for his conservative critics. Through his secretaries, the president sometimes asked the chair of the Federal Communications Commission (FCC) to reject petitions from applicants whom Roosevelt considered to be political opponents.[20]

After war broke out in Europe, the Roosevelt administration shifted the focus of its domestic media efforts toward building support for defense preparation; this, in turn, led to full-fledged propaganda programs after the United States was in the war. The president's main goal prior to American entry was to diminish and discredit isolationism and to convince the American public that the nation needed to prepare to defend itself in case of war. As was the case with information about the New Deal, Roosevelt was not afraid to slant output in order to present his policy and actions in the most favorable light possible. During 1941 the Division of Information in the Office of Emergency Management had a central press room that gave to the domestic press news releases, charts, pictures, and other materials culled from sixteen government agencies involved in defense preparation. The Office of Emergency Management produced daily between ten to twenty stories, and it distributed a glossy weekly magazine entitled *Defense*. After the 1940 election Roosevelt asked Secretary of the Interior Harold Ickes to help plan an agency that would not only provide information but also consciously seek to build loyalty and offset anti-American propaganda. The president even proposed asking George Creel to return to government service, a proposal that Ickes delicately (and successfully) resisted. In putting together his proposal, Ickes relied heavily on a report issued by a private organization known as the Committee for National Morale, which supported intervention. This committee argued that the job of swaying public opinion away from isolationism was too important to leave to an independent press or to news releases; instead, experts in polls and public opinion research needed to work from a centralized base to reshape prevailing attitudes. The agency that Roosevelt approved in May 1941, however, the Office of Civilian Defense, was more limited in scope and activity than Ickes had envisioned, and lacked the means to gather raw information about public opinion and to manipulate it. Its purpose was to coordinate state and local defense measures in case of attack or emergency, with heightened civilian morale

---

20. Richard W. Steele, *Propaganda in an Open Society: The Roosevelt Administration and the Media, 1933–1941*, 5–23; Barbara Dianne Savage, *Broadcasting Freedom: Radio, War, and the Politics of Race, 1938–1948*, 21–62.

being a hoped-for side effect. The Office of Facts and Figures, which was spun off from the Office of Civilian Defense in October 1941 and put under the direction of Roosevelt speech writer Archibald MacLeish, also had a limited purpose: to monitor public attitudes and to help established agencies formulate their own press and information releases. Neither agency was very effective, and considerable confusion existed over the duties and goals of each. By the fall of 1941 the Roosevelt administration had made clear its intention to use propaganda, but the precise aims and activities of this initiative were not yet defined.[21]

While Roosevelt and loyal subordinates such as Ickes and MacLeish were putting together the Office of Civilian Defense and the Office of Facts and Figures, the State Department was engaged in developing its first programs of public diplomacy. At the Inter-American Conference for the Maintenance of Peace, held in Buenos Aires in late 1936, the State Department had promoted the importance of cultural relations within the Western Hemisphere. With the creation of the Division of Cultural Relations (DCR) in May 1938 the State Department demonstrated a new willingness to support public diplomacy by helping private foundations and universities administer inter-American student and teacher exchanges, by overseeing distribution of American books to foreign libraries, and by providing advice to private broadcasters about the content of their programming. Supplementing the DCR was the Interdepartmental Committee on Scientific and Cultural Cooperation, also formed in 1938. The Interdepartmental Committee awarded grants to scientists, professors, and students in the Western Hemisphere, and it provided fellowships for specialized training in U.S. government agencies. Latin American governments selected employees from their own ranks to receive this training; the participants then returned to their posts to use their new knowledge. The Interdepartmental Committee also "loaned" U.S. government employees who were technical or scientific experts to Latin American governments; by 1945, sixty-three such specialists had been assigned to temporary positions in Latin America. Although the staffs of the DCR and Interdepartmental Committee did not perceive of their work as propaganda, they did consider their efforts to be a response to "the increasing threat posed by the cultural, information, and propaganda activities of European powers in Latin America during the late nineteen thirties."[22]

21. Steele, *Propaganda in an Open Society*, 67–95.
22. Ninkovich, *Diplomacy of Ideas*, 24–28; Charles A. H. Thomson, *Overseas Information Service of the United States Government*, 160–71.

With the outbreak of war, the need to offset Axis influence in the Western Hemisphere took on added importance. On August 16, 1940, the Office of the Coordinator of Inter-American Affairs (CIAA, later renamed the Office of Inter-American Affairs, or OIAA) was created and placed under the direction of liberal Republican Nelson Rockefeller. An independent executive branch agency, the CIAA had ample operating funds and a broad statement of purpose: its responsibilities included not only the organization of governmental and private cultural activities into a structured system but also the operation of its own programs, including radio, press liaison, film distribution, even teacher training. In many ways, the CIAA resembled the CPI, which had also set up or worked with schools in other nations, had formed a partnership with Hollywood studios to produce films, and had provided material to private press representatives. And like the CPI, the CIAA found that the State Department regarded its efforts with suspicion. Since the Division of Cultural Relations also coordinated government and private programs in Latin America, conflict between the two agencies resulted, and the State Department's jurisdiction over foreign policy added to the tension. In early 1941 Roosevelt entered the fray by supporting the State Department. A joint committee was formed in order to oversee work with private organizations, but it confused rather than defined the respective tasks of the Division of Cultural Relations and the CIAA.[23]

By the fall of 1941 a surprising and fairly quick development was complete; propaganda and public diplomacy agencies had proliferated throughout the layers of the federal government. While World War II provided much of the justification for these agencies, many of them predated the war, revealing two other major sources for government propaganda and public diplomacy in the 1930s: the Roosevelt administration's previous use of media to promote the New Deal and to discredit isolationism, and government coordination of cultural and scientific efforts in Latin America. Combined with the cultural effects of U.S. international business activity and the acquisition of control over international communication channels that had begun in the 1920s, the United States had never been better equipped to reach and mold foreign public opinion. The nation's entry into World War II in December 1941 then provided the final nudge needed to seek centralization of propaganda and public diplomacy efforts.

23. Ninkovich, *Diplomacy of Ideas,* 35–49; Thomson, *Overseas Information Service,* 117–51.

Given the mishmash of agencies that had developed, this would be no easy task. Furthermore, opposition to government media activities had not faded; indeed, conservative opposition revived as New Deal critics argued that the Roosevelt administration used these agencies to promote its political agenda. The struggle to justify and establish permanent information and cultural programs was far from over, as the directors of the Office of War Information discovered during and after the war.[24]

II. The Office of War Information

By the second half of 1941, two distinct but closely related strains of government-sponsored information or cultural programs existed: the first, manifested by the Office of Civilian Defense and the Office of Facts and Figures, targeted the American public; the second, represented by the Coordinator of Inter-American Affairs and the State Department's Division of Cultural Relations, focused on Latin American audiences. With the creation of the Office of the Coordinator of Information (COI) in July 1941, Roosevelt was one step away from blending the domestic and international propaganda strains together. The COI, under the leadership of the colorful William ("Wild Bill") Donovan, was directed to gather and examine material relating to issues of national security, and to present its findings to the president upon his request. In this regard, the COI was similar to several existing agencies. However, the COI was also instructed to spread propaganda abroad (excluding the Western Hemisphere) based on its intelligence efforts, which relied on espionage. In order to deliver its propaganda, the COI used its Foreign Information Service (FIS), headed by playwright and interventionist Robert Sherwood. A liberal, Sherwood wanted to disseminate truthful information, using various media to carefully explain the United States' dedication to democratic principles and to nurture morale among the enemies of the Nazis.[25] Donovan, however, perceived of propaganda as literally a weapon of war, and he began using the COI to carry out psychological warfare. These cross-purposes would contribute to the COI's demise just one year after its creation, but not before a crucial operation was added to the government's propaganda efforts. In February 1942 the FIS began mak-

24. The United States was not the only Allied power using overseas propaganda. Britain too carried out extensive propaganda operations, much of it aimed at drawing the United States into the war. See Nicholas Cull, *Selling War: The British Propaganda Campaign against American "Neutrality" in World War II*; Brewer, *To Win the Peace.*

25. Peter Buitenhuis, "Prelude to War: The Interventionist Propaganda of Archibald MacLeish, Robert E. Sherwood, and John Steinbeck," 1–30.

ing shortwave broadcasts abroad. This was the Voice of America, and during its first month on the air it broadcast programs in French, German, and Italian. Donovan granted latitude in hiring and broadcast subjects to Sherwood, who staffed the FIS and the VOA's language desks with liberals such as Joseph Barnes, James Warburg, and John Houseman, each of whom welcomed American entry into the war as a necessary step to crush forever the global forces of fascism, and who wanted to use the VOA to carry this message. At first the VOA transmitted its fifteen-minute programs over BBC relays while it worked to secure its own shortwave channels. Leases of privately owned shortwave transmitters were signed throughout 1942; by the end of the year fourteen U.S. transmitters were available to the VOA. By July 1944 the VOA was broadcasting twenty-four hours daily in more than forty languages.[26]

Since the COI was but one of several government agencies handling domestic and international media activities, confusion and conflict over specific responsibilities was rife during the hectic first months of America's entry into the war. Roosevelt sought to ease these tensions with the June 1942 creation of the Office of War Information, which was responsible for reaching both domestic and international audiences. The president's executive order authorized the OWI's director to use radio and other media to promote "understanding, at home and abroad, of the status and progress of the war effort and of the war policies, activities, and aims of the Government."[27] The FIS was separated from the COI and placed in this new agency, taking the VOA along with it, while the COI was folded into a new outfit, the Office of Strategic Services (OSS). Roosevelt explained that since the FIS carried out "essentially information and not espionage or subversive activity among individuals and groups in enemy nations," it did not belong in an agency dedicated to this sort of covert work. Donovan moved with the COI to the OSS, where for the duration of the war he carried out the espionage and psychological warfare that he preferred. For Sherwood and his staff the move to the OWI seemed logical, and 816 FIS employees joined that agency.[28]

26. Allan M. Winkler, *The Politics of Propaganda: The Office of War Information, 1942–1945*, 26–29; Holly Cowan Shulman, *The Voice of America: Propaganda and Democracy, 1941–1945*, 13–33; Clayton D. Laurie, *The Propaganda Warriors: America's Crusade against Nazi Germany*, 67–87; Pirsein, "Voice of America," 91–92.

27. Franklin D. Roosevelt, Executive Order 9182, June 13, 1942, in *The Public Papers and Addresses of Franklin D. Roosevelt*, vol. 11, *Humanity on the Defensive: 1942*, 275.

28. Laurie, *The Propaganda Warriors*, 110–11.

Although the creation of the OWI and the OSS provided a division between the different types of U.S. wartime propaganda, it did not mean that consensus now existed on the purposes of that propaganda.

OWI administrators and policy makers discovered quickly that explanation of U.S. war policies and aims invited controversy. Sherwood, who was joined in the OWI by journalist Elmer Davis and former Office of Facts and Figures director Archibald MacLeish, adopted part of the Atlantic Charter, which Roosevelt and British Prime Minister Winston Churchill had drafted at their August 1941 meeting off the coast of Newfoundland, as the basic statement of American war goals: the United States fought to destroy the forces of fascism in Europe and Asia and to promote self-determination for all peoples. This was a vague, broad definition of mission, and it conflicted with the priorities of other U.S. government agencies and officials. General Dwight D. Eisenhower, the War and State Departments, and Roosevelt himself sought first and foremost an expedient end to the war, even if that meant striking deals with fascists. In July 1943 the VOA criticized harshly Allied dealings with newly appointed Marshal Pietro Badoglio, the prime minister of Italy, referring to the fascist party leader as "a moronic little king." The *New York Times* and other domestic media denounced the broadcast for interfering with the war effort, and Roosevelt said publicly that the commentary should not have aired. For the war's duration, the OWI's administrators reconciled their liberal reading of U.S. war aims with the prevailing goal of swift military victory.[29]

The OWI's coverage of domestic affairs also caused trouble, especially with congressional conservatives who suspected that the agency promoted another brand of liberalism, the New Deal. During appropriations hearings in 1943 the OWI pamphlet *Battle Stations for All* drew criticism for describing favorably the president's rationing plan and tax increase before Congress had approved the measures. Senator Henry Cabot Lodge, Jr. (R–Mass.) questioned OWI Director Elmer Davis about another pamphlet,

29. Winkler, *The Politics of Propaganda*, emphasizes the reluctance, even refusal of the OWI liberals to set aside their guiding principles after early 1944, which led to their dismissal or departure from the OWI, thus leaving the agency in the hands of those willing to work with the State and War Departments. Cowan Shulman, *The Voice of America*, demonstrates that the OWI liberals more willingly accepted the limits placed on the OWI's message as it became apparent that victory for the Allies was nearing. For a summary of each author's argument, see Winkler, 1–7, and Cowan Shulman, 3–12, 205, note 17.

Negroes and the War, which indicated that blacks thought social security was a good idea. Did Davis agree with this statement? Lodge asked. Davis said yes. (To Southern members of Congress, the pamphlet seemed to favor integration, a suspicion that resulted in drastic reductions for the OWI's 1944 budget.) Several Republicans complained that an article in the OWI magazine *Victory,* "Roosevelt of America—President, Champion of Liberty, United States Leader in the War to Win Lasting and Worldwide Peace," was shameless publicity for the president's fourth term. Davis observed that the article was apt to win few votes for Roosevelt since it was distributed overseas, but the article's critics were not mollified.[30] Conservatives also attacked the OWI for disrupting the free press. In February 1945 Representative John Taber (R–N.Y.) stated that the OWI "is attempting to destroy the freedom of the press." The NBC and CBS broadcasting corporations were "under the absolute domination and control of the New Deal Administration," Taber added. In May 1945 an OWI ban on American newspapers and magazines in Germany brought widespread denunciation. After noting that the ban also applied to foreign businesses, Representative Paul W. Shafer (R–Mich.) accused the OWI of using the prohibition of print media as a "clever New Deal method" to mask "a move that will cost the American people hundreds of millions of dollars."[31] For Taber and Shafer, the OWI represented a far graver threat—the proliferation of unnecessary government programs.

As the war drew to a close, the OWI's raison d'etre appeared to end, but in hearings before the Appropriations subcommittees Elmer Davis lobbied to set up a postwar international information program, emphasizing that the need to keep the world accurately informed about the United States and its desire for peace everywhere was not limited to wartime. Indicating that active American involvement in postwar global affairs seemed inevitable, Davis said in April 1944, "we want to win friends and influence people." Seeking to deflect the charge that government-sponsored media ran counter to the principles of a free press, he also stressed that a government information program would not interfere with private media. At hearings before the House subcommittee in May 1945, just days after Germany's surrender, Davis stated, "[i]t is our job to give foreign peoples the truth about

30. Winkler, *Politics of Propaganda,* 66–67; Senate Subcommittee of the Committee on Appropriations, *Hearings on the National War Agencies Appropriations Bill for 1944,* 78th Cong., 1st sess., June 26, 1943, 173–92.

31. *Congressional Record,* 79th Cong., 1st sess., February 27 and May 11, 1945, vol. 91, 1538, A2219.

American policies, American life, and American character." Such a program, he continued, should not compete with but supplement private American news services.[32] In his bid to keep the OWI alive, Davis received support from Assistant Secretary of State for Public Affairs Archibald MacLeish (who had left the OWI in January 1943) and some Democrats in Congress. In February 1945 MacLeish told the House Appropriations Subcommittee on the State Department that the U.S. government needed to keep its information and cultural programs operating after the war in order to extend a "life line" to the liberated nations. In May 1945 Representative Louis Ludlow (D–Ind.) placed in the *Congressional Record* newspaper articles advocating continuance of the OWI. In a June address on NBC radio Senator Elbert Thomas (D–Utah) urged that the OWI maintain its operations. Representative Daniel Flood (D–Pa.) also made the case for a postwar information program, quoting William Shirer that liquidating the OWI "would be tantamount to silencing the voice of America over most of the globe," and that "there is an American story to be told, too."[33]

The prevailing view of the OWI as a temporary agency, however, was difficult to change. In spring 1945 the House Appropriations Subcommittee cut $17 million from the OWI's 1946 budget, explaining that since the war in Europe had ended, the agency needed only to maintain operations in the Pacific theater. Some legislators wanted to dismantle the OWI entirely. Shortly after the Nazi surrender Representative Leon Gavin (R–Pa.) said on the House floor that the OWI "should be abolished to save $50,000,000 for the taxpayers and a lot of headaches for the American people." In June Representative Richard Wigglesworth (R–Mass.) proposed attaching an amendment to the National War Agencies Appropriation Bill for 1946 that would liquidate "the agency [OWI] as a whole at the earliest possible time." Congressional Republicans also questioned the need for the State Department's Division of Cultural Relations and Office of Public Affairs, both of which Archibald MacLeish now headed. In a line of questioning

32. House Subcommittee of the Committee on Appropriations, *Hearings on the National War Agencies Appropriations Bill for 1945*, 78th Cong., 2d sess., April 19, 1944, 9; *Hearings on the National War Agencies Appropriations Bill for 1946*, 79th Cong., 1st sess., May 14, 1945, 894.

33. House Subcommittee of the Committee on Appropriations, *Department of State Appropriation Bill for 1946, Hearings before the Subcommittee of the Committee on Appropriations*, 79th Cong., 1st sess., February 26, 1945, 276; Ernest Lindley, "Was Elmer Davis Right?" May 28, 1945, and "Tell the American Story," May 30, 1945, *Washington Post*; William Shirer, "Propaganda Front," May 27, 1945, in *Congressional Record*, 79th Cong., 1st sess., vol. 91, A2619–20, A2652–53, A3042.

that would soon prove common, Representative Karl Stefan (R–Nebr.) asked MacLeish whether or not the State Department tried to sell its policies to the American public through publicity efforts. On August 31, 1945, President Truman settled the fate of the OWI. Executive Order 9608 liquidated the agency but transferred its functions, including the VOA, to the Interim International Information Service (IIIS), which was set up within the State Department. Truman declared that the United States "will endeavor to see to it that other peoples receive a full and fair picture of American life and of the aims and policies of the United States Government," and he asked the secretary of state to propose a permanent program by the end of the year. The president emphasized that the government would not interfere with privately run media, which would remain the primary means of telling the world about America, but rather would target only geographical areas where private companies did not yet operate. The executive order echoed the suggestions of Dr. Arthur W. MacMahon, a political science professor hired by the Department of State to study international information activities. In his report MacMahon had concluded that such activities were necessary in foreign affairs and should promote full and fair knowledge about the United States without competing with private media. MacMahon concluded that government-sponsored information activities would increase knowledge about the United States, promote international alliances, and facilitate trade.[34]

MacMahon's report and Truman's executive order advanced the belief that the sharing of information among the nations of the world fostered peace. In the months following World War II many prominent scholars, editors, and writers also put forth this idea. "If the nations are to become less quarrelsome, they must become more informed," wrote Herbert Agar in the *Saturday Review of Literature*. "Must We Tell the World?" asked *Harper's* editor Frederick Lewis Allen, answering yes. The Commission on Freedom of the Press, whose members included Harold Lasswell, Archibald MacLeish, and Arthur Schlesinger, Sr., advised that "[t]he surest antidote for ignorance and deceit is the widest possible exchange of objectively realistic information—*true* information, not merely more informa-

---

34. Pirsein, "Voice of America," 107–8; *Congressional Record,* 79th Cong., 1st sess., May 18, 1945, and June 7, 1945, vol. 91, 5739, A2378; House Appropriations Subcommittee, *Hearings for 1946,* 290–92; *Department of State Bulletin* 13 (September 2, 1945): 306–7; Arthur MacMahon, *Memorandum on the Postwar International Information Program of the United States,* xi–xiii, 2–4.

tion" [emphasis in original].[35] The commission's emphasis on truth indicates an essential part of the American faith in international information exchange. "True information" stuck to the facts, good or bad, allowing listeners to draw their own conclusions and opinions. By remaining objective and truthful, the taint of propaganda was avoided. Within this context, Truman's phrase "full and fair picture" (a paraphrase of the language in MacMahon's report) took on added significance. The State Department was to tell the facts about the United States without shirking from embarrassing or negative revelations.

Truman's approval of a postwar international information program also exemplified the developing corporatist strategy that linked together the international interests of American businesses and their government. By promising that government-run media would fill only a supplementary role, bypassing areas where American private media already operated abroad, Executive Order 9608 sought to establish a cooperative rather than competitive relationship between government and business. Ideally, such a partnership pleased both parties: the government made sure the peoples of the world were kept informed about the United States without taking markets away from American businesses. The viability of government and business cooperation and the international responsibility of the United States to promote world peace were distinctly liberal propositions. Because the VOA synthesized the international and domestic strains of these propositions, it became a prominent target in the postwar assault on the liberal ascendancy. Conservatives resisted government and business partnership, and they dismissed the proposition that government-run media would supplement rather than compete with private media. They also questioned the idea that international information exchange promoted peace, countering that government media could only be trusted to promote the policies of the incumbent administration. In order to legitimize the VOA, its administrators thus had to also justify its underlying liberal premises.

The official responsible for the VOA was the Assistant Secretary of State for Public Affairs (ASPA), who also oversaw domestic information operations and media relations for the State Department. In September 1945 Secretary of State James Byrnes asked William Benton to serve as ASPA after Archibald MacLeish stepped down. Though Benton had no back-

35. Herbert Agar, "They Want to Know"; Frederick Lewis Allen, "Must We Tell the World"; Llewellyn White and Robert D. Leigh, *Peoples Speaking to Peoples: A Report on International Mass Communication from the Commission on Freedom of the Press*, 2.

ground in diplomacy or government work, his accomplishments in advertising and public relations were impressive. Benton's pioneering work in radio advertising and consumer surveys made advertising agency Benton and Bowles one of the world's largest by 1935. As head of public relations for the University of Chicago, Benton helped dispel the popular belief that communists dominated the faculty. Benton was also a savvy entrepreneur. In 1939 he bought the bankrupt Muzak Corporation and made it profitable by targeting new markets such as elevators and offices. As chairman of *Encyclopedia Britannica,* Benton aided in development of the Great Books curriculum. Benton initially declined Byrnes's offer, believing that his career experiences did not qualify him for the position, but then accepted the job after the secretary dismissed his concerns.[36] If familiarity with the ways of Washington counted as a job qualification, then Benton's self-doubts were justified. Though earnest and hard-working, Benton frequently alienated members of Congress and other State Department officials. In November 1946 Benton's gift of *Encyclopedia Britannica* angered incoming House Appropriations Committee Chair John Taber, who thought Benton was trying to influence his vote on VOA funds. On Capitol Hill, Benton had a reputation as a "publicity man and a propaganda man." Within the State Department, Benton's fondness for frequent and lengthy memoranda made him unpopular with busy superiors such as Undersecretary Dean Acheson and George C. Marshall, Byrnes's successor as secretary of state.[37]

Consistent with the task before him, Benton touted the benefits of international exchange of information. Just after his appointment, Benton declared that the people of the world needed to use mass media to maintain contact with one another and that the United States should try to understand foreigners. In October 1945 he told the House Foreign Affairs Committee that the information programs, including the VOA, "hold some reasonable hope and promise that the world can learn to live together in

---

36. Sydney Hyman, *The Lives of William Benton,* 129–54, 170–85, 211–62, 308–13.

37. Benton to Taber, November 28, 1946, box 17, folder 152, Karl Stefan Papers, Nebraska State Archives, Lincoln; the quote is from Sen. H. Alexander Smith (R–N.J.), who made the statement during a Senate Foreign Relations Committee discussion held June 16, 1948. *Executive Sessions of the Senate Foreign Relations Committee,* vol. 1, 80th Cong., 1st and 2d sess., 1947–1948, 304. In May 1947 Benton complained that his memoranda to Marshall and Acheson were screened and held back so that neither man paid more than five minutes of attention per week to them. Benton to Carlisle Humelsine, May 8, 1947, drawer 24, Murray G. Lawson History Card File, United States Information Agency Historical Collection, Washington, D.C. (hereafter cited as Lawson File).

peace and understanding." Like other supporters of international exchange of information, Benton expressed abiding faith in truthful presentation. We only supply the facts, Benton wrote in a report that the secretary of state submitted to the president at the end of 1945. When questioned about the ability of the government to resist propagandizing, Benton answered that "truth" would prevent this possibility.[38]

According to Benton, peoples of the world were keenly interested in the United States. During a January 1946 radio broadcast called "America—As Others See Us," Benton repeated some of the questions that the daily half-hour VOA broadcast "At Your Service" drew from French and Italian listeners: Do gangsters infest the U.S.? Could I live in America on ten thousand francs a month? What sort of guns do American police carry? Benton also observed that foreigners held derogatory opinions about the United States—self-serving capitalists controlled all media and monopolies belied the existence of free enterprise. In a magazine article Benton wrote that abroad, America was seen as an industrial giant, dumping its goods on the world, or else as the lawless Wild West. By vividly describing these negative images, Benton sought to demonstrate the need for an international information program. In order to rebut the view that private media should correct foreigners' negative opinions of the United States, Benton emphasized that the VOA filled a niche that private media did not, and he promised that the State Department would work with private media.[39] However, separate conflicts between the VOA and the Associated Press

38. Benton press statement, September 17, 1945, in *Department of State Bulletin* 13 (September 23, 1945): 430; House Committee on Foreign Affairs, *Interchange of Knowledge and Skills between the People of the United States and Peoples of Other Countries, Hearing before the House Committee on Foreign Affairs on H.R. 4368 and H.R. 4982,* 79th Cong., 1st and 2d sess., 1945 and 1946, 7 (hereafter cited as *Bloom Bill Hearings*). Byrnes to Truman, December 31, 1945, box 375, folder 1, William Benton Papers, University of Chicago; Benton statement before the House Committee on Appropriations, October 4, 1945, in *Department of State Bulletin* 13 (October 21, 1945): 593–95; Benton statement before the American Society of Newspaper Editors, April 18, 1946, in *Proceedings of the 23rd Annual Convention of the American Society of Newspaper Editors,* 60.

39. "America--As Others See Us," radio broadcast, January 3, 1946; William Benton, "The Voice of America"; Benton, "Our International Information Service," 8; Benton, "Self Portrait—By Uncle Sam"; House Subcommittee of the Committee on Appropriations, *Department of State Appropriation Bill for 1947, Hearings before the Subcommittee of the Committee on Appropriations,* 79th Cong., 2d sess., 1946, 493; Senate Subcommittee of the Committee on Appropriations, *Departments of State, Justice, Commerce, and the Judiciary, Hearings before the Subcommittee of the Committee on Appropriations for 1947,* 79th Cong., 2d sess., 1946, 21–33; Benton statement to the House Committee on Appropriations, October 4, 1945.

(AP) and the World-Wide Broadcasting Foundation (WWBF) during 1946 undermined Benton's position and impeded passage of enabling legislation providing permanent standing for the VOA, one of Benton's top priorities. Without enabling legislation, the VOA and other programs (press and publications, motion pictures, exchange of persons, and overseas libraries) operated only on the authority of Truman's executive order and were vulnerable to liquidation through congressional elimination of appropriations.

In October 1945 Benton asked Representative Sol Bloom (D–N.Y.), chair of the House Foreign Affairs Committee, to introduce enabling legislation that Benton's office had drafted. H.R. 4368 (79th Cong., 1st sess.) authorized the State Department to maintain international information and cultural exchanges abroad. Appearing before the Foreign Affairs Committee in support of the bill, Benton promised that the State Department's programs would not interfere with the activities of private news services, broadcasters, and filmmakers, stressing that the department intended only to take a supplemental role in disseminating information abroad about the United States. Representative John Vorys (R–Ohio) expressed concern, however, that the bill did not clearly explain the extent to which the State Department would operate news services, libraries, and cultural exchanges in areas where private companies or organizations were already in place. Indeed, the Bloom bill lacked provisions preventing government overlap or interference with private media. The bill also made no mention of the VOA. Benton's assistant Haldore Hanson admitted this conspicuous omission and stated that recommendations for radio would be given to Congress within the next year. The Bloom bill underwent so many modifications that it was reintroduced as H.R. 4982 on December 13, 1945. The new bill authorized government shortwave broadcasts, instructing the secretary of state to disseminate abroad information about the United States and its people and policies. The revised bill still did not, however, specifically prohibit competition with private or other government broadcasters, instead giving the secretary of state the power to give monetary, service, or property grants to nonprofit public and private corporations for "preparation and dissemination of informational materials abroad."[40]

An unexpected clash with the AP and UP disrupted Benton's efforts to convince critics that the information programs, particularly the VOA, would not interfere with private media. On January 16, 1946, the AP ceased

40. House Committee on Foreign Affairs, *Bloom Bill Hearings,* 1–10, 92–93, 151, 182–89, 210.

service to the VOA, claiming that continued association with the government would give outside observers the impression that the AP was not impartial. According to an AP press release, the "government cannot engage in newscasting without creating the fear of propaganda which necessarily would reflect on the objectivity of the news services from which such newscasts are prepared." On January 27 the UP dropped its service to the VOA, citing the same concern. Both agencies also worried that the government might try to manipulate their output. With budget hearings just a month away and the Bloom bill still in committee, the timing of the AP and UP action could not have been much worse. The news agencies' justifications for dropping service gutted Benton's assertion that the State Department's information programs did not interfere with private media. Benton responded with a flurry of public statements denying the charges of government propagandizing. In an open letter to AP head Robert McLean he criticized the AP for not consulting him beforehand and claimed that AP directors were not familiar with VOA programming. Complaining that the AP and UP action crippled the State Department's ability to provide news to areas the news wires did not service, Benton promised that the department would cease wireless news bulletins once private agencies set up operations in these areas. Finally, Benton called for an outside panel to study the objectivity of VOA broadcasts and issue a report to Congress and the AP. But the damage was already done. Representatives Karl E. Mundt (R–S.D.) and John Vorys, members of the House Foreign Affairs Committee, delayed hearings on the revised Bloom bill because of the controversy. Mundt sided with the news services. In a letter to AP General Manager Kent Cooper, Mundt stated that "a number of the members of our Committee are reluctant to have this legislation considered on the floor until we have an opportunity to know precisely the position of the Associated Press and the United Press on this matter." The Bloom bill was undermined further when the American Society of Newspaper Editors (ASNE) issued a statement supporting the AP and UP.[41]

41. "Include AP Out," *Newsweek* 27, no. 4 (January 28, 1946): 74–75; Pirsein, "Voice of America," 116–17. Privately, Benton admitted that the MacMahon report, which was sponsored by the State Department, might have prompted the AP's decision. The report claimed that the news service Reuters was affiliated with the British government; the AP feared it too might be linked to its home government. MacMahon, *Memorandum on the Postwar International Information Program*, pt. 3. Benton's admission was reported by his assistant Alice Curran to John Howe, January 19, 1946, box 372, folder 2, Benton Papers. For Benton's defense of the VOA, see Department of State Bulletin 14 (January 27, 1946): 92–95; *Department of State Bulletin* 14 (February 10, 1946):

In order to prove that the VOA did not threaten freedom of the press, Benton asked his assistants to draft a proposal for an International Broadcasting Foundation (IBF). To be composed of prominent figures from the radio industry, the IBF was to oversee operation of the VOA. The IBF's suggested powers included language selections, the setting of program patterns, allocation of funds, and "[d]aily and weekly policy suggestions on the handling of major news stories affecting the U.S. foreign policy." Essentially, Benton was proposing the creation of a private corporation to operate the VOA for the government, a plan that co-opted opponents' arguments. If the government could not be objective (an assertion that Benton continued to deny), then a private operation would ensure objectivity for the VOA. Years later Benton admitted that the IBF was a desperate ploy to keep the VOA on the air. Although the IBF was never established, OIC officials worked on the foundation plan throughout 1946 and early 1947, and Benton lobbied strenuously for its approval by Congress and his superiors in the State Department. According to Benton, Republican members of Congress expressed interest in the IBF; however, they also questioned how it would resist political pressures on VOA programming.[42] Many worried that the VOA might be coerced into slanting broadcasts to the favor of the administration and the Democratic party.

With hearings on the 1947 budget only weeks away, the IBF was too little, too late. Benton assured the House Appropriations Subcommittee that the VOA did not interfere with domestic media and emphasized the niche filled by the VOA: "this is the only major way people of many other countries can be sure to get news of America from American sources." Unconvinced, the subcommittee approved only $10 million of the $19 million requested. "[A] concerted effort must be made by all concerned to reduce the cost and limit the size of our Government," read the

---

217–18. For the delay of hearings on the Bloom bill, see unsigned staff memorandum to Benton, February 28, 1946, box 7, folder "Congressional," RG 59, Records of the Assistant Secretary of State for Public Affairs, Office Symbol Files, National Archives, College Park, Md. (hereafter cited as Records of the ASPA); *Congressional Quarterly Almanac,* vol. 2, 477–78; Mundt to Cooper, February 18, 1946, box 454, folder 5, Karl E. Mundt Papers, Karl E. Mundt Archives, Madison, S.D.; statement from Wilbur Forrest, *Bulletin of the American Society of Newspaper Editors* 271 (February 1, 1946).

42. Haldore Hanson to William T. Stone, February 6, 1946, box 9, folder "Radio Legislation," RG 59, Records Relating to International Information Activities, 1938–1953 (hereafter cited as RIIA); William Benton, interview by Robert Pirsein, September 11, 1965, in Pirsein, "Voice of America," 131; Benton to James Byrnes, April 13, 1946, 811.42700(R)4–1346, RG 59, Central Decimal File (hereafter cited as CDF).

report. In order to force the State Department to use private media, the subcommittee eliminated funds for filmmaking and publication of the magazine *Amerika*. It also cut the VOA's budget to limit broadcasts to straight news, but the amount approved for radio operations was not enough to even keep the VOA on the air.[43]

While the Bloom bill remained in committee, Republicans in Congress expressed doubts over the State Department's ability to operate the VOA. In April 1946 House Foreign Affairs Committee Member John Vorys stated that the AP/UP controversy showed the State Department was dragging its feet on setting up permanent standing for the VOA. In May Vorys complained that the department was contemplating setting up a monopoly on overseas information programs. Representative Robert F. Jones (R–Ohio) offered an amendment to the appropriations bill striking out all funds for the information programs, including the VOA, stating that private media did a better job than the State Department. Jones also expressed his concern that the State Department might use the information programs to glamorize the administration in power. Representative Noah Mason (R–Ill.) was more direct than Jones, declaring that the State Department could not be trusted to tell the truth because it had lied about the partition of Poland.[44]

Problems with a radio transmitter owner further undermined Benton's position that the VOA did not interfere with private media. During World War II the government had leased seven privately owned international shortwave transmitters to carry the VOA. The contracts expired June 30, 1946. Because the House Appropriations Subcommittee had not approved funds to build or buy VOA transmitters and Congress had not voted on the Bloom bill, the State Department needed to renew the contracts. With the exception of the World-Wide Broadcasting Foundation (WWBF), the transmitter owners signed new contracts. Founded by Walter Lemmon, a wealthy Christian Scientist, the WWBF had broadcast before the war cultural, educational, and spiritual programs about the United States. Lemmon was eager to resume operations, but due to a lack of international frequencies, the VOA's output would have been reduced had the

43. House Subcommittee of the Committee on Appropriations, *Hearings for 1947*, 435; *State, Justice, Commerce, and the Judiciary Appropriation Bill, Fiscal Year 1947*, 79th Cong., 2d sess., April 9, 1946, 3–8.

44. *Congressional Record*, 79th Cong., 2d sess., April 10 and May 2, 1946, vol. 92, 3472, 4348, 4354–56.

WWBF regained its transmitter. The WWBF thus presented Benton with a dilemma. Action on the Bloom bill was suspended because of concerns about VOA interference with private media, but without the WWBF transmitter, the VOA would lose air time. At the American Society of Newspaper Editors (ASNE) convention in April 1946 many in attendance criticized the government's hold on the WWBF transmitter. Defending the VOA, Benton asserted that the WWBF was not capable of broadcasting in twenty-four languages for four hundred hours a week, but he had no immediate answer when *Christian Science Monitor* editor Erwin Canham rejoined that the State Department should at least let one station have a free voice. Within the State Department an official objected to the "undue pressure put upon him" to renew transmitter contracts, and the chair of the Federal Communications Commission advised Benton to at least offer the WWBF partial use of its transmitter.[45]

On June 17, 1946, Walter Lemmon appeared before the Senate Appropriations Subcommittee to complain of the State Department's hold on the WWBF transmitter. After listening to Lemmon's statement, Senator Walter White (R–Maine) stated that "there is no legal authority whatsoever for the action the State Department is taking." After the hearings the subcommittee required the State Department to give the WWBF three hours daily of broadcast time. Although Benton was unhappy with the decision, it helped smooth the way for restoration of the $9 million that the House had cut from the information and cultural programs' budget, thus allowing the VOA to stay on the air. In its report the subcommittee stated that "short-wave radio is one way, and possibly the only way, by which accurate information concerning the U.S. may be gotten to peoples of the world."[46] Although the arrangement with the

---

45. The owners were RCA, NBC, CBS, the Crosley Corporation, Westinghouse, General Electric, and the World-Wide Broadcasting Foundation. Benton defended the government's hold on the WWBF transmitter at the American Society of Newspaper Editors convention in April 1946 and at the hearings on the Bloom bill in May 1946. See *Proceedings of the 23rd Annual Convention of the American Society of Newspaper Editors*, 58–59; House Committee on Foreign Affairs, *Bloom Bill Hearings*, 182–89. On the pressure to renew transmitter contracts, see Charles Hulten to William Benton, April 2, 1946, box 375, folder 2, Benton Papers; the view of the FCC's chairman was reported by Forney A. Rankin to William Stone, August 16, 1946, box 1, folder "IBD 1946," RG 59, Records of the ASPA.

46. Senate Subcommittee of the Committee on Appropriations, *Departments of State, Justice, Commerce, and the Judiciary for 1947, Hearings Part 2, State Department-- Informational and Cultural Program, World Wide Broadcasting Foundation*, 79th Cong., 2d sess., June 17, 1946, 11; *Departments of State, Justice, Commerce, and the Judiciary Appropriation Bill, Fiscal Year 1947*, 79th Cong., 2d sess., June 18, 1946.

WWBF seemed to settle the issue of monopoly for the Senate Appropriations Subcommittee, Republicans still sought tighter guarantees of noninterference. Because of the AP/UP controversy and the conflict with the WWBF, Representative John Vorys introduced an amendment to the Bloom bill that specifically prohibited State Department monopolization of information activities and required the use of private services wherever possible. Only after the Vorys amendment was written into the Bloom bill did it come up for a vote, and on July 20, 1946, the House passed it by a voice vote.[47]

The Vorys amendment and compromise with the WWBF were not enough, however, to ensure passage of the Bloom bill in the Senate. In addition to interference with private media, the backgrounds of VOA and State Department personnel aroused the suspicions of Republicans and Southern Democrats. Combined with the issue of noninterference, these concerns spelled the Bloom bill's defeat. When the Senate version of the bill came up for consideration on July 29, several Republican senators asked that the bill be passed over.[48] When the House bill was called, Senator Robert Taft (R–Ohio) asked to pass it over, also blocking a vote on August 2, the last day of the session. Taft distrusted the State Department, and he was not alone.

III. Domestic Subversion and the VOA

Accusations that the State Department and the VOA employed subversives and communist sympathizers resounded throughout Washington after World War II. Representative Chester Merrow (R–N.H.) introduced a resolution for a House committee to undertake a comprehensive study of American foreign policy and to investigate the presence of pro-communist and pro-British cliques within the State Department. In November 1945 Representative Paul Shafer referred to the "Stalining" of the department, meaning "the process of making changes in personnel and policy with a view to their acceptability in the eyes of Joseph Stalin." Also in November, the House Un-American Activities Committee (HUAC) indicated that it would ask Patrick Hurley

---

47. At hearings on the revised Bloom bill on May 14, 1946, Vorys said, "the State Department plans a monopoly of all time on all international shortwave stations." House Foreign Affairs Committee, *Bloom Bill Hearings*, 181; *Congressional Quarterly*, vol. 2, 478.

48. *Congressional Quarterly*, vol. 2, 478; *Congressional Record*, 79th Cong., 2d sess., 1946, vol. 92, 10340.

to identify the "red sympathizers" in the State Department who had purportedly undermined his work in China. Mincing no words, Representative Eugene Cox (D–Ga.) declared that the State Department was "chock full of Reds" and was "the lousiest outfit in town." The department's takeover of the OWI in fall 1945 only enhanced these suspicions. Republicans on the House Foreign Affairs and Appropriations Committees "insist that the State Department is harboring Communists and fellow travelers brought over from the OWI," reported the *Christian Science Monitor* on April 17, 1946. "Shaken out of the OWI and the Army's intelligence divisions, they have crawled into the State Department's information agencies, these legislators charge." During hearings on the State Department's 1947 budget, Senator Styles Bridges (R–N.H.) asked a State Department official to tell the Appropriations Committee "the procedure you have followed, first, to absolutely screen those employees, what agencies they come from, and also what you are doing now to determine their loyalty, and to rid the Department of any Communists?" Kenneth Wherry (R–Nebr.) was more blunt than Bridges: "Are you paying salaries to anyone in the State Department whom you know to be a communist?"[49]

Concerns over the political allegiances of State Department and OWI personnel unavoidably spilled onto the VOA. In February 1946 House Rules Committee members Eugene Cox and Clarence Brown (R–Ohio) listed security concerns along with the AP/UP clash as the reasons why they refused to report out the Bloom bill. Cox also characterized the bill as an effort to "revitalize the OWI." During hearings Cox repeatedly raised doubts about the loyalty of State Department personnel and told Benton that ten of the twelve Rules Committee members opposed the bill because of security concerns. In May Representative Richard Wigglesworth questioned why more than thirty-five hundred persons from the OWI and other wartime agencies were transferred to the State

49. *Congressional Record,* 79th Cong., 2d sess., January 22, 1946, vol. 92, 223; 79th Cong., 1st sess., November 6, 1945, vol. 91, A4730; "Check Shows '2 Dozen' Leftists in State Department," *Los Angeles Examiner,* November 30, 1945; "State Dept. News Called a New OWI in Stormy Hearing," *New York World-Telegram,* February 14, 1946; Senate Subcommittee of the Committee on Appropriations, *Hearings on the Second Deficiency Appropriation Bill for 1946,* 79th Cong. 2d sess., April 17, 1946, 186–90. Republicans also received the FBI's help in substantiating their charges. Throughout 1945 and 1946, FBI Director J. Edgar Hoover leaked derogatory information about State Department employees from FBI files. See Kenneth O'Reilly, *Hoover and the Un-Americans: The FBI, HUAC, and the Red Menace.*

Department without proper clearance. Also with regard to the OWI transfer, Senator Kenneth Wherry pointedly asked William Benton whether or not he had purged leftists in the process.[50] In June the Senate included in the State Department appropriation bill a provision giving Secretary of State Byrnes the power to fire personnel without following Civil Service rules, an option intended in part for the dismissal of VOA staff. "Some members of the [Appropriations] committee would have voted against any money for the International Information Service unless there was some protection against it getting into the hands of the wrong kind of people," explained Senator Richard Russell (D–Ga.).[51]

Wherry's use of the term "leftists" and Russell's reference to "the wrong kind of people" provide strong clues as to why Republican and conservative Democratic members of Congress charged the State Department and the VOA with employing communists. These accusations preceded the Truman administration's March 1947 request for aid to Greece and Turkey, so legislators were not yet redirecting nascent containment policies to the homefront. But charges that the federal government employed communists and fellow travelers were hardly new in 1945 and 1946. Formed in 1938, the House Un-American Activities Committee had investigated the possible presence of communists in various government programs. By targeting controversial and vulnerable programs such as the WPA's Federal Theater and the Writers' Project, HUAC chair Martin Dies (D–Texas) and his conservative colleagues sought to discredit and weaken the New Deal. After World War II, charges that communists were on the federal payroll continued the goal of ending the New Deal and unseating its advocates. It is useful to view the mixed charges about domestic communists and leftists as part of an incomplete syllogism: communism took control of all property, production, and resources; the New Deal encroached upon democratically guaranteed property rights and the free marketplace; therefore, the New Deal and its executors were friendly to communists. Left dangling was the implication that New Dealers might become too cozy with communists or actually become communists, thus resulting in the destruction of

50. *New York World-Telegram*, February 14, 1946; Haldore Hanson to James Byrnes, March 13, 1946, box 4, folder "Secretary Byrnes," RG 59, Records of the ASPA; Benton to Acheson, box 4, folder "Dean Acheson 1946," RG 59, Records of the ASPA; *Congressional Record*, 79th Cong., 2d sess., May 2, 1946, vol. 92, 4366–67; Senate Appropriations Subcommittee, *Hearings for 1947*, 36.

51. "Senate Votes Byrnes Power to Oust Reds," *Washington Daily News*, June 22, 1946.

American democracy. This syllogism served Republicans well during the 1946 midterm elections. Scores of Republican candidates and incumbents linked strikes, inflation, and price controls to supposed communist infiltration of the Democratic party, a tactic that wrested votes from traditional Democratic blocs such as urban Catholics and gave the GOP control of Congress for the first time since 1928. As Representative Karl Stefan put it in his campaign literature, "[w]hat do you want: Our Country and Our Constitution, or Communism and Regimentation? There can be no compromise."[52]

Pre-containment attacks on the VOA and State Department personnel fit into this syllogism and served the goal of rolling back the New Deal. Occurring before the introduction of President Truman's loyalty program, the attacks also prompted State Department officials to take independent measures to convince their critics that neither the VOA nor the department leaned left. Members of Congress were particularly interested in the security files of Haldore Hanson and William Stone, both of whom worked for the Office of International Information and Cultural Affairs (OIC, the outfit within the State Department responsible for the VOA and the other information and cultural programs). Hanson and Stone also had previous connections to the journal *Amerasia*. (In 1945 editor Phil Jaffe, Foreign Service Officer John Stewart Service, and two other government employees were arrested after the FBI found classified government documents in *Amerasia*'s office). In March 1946 Benton's assistant Haldore Hanson described to his superior the items that might cause trouble for himself and the department. In 1939 he had written numerous articles about the Chinese communists; some of these pieces appeared in *Amerasia*. While stationed in China as an AP war correspondent, Hanson had roomed with

---

52. For the argument that Republicans' public complaints about subversion left Truman no choice but to set up a loyalty program, see Francis H. Thompson, *The Frustration of Politics: Truman, Congress, and the Loyalty Issue, 1945–1953;* Alan D. Harper, *The Politics of Loyalty: The White House and the Communist Issue, 1946–1952.* For the counter-argument that Truman's efforts to rally support for containment abroad facilitated McCarthyism, see Athan G. Theoharis, *Seeds of Repression: Harry S. Truman and the Origins of McCarthyism;* Richard M. Freeland, *The Truman Doctrine and the Origins of McCarthyism: Foreign Policy, Domestic Politics, and Internal Security, 1946–1948.* On HUAC, see Walter Goodman, *The Committee: The Extraordinary Career of the House Committee on Un-American Activities,* 24–58. On the 1946 election, see James Boylan, *The New Deal Coalition and the Election of 1946,* 136–38; Richard Gid Powers, *Not without Honor: The History of American Anti-Communism,* 197; Campaign pamphlet, box 31, folder 39, Karl Stefan Papers.

Service and had given Service fifty dollars after the department suspended him from his post following his arrest. OIC General Manager William Stone had served on *Amerasia*'s editorial board. However, neither man was implicated in the charges resulting from the *Amerasia* case. Benton personally asked that they not be terminated, and Assistant Secretary of State for Administration Donald Russell granted his request.[53]

Such decisions did not help congressional relations. After warning that Senator Styles Bridges and Representative Bartel Jonkman (R–Mich.) were upset that State Department security checks were taking so long, administrative official Joe Panuch advised Donald Russell to investigate "suspicious personnel and get rid of some of the State Department members who have received 'disloyalty' publicity in the press and on the Hill." Also writing to Russell, William Benton complained in August that it was unfair to subject his personnel to continuing loyalty investigations, but that Senators Bridges, Wherry, and Pat McCarran (D–Nev.) "stated frankly that their whole question on my budget revolved around their fears of disloyalty."[54] Indeed, in its otherwise supportive report on the 1947 State Department budget, the Senate Appropriations Subcommittee had advised that the department needed to subject each information and cultural program employee to thorough background checks.

After the strong Republican showing in the 1946 congressional elections, pressure to eliminate suspected left-leaning personnel from the VOA intensified. In December Representative Christian Herter (R–Mass.) confided to a State Department official that though he was sympathetic to the information program, Republicans needed to be persuaded that the VOA

53. Hanson to Benton, March 25, 1946, box 73, folder "H," RG 59, Miscellaneous Records of the Bureau of Public Affairs, Subject Files of the Policy Plans and Guidance Staff. One of the accused, Jimmy Larsen, was a former Office of Naval Intelligence employee who was working for the State Department when he was arrested for spying. For a full account of the case, including evidence that Service and his co-defendants did steal or receive classified government documents, see Harvey Klehr and Ronald Radosh, *The Amerasia Spy Case: Prelude to McCarthyism.* For substantiation of communist infiltration of the OWI, see Harvey Klehr, John E. Haynes, and Fridrikh Igorevich Firsov, *The Secret World of American Communism,* 110–18, 229, 281–82, 307–8, 317–21. For Benton's request that Stone and Hanson not be fired, see Benton to Russell, August 14, 1946; Russell to Benton, August 17, 1946, box 73, folder, "Security," RG 59, Miscellaneous Records of the Bureau of Public Affairs, Subject Files of the Policy Plans and Guidance Staff.

54. Panuch to Donald Russell, July 19, 1946, box 7, folder "General Memoranda, 1945–1947," J. Anthony Panuch Papers, Harry S. Truman Presidential Library, Independence, Mo., 5; Benton to Russell, August 22, 1946, box 375, folder 3, Benton Papers.

"is not being used as a vehicle for distribution of left-wing philosophy and social and other ideas that many Republicans regard as dangerous." Eugene Cox, who had bottled up the Bloom bill because of his suspicions about personnel, confidentially advised Benton that the State Department needed to "convince Congress that the Marxists are being put out of the Department." Soon after the Eightieth Congress convened, Representative Karl Mundt told Benton that he should submit the names of every OIC employee to HUAC for background checks. According to Benton, Mundt and other Republicans indicated that if HUAC cleared the employees, it would help result in favorable action on legislative and appropriations requests. In February 1947 Representative Bartel Jonkman complained of constantly receiving misleading statements about forty questionable State Department officials, misinformation that he claimed was a deliberate policy of the New Deal administration. (The State Department had, however, sent Jonkman a brief summary of the employment status of twelve former and present State Department employees, including William Stone and Haldore Hanson).[55]

The VOA was also singled out as a security risk because it employed aliens. In order to write, edit, and air programming in more than twenty languages the VOA required highly skilled, bilingual or multilingual speakers. Announcers in particular had to be comfortable with the idioms, slang, and cadences of their respective broadcast languages. Naturalized citizens and bilingual native-born Americans often did not have the proper "ears," so the VOA relied on aliens and recent immigrants. In both versions of the Bloom bill, State Department officials made sure to include provisions permitting the employment of aliens. Members of Congress made it clear, however, that they did not want the VOA to employ aliens. At the 1946 House budget hearings, William Benton was asked how many foreigners worked for the VOA. Benton assured the committee that the department conducted background checks and that Americans proofread all scripts written by aliens. But soon the State Department began terminating alien employees in order

---

55. Oliver McKee to William Benton, December 16, 1946, box 121, folder "Congressional Relations," RG 59, RIIA; Cox to Benton, January 27, 1947, drawer 21, Lawson File; Benton to Dean Acheson, January 27, 1947, box 4, folder "Discuss with Lovett," RG 59, Records of the ASPA. For Jonkman's complaints, see *Washington Times-Herald*, February 26, 1947; John Peurifoy to Bartel Jonkman, February 4, 1947, box 7, folder "Misc. Security Materials," RG 59, Records of the Office of Security and Consular Affairs, Reading Files of Samuel Boykin.

to appease concerned members of Congress. The case of Karel Mazel, a Czech national who headed the VOA's Czech language desk, is instructive. Mazel cleared two security checks, the first conducted by the Civil Service Commission in 1943, the second carried out by the State Department's own investigative unit in 1946. "However, later in 1946, when the Department began to attempt to get rid of alien employees in accordance with Congressional direction, steps were taken to terminate Mazel." Two reasons were offered for letting Mazel go: he and his wife had worked for the Czech Information Office in New York City, and he had not listed this information on his application for government employment. Mazel resigned his post in April 1947; his departure was part of the near total reduction of alien employees within the VOA's studios. In March 1947 the VOA employed twenty-four aliens in its New York studios as script writers or language experts; by fall 1947 only four aliens remained as full-time employees of the VOA.[56]

The 1945–1946 drive to purge the State Department and VOA of suspect employees distinctly affected congressional Republicans' and Southern Democrats' attitudes and actions toward the VOA in the years to come. As previously explained, proponents of the VOA recognized that their primary task was to convince dubious members of Congress that the U.S. government needed to help private media tell foreign audiences about the United States and its people. As William Benton and State Department administration officials realized during the summer of 1946, there was another priority: convincing these same legislators that the VOA's employees were loyal. Benton believed that this simply required a security procedure "that will win the confidence of Congress." To be sure, the Yalta Conference and *Amerasia* spy case proved to many that the State Department, and indeed the entire executive branch, was either unwilling or unable to screen suspect employees from their ranks. After the Republican sweep in the 1946 elections, Truman ordered work

56. R. E. Ward to Haldore Hanson, November 23, 1945, box 2, folder "OIC," RG 59, Records of the ASPA; Section 3, part (i) of H.R. 4368 and H.R. 4982, in House Committee on Foreign Affairs, *Bloom Bill Hearings*, 2, 212; House Appropriations Subcommittee, *Hearings for 1947*, 495. For the Mazel case, see Jesse MacKnight to George Allen, March 17, 1949, box 73, folder "M," RG 59, Miscellaneous Records of the Bureau of Public Affairs, Subject Files of the Policy Plans and Guidance Staff; "Report of House Subcommittee of the Appropriations Committee," box 7, unmarked envelope, RG 59, Records of the ASPA; Report for the Smith-Mundt Committee, box 117, folder "Special OIE Material for Smith-Mundt Committee," RG 59, RIIA.

begun on a comprehensive loyalty and security program for all federal employees. Even before the results of the midterm elections, though, the State Department had begun shoring up its security procedures after a spot check revealed that classified documents were not properly secured in locked cabinets or safes.[57] As President Truman and the State Department soon discovered, these efforts did little to stop charges that the administration was lax on domestic security. During the next few years events such as the trial of Alger Hiss, the Chinese Communists' victory over the Nationalists, the sudden rise of Joe McCarthy, and the Korean War would fuel continuing attacks on the administration's domestic security programs.

Because of conservatives' conflation of liberalism with communism, such charges also advanced the assault on the New and Fair Deals, and it is within this larger context that concerns about the VOA's employees are usefully evaluated. The VOA's proponents not only needed to convince critics that a government radio station was desirable for postwar international relations but also had to demonstrate that the men and women responsible for the VOA's message approached their task in a nonpartisan manner. Was this agency the voice of America, or the voice of the administration? For both congressional conservatives and the State Department, the meaning of loyalty began with allegiance to the United States and its government. But for conservatives, the definition of loyalty did not end there; it also crossed party lines. The VOA was an offshoot of the OWI, itself a controversial agency that had demonstrated to conservatives the excessive government spending and activities that they associated with the New Deal. Moreover, since the VOA's resources yielded its staff an opportunity to disseminate abroad information about domestic politics, critics wondered openly whether or not the true purpose of the VOA was to promote liberal policies. If so, then the VOA's employees were "disloyal" because they supported political principles

57. Benton to Joe Panuch, June 27, 1946, box 73, folder "Security," RG 59, Miscellaneous Records of the Bureau of Public Affairs, Subject Files of the Policy Plans and Guidance Staff. For Republican distrust, see Theoharis, *The Yalta Myths*, 1–9; Klehr and Radosh, *The Amerasia Spy Case*. For State Department security procedures, see S. R. Goodrich to Joe Panuch, August 15, 1946, box 4, folder "Security Survey"; Stanley Goodrich to Wright, November 1, 1946, box 4, folder, "Letters, Memoranda, Etc.," RG 59, Bureau of the Office of Security and Consular Affairs, Reading Files of Samuel Boykin; *New York World-Telegram*, February 14, 1946; Haldore Hanson to James Byrnes, March 13, 1946, box 4, folder "Secretary Byrnes"; Benton to Acheson, box 4, folder "Dean Acheson 1946," RG 59, Records of the ASPA.

that conservatives believed (or at least hoped) did not represent main-
stream America. Working from this logic, Eugene Cox thus complained
about the "Marxists," Kenneth Wherry asked whether the "leftists" had
been purged, and Christian Herter expressed concern that the VOA
might be used to spread "left-wing philosophy." These doubts persisted
even as the VOA benefited from the support that members of Congress
lent to the containment of communism abroad, articulated by Truman as
the basic principle of American postwar foreign policy in early 1947. In
the years to come, the VOA would find that it had two audiences, one
foreign, the other domestic. Pleasing the latter often proved a difficult,
even impossible, task. But first, Benton and other supporters needed to
finish convincing the VOA's critics that a genuine need existed for the
radio agency.

Chapter 2

Containment and the VOA

The November 1946 midterm elections increased the challenges confronting the VOA; Congress's incoming Republican majority promised budget cuts and the elimination of unnecessary government programs. As William Benton's executive assistant Haldore Hanson observed, the information programs made a vulnerable target. In order to build support for revised enabling legislation, officials in the Office of International Information and Cultural Affairs (OIC), which oversaw the VOA, sought the help of the House Foreign Affairs Committee, particularly from its Republican members. "I know we made mistakes in the last Congress and I would like to profit as much as we can from that experience," Hanson wrote to Congressman Karl Mundt. In November Mundt and other members were asked for improvements to the Bloom bill, which had failed to pass the Seventy-ninth Congress. After the Eightieth Congress convened, Representative John Vorys indicated that his Republican colleagues wanted to make changes in the bill in order to prove that it was not a Democratic proposal.[1] These changes included guarantees of noninterference with private media and stiffer security checks on personnel.

Securing appropriations for 1948 promised to be as tough as passage of enabling legislation. Two Republicans committed to cutting federal spending assumed leadership of the House committees that handled the VOA's budget. John Taber, who had once described VOA broadcasts as "putrid," now headed the House Appropriations Committee, while Karl Stefan took

1. Hanson to John Caldwell, November 19, 1946, box 2, folder "OIC," RG 59, Records of the ASPA; Hanson to Mundt, November 21, 1946, box 454, folder 5, Mundt Papers; Hanson to Benton, March 7, 1947, drawer 19, Lawson File.

over as chair of the House Appropriations Subcommittee on the State Department. After the election, Stefan asked Taber to fill the fourth Republican spot on the subcommittee with someone "sympathetic to certain cuts I have in mind for the entire State Department." In January 1947 Benton reported that Stefan had told him he felt obligated to reduce the VOA's budget because the party line called for drastic budget cuts across the board. One month later Stefan's subcommittee investigated the OIC's budget and operations. The report was highly critical: salaries were too high, employees arrived late to work, classified files were left unattended on desks, and security checks had not been made on all employees. These and other criticisms surfaced at the March budget hearings, which the subcommittee also conducted. The State Department had requested $31 million for the information and cultural programs, of which nearly $15 million was slated for the VOA. Representative Walt Horan (R–Wash.) complained that the VOA duplicated the work of private broadcasters and announced, "I personally shall attack the amount that is in here for this item." Reviewing a $230,000 line item request for VOA promotional materials and schedules, Stefan told Benton, "[t]hat is too much money, Mr. Secretary." Horan and Stefan continually asked why private media services could not be expected to keep the world abreast of American news and events. Subcommittee members also asked Benton to detail security check procedures.[2]

The subcommittee revealed its dissatisfaction with the OIC and VOA in its April budget report. Only $3 million was approved—for cooperative programs with Latin America. The subcommittee proposed elimination of the VOA, listing several reasons. The VOA lacked legislative authority for broadcasting, and government sponsorship of international broadcasting was "slightly out of tune with American precedents and American principles," the report stated. The latter point hinted at the subcommittee's primary justification, that private enterprise should fulfill broadcasting duties instead of the federal government, thus ending

2. Taber to James Byrnes, November 2, 1945, drawer 21, Lawson File; Stefan to Taber, November 29, 1946, box 25, folder 12, Stefan Papers; Benton to Russell, January 7, 1947, box 375, folder 4, Benton Papers. For the subcommittee's criticisms, see "Report of the House Subcommittee of the Committee on Appropriations," box 8, folder "A-P Peurifoy-Hulten," RG 59, Records of the ASPA; House Subcommittee of the Committee on Appropriations, *Department of State Appropriation Bill for 1948, Hearings before the Subcommittee of the Committee on Appropriations*, 80th Cong., 1st sess., March 3, 1947, 27, 404–5, 430–31, 440–41, 504.

unnecessary spending.[3] House Appropriations Chair John Taber supported fully the decision to strike all VOA funds. Unless the Senate Appropriations Committee restored the money that summer, the VOA was off the air.

I. The VOA and the Truman Doctrine

At the same time the House Appropriations Subcommittee sought to eliminate the VOA, the Congress as a whole debated the president's request for $400 million in economic and military aid for Greece and Turkey. Truman and the State Department hoped that the aid would help the two nations' governing powers quash domestic communist movements and stymie Soviet influence in the Near East. In his address in the Capitol on March 12, 1947, Truman declaimed "[a]t the present moment in world history nearly every nation must choose between alternative ways of life," and "I believe that it must be the policy of the United States to support free peoples who are resisting attempted subjugation by armed minorities or by outside pressures." These statements introduced the containment principle, otherwise known as the Truman Doctrine, as the nation's guiding foreign policy. The president deliberately scared Congress and the public in order to win approval of the aid bill, using ominous if indirect language to suggest that the Soviet Union was inexorably spreading communism across the globe. (Truman never mentioned the Soviet Union and referred only once to "Communists.") The Truman Doctrine established the basis for bipartisan foreign policy—Congress approved the aid by a nearly three-to-one ratio.[4]

---

3. House Subcommittee of the Committee on Appropriations, *State, Justice, Commerce, and the Judiciary Appropriation Bill, Fiscal Year 1948*, 80th Cong., 1st sess., May 5, 1947, 6.

4. At a meeting with a bipartisan group of members of Congress, George Marshall and Dean Acheson phrased the need for the aid in terms of stopping Soviet expansion in the Near East. See John Lewis Gaddis, *The United States and the Origins of the Cold War, 1941–1947*, 348–49. For Truman's speech, see "Special Message to the Congress on Greece and Turkey: The Truman Doctrine," *Public Papers of the Presidents of the United States: Harry S. Truman: 1947*, 176–80. The policy of containment articulated by the Truman Doctrine was actually decided upon in 1946, as administration officials grew increasingly doubtful that cooperation with the Soviet Union was possible. See John Lewis Gaddis, "Was the Truman Doctrine a Real Turning Point?"; Melvyn P. Leffler, "Was 1947 a Turning Point in American Foreign Policy?" On Truman's scare tactics, see Melvyn P. Leffler, *Preponderance of Power: National Security, the Truman Administration, and the Cold War*, 144–46; Gaddis, *The United States and the Origins of the Cold War*, 346–52.

Many Republicans initially expressed suspicion at Truman's request for aid, however, characterizing it as a transparent attempt to deflect Congress's attention away from its domestic priorities. The day after the president's address Representative Clare Hoffman (R–Mich.) admonished his Republican colleagues to concentrate on stopping domestic communism and the New Deal. Describing the aid as an attempt to revive the New Deal through wasteful expenditures, Representative Howard Buffett (R–Nebr.) asked why "leftists" were suddenly champions of anticommunism. Indeed, many conservatives countered Truman's foreboding request with calls for the containment of domestic communism. Paul Shafer observed, "at the time we are being asked, in effect, to declare economic war on Russia in Greece and Turkey, we are allowing . . . 25,000 members of the Communist Party of America—who are, in effect, agents of Russia—to run loose in the United States." During the House Foreign Affairs Committee's hearings on the aid, former Representative Hamilton Fish (R–N.Y.) stated, "[c]ommon sense would seem to dictate that first we stop it [communism] here at home. That means that every Communist, every fellow traveler, be cleared out of our own State Department." Some influential Democrats agreed. Declared Senator Walter George (D–Ga.), a member of the Foreign Relations Committee and key supporter of the aid, "[i]f I am going to pursue the Communists all over Greece and Turkey, I want to get after them here, too."[5]

Concern also arose that the aid to Greece and Turkey might establish a dangerous, limitless precedent. Representative Lawrence Smith (R–Wisc.) quoted Undersecretary of State Dean Acheson's statement that the proposed help was not a war against any ideology. If that was the case, Smith asked Acheson, why did the president refer to free peoples and what cri-

---

5. *Congressional Record*, 80th Cong., 1st sess., March 13 and 17, 1947, vol. 93, 2036, 2215–17, A1073. Fish was respected among Republicans as an expert on domestic communism. While in Congress he chaired a special committee (1930–1931) investigating communist activities in the United States. See Powers, *Not without Honor*, 87–91. Fish's statement is from the House Committee on Foreign Affairs, *Assistance to Greece and Turkey, Hearings before the Committee on Foreign Affairs on H.R. 2616*, 80th Cong., 1st sess., March–April 1947, 196. For concerns about domestic communism, see Senate Committee on Foreign Relations, *The Legislative Origins of the Truman Doctrine, Hearings Held in Executive Session before the Committee on Foreign Relations*, 80th Cong., 1st sess., 1947, 185. The administration was not oblivious to these complaints about domestic subversion. After the 1946 elections Truman ordered work begun on a federal employee loyalty program, which Executive Order 9835 implemented on March 22, 1947, ten days after the Doctrine speech. See David Caute, *The Great Fear: The Anti-Communist Purge under Truman and Eisenhower*, 27, 268–69.

teria would be used to deny or extend aid to them? At the Senate Foreign Relations Committee hearings on the aid, H. Alexander Smith (R–N.J.) queried Acheson if the aid would become a doctrine, guaranteeing help to other nations in similar situations in the future. Acheson said no, later stating that the president was not embarking on an ideological crusade. At the House hearings Representative Walter Judd (R–Minn.) worried that the help for Greece and Turkey would set up "an international WPA."[6] On the Senate floor Charles Brooks (R–Ill.) stated that the aid would start "a chain reaction," dragging the United States into conflicts all over the world. There will be no end to the spending, warned Senator Kenneth Wherry, resulting in the return of wartime price controls. Such concerns led the Senate Foreign Relations Committee to include the following statement in the aid bill: "it is not to be assumed that this Government will be called upon, or will attempt, to furnish to other countries assistance identical with or closely similar to that proposed for Greece and Turkey in the present bill."[7]

Considering the Truman Doctrine's enormous influence on subsequent American foreign policy, these worries about precedent and ideology now appear prescient. At the time they signified concern over Congress's control of foreign policy. The urgency with which the administration pressed for the aid suggested a fait accompli rather than an equitable proposal. Describing opposition to the aid, Brooks said, "[i]t may be that momentarily we are weakening the hand of the President of the United States, but we are strengthening representative government; and we may have to fight for it harder than we ever have fought before in our lives, if a program of this kind goes into effect." Wherry complained that the Truman administration consistently refused "to take the either the U.S. Congress or the American people into its confidence." "[F]ighting communism is only a cloak for the more fundamental and underlying power politics which is being played," warned Representative Robert Rich (R–Pa.), while his House colleague Clare Hoffman claimed that the aid request was practically a declaration of war—a power of Congress. Even Senate Foreign Relations Committee chair Arthur Vandenberg (R–Mich.),

---

6. House Committee on Foreign Affairs, *Assistance to Greece and Turkey*, 43, 153; Senate Committee on Foreign Relations, *Assistance to Greece and Turkey, Hearings before the Committee on Foreign Relations*, 80th Cong., 1st sess., March 1947, 19, 30.

7. *Congressional Record*, 80th Cong., 1st sess., April 16 and 21, 1947, vol. 93, 3467, 3737–45; Senate Committee on Foreign Relations, *Legislative Origins of the Truman Doctrine*, 220–21.

a crucial supporter of the aid, complained that the president delayed consulting members of Congress until a crisis was at hand.[8]

Both the Truman Doctrine and conservatives' worries about legislative prerogative in foreign affairs spilled over into debate on the VOA. Recognizing an opportunity to rescue the VOA, William Benton linked it to the containment principle. The day of Truman's speech, Benton wrote to Acheson that in light of the proposed aid to Greece and Turkey, "[w]e should give high priorities to the development of adequate facilities for the 'Voice of America.'" On April 8, 1947, OIC General Manager William T. Stone submitted plans to Benton on supplementing the information programs with the proposed aid to Greece. Resumption of VOA broadcasts to Greece was proposed along with an increased budget request of $1.1 million for information and cultural activities in Greece and Turkey, and a request for an additional $10 million for programs in France, Hungary, Czechoslovakia, Italy, and the Far East. Writing to Acheson after the House Appropriations Subcommittee issued its report, Benton suggested that efforts to secure the aid to Greece and Turkey also be used to build support for the OIC. The VOA went on the air to Greece in early May, and Benton lined up Senator Vandenberg to deliver the inaugural program.[9]

Benton was not the only government official who connected the VOA to anticommunism abroad. "The VOA program is nothing more or less than the propaganda arm of the Truman Doctrine," said Representative George Bender (R–Ohio). Others made positive links. In March Vandenberg had stated, "[i]f we are now in an ideological contest with the Russians, I think we have to use all of our available ideological resources too, and I do not think we do." At hearings on the aid to Greece and Turkey, Senator Henry Cabot Lodge, Jr. (R–Mass.) declared that the United States needed to also begin an ideological crusade against communism. Shortly after the president's Doctrine speech, Walt Horan said about the VOA, "[i]f we are going to compete with the Russians, I think you are on the right track."[10] For Karl

8. *Congressional Record*, 80th Cong., 1st sess., April 1, 16, and 21, and May 9, 1947, vol. 93, 2993–94, 3469, 3741, 4920; Vandenberg memorandum, March 24, 1947, in *The Private Papers of Senator Arthur Vandenberg*, 342.

9. Benton to Acheson, March 12, 1947, box 4, folder "Undersecretary Acheson 1947," RG 59, Records of the ASPA; Stone to Benton, April 8, 1947, 811.42700/4–1447; Benton to Vandenberg, May 15, 1947, 811.42700(R)/5–1047, RG 59, CDF; Benton to Acheson, April 29, 1947, drawer 24, Lawson File.

10. *Congressional Record*, 80th Cong., 1st sess., June 6, 1947, vol. 93, 6575–76; Senate Committee on Foreign Relations, *Legislative Origins of the Truman Doctrine*, 14, 187; House Appropriations Subcommittee, *Hearings for 1948*, 441.

Mundt, the VOA's potential dual role in serving containment was promising enough to take direct action. On May 6, 1947, Mundt introduced H.R. 3342, a bill providing legal authority for the State Department to distribute overseas publications and films, administer international exchanges of college students and professors, and operate the VOA.

Mundt seemed an unlikely sponsor of such legislation. The five-term Republican from South Dakota began his career as an isolationist and generally voted against New and Fair Deal legislation. Though he had voted for the aid to Greece and Turkey, during debate Mundt had called for the State Department to publish the unexpurgated transcripts of the February 1945 Yalta Conference, declaring that the department was trying to hide evidence that its own officials had aided the Soviet Union.[11] Mundt also believed that domestic communism was a serious and ignored problem. Beginning in 1943 he served on the House Un-American Activities Committee (HUAC). In 1945 he asked one hundred prominent Americans for their definition of "UnAmerican Activities" in order to help direct the committee's investigations. Just before Truman delivered his Doctrine speech, Mundt wrote to a friend that he hoped the president would make it clear that "the program of international communists combined with its American agents in this country and even in positions on our public payroll is a genuine menace."[12] Considering the VOA's reputation among conservatives as a haven for communists and as a prime example of unnecessary government spending, Mundt's effort to save the program is puzzling.

Mundt's bill represented an attempt, however, to establish congressional control over this newly established part of the nation's foreign policy—information about that policy. Mundt agreed with the liberal viewpoint that news and information were important components in the nation's foreign policy. At the same time, he wanted to carefully regulate the formulation and presentation of that information. Responding to criticisms of the VOA, the former college speech instructor declared on the House floor, "[c]olleagues, if the VOA has had a faulty lisp at times or a foreign accent, let us not cut the throat of the VOA to correct either its diction or direction. Let us rather guide it by Congressional mandate and supervision to make certain it develops the sturdy American twang which we all desire it to demonstrate."[13] Accordingly, H.R. 3342 contained provisions for security of

11. House Committee on Foreign Affairs, *Assistance to Greece and Turkey,* 33.

12. Memorandum, January 20, 1945, box 678, folder 3; Mundt to Henry Schmitt, March 10, 1947, box 681, folder 3, Mundt Papers.

13. *Congressional Record,* 80th Cong. 1st sess., May 14 and June 23, 1947, vol. 93, 5286, A3071–75.

personnel and guarantees of noninterference with private media. The act required each current and prospective employee to receive a background check by the FBI determining that "such individual is loyal to the United States and such employment or assignment is consistent with the security of the United States." With regard to private media, the act prohibited monopoly by the State Department of international shortwave radio broadcasts or any other medium.[14] Both stipulations sought to strip away or at least reduce the VOA's liberal features. The FBI, one of the few executive agencies that conservatives trusted, was to serve as a gatekeeper, screening out potentially subversive applicants and employees. By prohibiting a government monopoly in broadcasting, the Mundt bill tried to reconcile conservative opposition to government-sponsored media with liberal advocacy of an international information program. In effect, the bill set limits within the corporatist notion of government and business partnership. Although Benton had continually declared that the VOA did not interfere with private media, the 1946 clashes with the AP, UP, and the WWBF had seemed to indicate otherwise, and the Mundt bill sought to prevent such interference.

The House Foreign Affairs Committee held hearings on Mundt's bill between May 13–20; at the same time the Appropriations Subcommittee's liquidation of the VOA's budget was debated. Without operating funds for the VOA, passage of H.R. 3342 mattered little. Appearing on an NBC broadcast forum about the VOA, House Appropriations Committee Chair John Taber criticized Benton and stated that private broadcasters could do a more efficient and effective job than the VOA. Though Taber later gave the Foreign Affairs Committee cautious approval of a reduced VOA that contracted services with private broadcasters, he indicated that the Appropriations Committee would still withhold the VOA's funds until enabling legislation was actually passed.[15]

In order to secure passage of the Mundt bill and restore appropriations, State Department officials strengthened the connections between the VOA and the burgeoning containment policy. Walter Bedell Smith told the House Foreign Affairs Committee that the United States needed to explain democracy to Europeans who were now groping toward it. In a letter to

14. *United States Information and Educational Exchange Act of 1947*, in House Committee on Foreign Affairs, *Hearings on H.R. 3342*, 80th Cong., 1st sess., 3–4, 6, 8.

15. "Taber Expresses Partial Approval of U.S. Broadcasts," New York Times, May 18, 1947.

Congress, Secretary of State Marshall wrote, "I consider American security to rest not only on our economic and political and military strength, but also on the strength of American ideas—on how well they are presented abroad." Congressional supporters of the VOA contributed to this justification. On the House floor Representative Robert L. F. Sikes (D–Fla.) said that information activities provided necessary explanations of why the United States was providing aid to Greece and Turkey. Referring to that aid, Mundt stated that it should be accompanied by "revitalization of an American information program abroad."[16]

The VOA's potential in aiding containment provided a raison d'etre, but another possible connection provided reason to liquidate the program: was the VOA the voice of liberalism? A radio program about Henry A. Wallace seemed to show conservatives that it was. Twice in April 1947 the VOA broadcast to Austria and Germany a review of Russell Lord's book *The Wallaces of Iowa*. Senator Walter George accused the broadcast of being "laudatory" toward the former vice president, who was a vigorous proponent of conciliation with the Soviet Union and a sharp critic of the Truman Doctrine. Taber used the incident to justify the liquidation of the VOA's budget, and on April 30 the State Department barred rebroadcast of the review over any VOA desk. The review did describe in detail Lord's praise for the Wallaces' contribution to American agriculture; however, the review said very little about Henry Wallace's political activities, even observing that this was "perhaps the least interesting part of the book." Moreover, VOA commentary broadcast to Germany on the same day as the Wallace review criticized harshly Wallace's opposition to the aid package for Greece and Turkey, emphasizing that Wallace did not speak for the majority of the American people. This criticism and the review's distinction between agriculture and statesmanship received little press coverage, though. And as Representative Clarence Kilburn (R–N.Y.) pointed out, the simultaneous broadcast of the Lord review and the commentary meant that the VOA appeared to be praising Wallace at the same time it criticized him.[17]

16. House Committee on Foreign Affairs, *Hearings on H.R. 3342*, 46; *Congressional Record*, 80th Cong., 1st sess., May 6 and June 20, 1947, vol. 93, 4316, 4638, 7515.

17. Translation, Ruby Parson to Benton et al., April 25, 1947; MacKnight to Benton, April 25, 1947, box 125, folder "Wallace Story," RG 59, RIIA; "Senate Is Told U.S. Broadcast Lauds Wallace," *New York Herald Tribune*, April 26, 1947; State Department to Vienna, April 30, 1947, 811.42700(R)/4–3047, RG 59, CDF; Jesse MacKnight to William Benton, April 27, 1947, box 375, folder 4, Benton Papers. Kilburn's observation was reported by John Howe to Oliver McKee, April 27, 1947, box 80, folder "Congressional—General," RG 59, RIIA.

Conservatives continued to question whether or not the State Department and VOA could be impartial, that is, not promote liberalism. The VOA needed to "reflect the best attitudes of all our people, acting through their regularly elected Representatives," said Walt Horan on May 13, 1947. Representative Fred Busbey (R–Ill.) accused OIC General Manager William T. Stone of being a communist because of his previous affiliation with the journal *Amerasia,* while Representative Arthur Miller (R–Nebr.) stated that the nation did not need the "voice of radical left-wingers." Calling for an immediate end to the VOA, John Taber read excerpts from broadcasts he found objectionable for either portraying favorably Truman and organized labor or else for discussing art and literature, and he indicated that he did not believe H.R. 3342's security provision could prevent broadcasters from airing their opinions and biases over the VOA. Representative Walter Judd expressed concern that scriptwriters would misrepresent the policies handed down to them and accused the VOA of having a liberal bias for broadcasting commentary by Raymond Swing that was critical of the Taft-Hartley bill, thus revealing "the voice of the Democratic administration." In reference to Judd's and other Republicans' criticisms, Mundt said the main concern of his colleagues' opposition seemed to be "the product which is being turned out and the personnel who are in charge of the program." Mundt himself fell into this group. On May 31, 1947, he wrote to Benton that three employees of the VOA's Indonesian desk "are highly UnAmerican [*sic*] in their activities and comments, *at least when they are not working on their jobs . . .*" (emphasis added). Mundt asked Benton to investigate the individuals; he also told Benton that he was having HUAC's chief investigator Robert Stripling conduct background checks.[18]

Worries about political slant carried over to the State Department's domestic information activities. The House Committee on Expenditures in the Executive Departments seemed determined to show that the State Department was violating a law prohibiting the use of federal funds to influence congressional votes. The day after the Truman Doctrine speech, members of the Subcommittee on the State Department questioned two

18. *Congressional Record,* 80th Cong., 1st sess., May 13–14 and June 6, 1947, vol. 93, 5205, 5217, 5296–300, 6577; "3 Officials Call U.S. Radio Voice Vital to Policy," *New York Herald Tribune,* May 14, 1947; House Foreign Affairs Committee, *Hearings on H.R. 3342,* 71–76, 92, 185–86. Judd was wrong; the VOA did not carry the Swing broadcast. For Mundt's suspicions, see Mundt to Benton, May 31, 1947, box 68, folder "Benton, January 1951," RG 59, RIIA.

State Department officials at length about whether or not the department promoted its views and policies to the American public. According to the officials' record of the meeting, "[i]t was apparent that the Committee was fishing around for openings and that it does not yet have a definite plan of attack." The next month subcommittee chair J. Edgar Chenowith (R–Colo.) pointedly asked Benton "[t]o what extent [are] appropriations of the State Department being used to propagandize the American people on certain controversial issues on which the Congress will eventually have to decide?" And in May the *Washington Times-Herald* published a confidential department memorandum telling staff members about a meeting being held by former OWI employees now working in radio and publishing. In Benton's opinion, the conservative newspaper was trying to show that the State Department was lobbying for help in persuading Congress to restore appropriations.[19]

Concerns about liberal bias within the VOA and State Department did not prevent the Foreign Affairs Committee from favorably reporting Mundt's bill in late May, and floor debate on H.R. 3342 opened on June 6, 1947. Also during June, the Senate Appropriations Committee began reviewing the House's budget report. With its 1948 appropriations and the third attempt to pass enabling legislation hanging in the balance, the VOA faced its most crucial test yet. In the House, H.R. 3342 met fierce resistance from Republicans and conservative Democrats who opposed its teacher and student exchange program. These legislators echoed the concerns about the VOA casting itself as the voice of liberalism and the New Deal. Clare Hoffman declared that the bill would let teachers of communism into the United States at a time when Republicans needed to end the spending of millions of dollars on foreign governments, New Dealers, and left-wingers. Representative John Rankin (D–Miss.) stated that the exchange would channel communists into American colleges where they would "poison the minds of the students of this nation." Representatives Howard Buffett, Fred Busbey, Noah Mason (R–Ill.), and Arthur Miller joined Hoffman and Rankin in denouncing the bill, and the group deployed a variety of measures to prevent a vote. On the first day of debate Hoffman introduced a resolution to kill the bill, which the

19. Charles Hulten and Jack Peurifoy, March 13, 1947, 811.42700(R)/6–1747, RG 59, CDF; Transcript, vol. 1, Hearings of the Subcommittee of the Committee on Expenditures in the Executive Department, April 22, 1947, box 475, folder "HR80A F6.8," RG 233, file HR80A-F6.7, National Archives, Washington, D.C., 53; Benton to Marshall, May 27, 1947, box 4, folder "Secretary Byrnes," RG 59, Records of the ASPA.

House rejected by voice vote. Using repeated points of no quorum, adjournment calls, and motions to strike the enacting clause of the bill, the opposition delayed action on H.R. 3342 until June 24, 1947.[20]

During this delay, amendments were introduced that buttressed congressional oversight and security measures. Representatives Richard Simpson (R–Pa.) and Clarence Brown (R–Ohio) drafted a provision worked into the final bill that required the VOA to provide members of Congress with English translations of scripts upon request. Representative Everett Dirksen (R–Ill.) proposed an Advisory Commission for the information programs. To be composed of leaders from the press and broadcasting industries, the commission was to issue quarterly reports to Congress on the program and to advise it on appropriations and policy decisions. Both amendments were prompted by concerns that the administration rather than the legislators would have preponderant influence and control over the VOA and related programs. For the same reason, a clause was written into the bill giving Congress the right to terminate for any reason the programs authorized by H.R. 3342. In order to assuage concerns about security, an additional safeguard was written into the bill by the Foreign Affairs Committee. Section 701 limited the employment of aliens to "the translation or narration of colloquial speech in foreign languages *when suitably qualified United States citizens are not available*" [emphasis added]. Mundt lobbied intensely during June to persuade critics that the program would be cleaned up and that the FBI checks would be sufficient; many legislators distrusted William Benton's administration of the OIC and suspected him of failing to rid his personnel ranks of New Deal partisans. "Neither Assistant Secretary of State Benton nor any of his associates or employees are continued in authority by the passage of H.R. 3342," Mundt assured his colleagues. Mundt also reiterated that the bill's security provision would ensure "that no Communists, or parlor pinks, or crypto-communists, or fellow travellers will have any part in this program in any way, shape, or form."[21]

On June 24, 1947, H.R. 3342 finally came up for a vote after a motion to recommit was defeated. The bill passed by a voice vote of 272 to 97, with

20. *Congressional Record,* 80th Cong., 1st sess., June 6, 1947, vol. 93, 6566; "Mundt Bill Gains in House Test," *New York Times,* June 7, 1947; "'Voice of America' Bill Is Delayed by Tactics of House Opponents," *Washington Star,* June 7, 1947; Memorandum, "Congressional Debate on Mundt Bill, June 9–10, 1947," Jesse MacKnight to William Benton, June 11, 1947, box 78, folder "Smith-Mundt," RG 59, RIIA; *Congressional Quarterly,* vol. 3, 267–68.

21. *Congressional Record,* 80th Cong., 1st sess., May 14 and June 23, 1947, vol. 93, 5296–300, A3073.

152 Democrats and 120 Republicans voting yes. Ninety Republicans voted against, joined by seven Southern Democrats. According to Mundt, the bill's amendment allowing members of Congress to review scripts helped win many of the needed votes.[22] That same day the Senate Appropriations Subcommittee on the State Department granted $11.5 million for continuation of the information and cultural programs. The decision followed vigorous lobbying by both Benton and Mundt, as well as personal appeals by Secretary of State George Marshall and President Truman. However, subcommittee chair Joseph Ball (R–Minn.) stipulated that two-thirds of the funds slated for the VOA were to be used to pay private broadcasters to write and air VOA broadcasts. Ball insisted that NBC and CBS did a better, cheaper job than did the State Department. The subcommittee also required the VOA to drastically cut its staff and end plans to build two relay stations designed to improve reception in Eastern Europe and the Far East.[23]

The House's passage of H.R. 3342 and the Senate's restoration of the VOA's funds marked both a victory and a setback for the VOA. The agency was on the air for another year at least, and if the Senate as a whole passed the Mundt bill, it would have long-term legitimacy. However, the price paid in terms of the VOA's autonomy was high. Because of the Senate's stipulation that NBC and CBS produce the majority of programming, the VOA and the State Department had little control over what went over the air while remaining responsible for every word uttered in the name of the U.S. government.[24] Stringent security checks were required, and the use of aliens was curtailed. Script review, the Advisory Commission, and the termination clause gave Congress and individual members oversight over the program. Added to Congress's standing power of appropriations, these measures gave legislators considerable power and influence.

22. As reported by Howland Sargeant to Benton, June 13, 1947, box 86, folder "Old Correspondence," RG 59, RIIA.

23. Senate Subcommittee of the Committee on Appropriations, *Departments of State, Justice, Commerce, and the Judiciary, Hearings before the Subcommittee of the Committee on Appropriations for 1948*, 80th Cong., 1st sess., June 24, 1947, 3; Memorandum of conversation, Charles Bohlen and Joseph Ball, June 18, 1947, 811.42700(R)/6–1847, RG 59, CDF; "'Voice of U.S.' Radio Program Voted by House," *New York Times*, June 25, 1947.

24. Charles Bohlen noted this liability in a memorandum to Robert Lovett and Dean Acheson, June 19, 1947, 811.42700(R)/6–1947, RG 59, CDF.

II. The Smith-Mundt Subcommittee in Europe

A subcommittee of the Senate Foreign Relations Committee opened hearings on the Mundt bill in July. Chaired by bill co-sponsor H. Alexander Smith (R–N.J.) and Carl Hatch (D–N.M.), the subcommittee listened as supportive letters from Dwight D. Eisenhower and several U.S. ambassadors were read aloud. Appearing before the subcommittee, Karl Mundt detailed the extensive oversight his bill granted Congress; by his count, there were twenty-five separate controls. Already predisposed to the bill, the subcommittee reported it favorably on July 16. Added to the draft was a section authorizing a study of the overseas program by a joint congressional committee. The investigation was Hatch's idea, which he had already proposed in April 1947 as S.R. 16. Aimed at easing the concerns of the OIC's opponents, the study was to determine the qualifications of personnel, justifiable costs, and which information and cultural activities should be carried out by the State Department. Rather than help secure the Smith-Mundt bill's passage, Hatch's proposal impeded efforts. As the Eightieth Congress's first session moved toward recess, Hatch struggled to bring the bill to the Senate floor. Republicans Kenneth Wherry (Nebr.), Bourke B. Hickenlooper (Iowa), and Leverett Saltonstall (Mass.) stymied him by making points of order and continually asking Hatch to yield the floor. Robert Taft (R–Ohio) argued that it was illogical to simultaneously grant the OIC programs permanent status and to authorize an investigation of them. Taft proposed placing the bill on the next session's calendar in order to carry out the proposed investigation. Despite long debate with the Republican Senate leader, Hatch failed to change Taft's mind. The Smith-Mundt bill was not put on the calendar before adjournment.[25]

During August Smith and Mundt organized a subcommittee of representatives and senators to investigate the OIC programs. All were members of either the House Foreign Affairs Committee or the Senate Foreign Relations Committee. Joining Smith from the Senate were Hatch, Alben W. Barkley (D–Ky.), and Bourke B. Hickenlooper. From the House came Republicans Lawrence Smith (Wisc.), John Davis Lodge (Conn.), and

25. Senate Subcommittee of the Foreign Relations Committee, *Hearings on H.R. 3342*, 80th Cong., 1st sess., July 1947, 15–16; Senate Concurrent Resolution 16, 80th Cong., 1st sess., April 21, 1947; *Congressional Record*, 80th Cong., 1st sess., July 25, 1947, vol. 93, 10129–31; *Congressional Quarterly*, vol. 3, 449. In April 1947 Taft had given William Benton the impression that he supported passage of enabling legislation. Benton to Oliver McKee, April 18, 1947, box 13, folder "T Jan–Sept 1947," RG 59, Records of the ASPA.

Walter Judd. House Democrats were Pete Jarman (Ala.), Mike Mansfield (Mont.), and Thomas Gordon (Ill.). Most members of the subcommittee were already supporters of the VOA and the other programs. All of the House members except Lawrence Smith had voted for Mundt's bill on June 24, 1947, and of the Senate contingent, only Hickenlooper remained unconvinced of the need for the VOA.

The Smith-Mundt group left Washington for London on September 5, 1947. Three members—H. Alexander Smith, Lawrence Smith, and John Davis Lodge—traveled separately, joining their colleagues later in the month. The itinerary was challenging; the group visited twenty-two countries in five weeks. After Britain, the subcommittee traveled across central Europe, visited the Scandinavian countries, made stops in Czechoslovakia, Poland, Bulgaria, and Romania, then concluded their travels in the Near East and Mediterranean. The stated purpose of the trip was as ambitious as the schedule. In addition to studying the effectiveness of the information service, the group intended to survey "necessity for the Marshall Plan; education and labor; displaced persons problems."[26] The Marshall Plan, outlined by the Secretary of State in a speech on June 5, 1947, proposed a massive program of American aid to help rebuild Europe. Though justified on humanitarian grounds, the plan also aimed at curtailing communist influence in Western Europe. Marshall warned that unless the United States provided help, serious social, economic, and political problems were sure to ensue in Europe.

State Department personnel in the United States Information Service (USIS) went all out to impress the subcommittee. (The USIS comprised the field offices of the OIC. Attached to the American embassy, the USIS centers maintained libraries, distributed releases to the local press, gave out VOA schedules and monitored its reception, and arranged lectures and cultural events.) William Benton had even considered conducting an advance check of the USIS centers, but he rejected the plan out of concern that the congressional group would find out. Before leaving the United States, Smith and Mundt had written a questionnaire for the subcommittee to help determine the effectiveness of the USIS programs. The paper asked for evidence of misunderstanding about the United States, comparison with the information programs of other nations, and what steps were needed to strengthen the USIS, among other points. Before the group arrived at

26. Smith-Mundt subcommittee itinerary, August 27, 1947, box 470, folder 3, Mundt Papers.

an embassy, detailed answers to the questionnaire had often already been prepared. For example, USIS employees at The Hague emphasized in their report the common misperceptions about the United States in the Netherlands and detailed the information programs of France, Britain, and the Soviet Union. The report urged immediate passage of the Smith-Mundt bill and the granting of sufficient appropriations.[27]

The USIS in Romania greeted the Smith-Mundt group with an eighty-eight-page report addressing the questionnaire, including a section detailing the effects of budget cuts. During a briefing the Chief of Mission for the United States told the subcommittee, "[u]nless we devise some special technique, we are in grave danger of being forgotten in this country. Knowledge of the United States is being systematically blotted out." In Turkey, the USIS described Radio Moscow's attacks on the American aid program and the proposed Marshall Plan, reminding the subcommittee that the VOA did not broadcast to that area.[28] The reference to the Marshall Plan is significant. Although the subcommittee had given itself the goal of surveying the need for the plan, it had not included questions about it on its questionnaire. Nevertheless, ambassadors, USIS personnel, and officials of the nations visited sought to show the congressmen and senators the pressing need for the Marshall Plan. They also described the usefulness of the information programs in telling affected populations about the plan and the motives of the United States. In short, the State Department positioned the USIS to sell the Marshall Plan to eleven members of the Foreign Affairs and Foreign Relations Committees. The tactic worked.

In Paris Ambassador Caffrey warned the subcommittee members that France was crucial to keeping Western Europe free. The French Communists were well organized, Caffrey said, and without help, France would run out of bread and coal by December 1947. The Chief of the American Mission in Greece, Dwight Griswold, was more direct than Caffrey. If funds for the Greek army were not continued after July 1948, "the country will become Communistic," Griswold told the subcommittee. The ambassador to Italy made the same prediction about his host nation,

27. Benton to Luther Reed, July 29, 1947; "Study of United States Foreign Information Service," box 121, folder "Smith-Mundt Investigating Committee," RG 59, RIIA; "Memorandum Answering Questions Posed by the Smith-Mundt Committee," box 468, folder 8, Mundt Papers.

28. "Transcript of the Discussion of the Smith-Mundt Congressional Committee with the Legation Staff," September 28, 1947, box 473, folder 7; "OIE Operations in Turkey," box 471, folder 3, Mundt Papers.

telling Congressman Mike Mansfield that without U.S. aid, communists would take control of the Italian government. Members of the subcommittee also raised the issue of takeover, asking Belgian and Dutch government officials if their countries could resist communism if France or Italy became communist. Prince Charles, the Regent of Belgium, said that U.S. aid would be needed.[29]

In order to link the USIS to the Marshall Plan, State Department officials emphasized two related points to the subcommittee: Europeans misunderstood American motives behind the aid plan, and the Soviets were maligning the United States. The USIS in Norway told the Smith-Mundt group that Norwegians believed the United States was materialistic, devoid of culture, and that the Marshall Plan was designed to stop an impending economic depression in the United States. During a conference with the subcommittee, Norwegian press representatives reiterated this last point and suggested that the U.S government deliver more news service to Norway, including radio broadcasts. The head of Information Control in Germany told the subcommittee that Russian propaganda was active and vigorously anti-American, adding that the VOA was popular in Germany. Discussing Soviet motives in Germany and the rest of Europe, the First Secretary of the American Embassy in Moscow, Fred Reinhardt, warned that traditional Russian imperialism had combined with the Marxist impetus to spread revolution. The United States needed to enact the Marshall Plan, prepare to meet the Soviets militarily, and strengthen the USIS, Reinhardt told the subcommittee.[30]

Members of the subcommittee returned to the States thoroughly convinced of the need for both the Marshall Plan and the information and cultural programs. In a letter to New York Governor Thomas Dewey, Senator Bourke Hickenlooper wrote that the proposed Marshall Plan had stimulated hope among Europeans and could encourage intra-European

29. "Summary of Conferences and Meetings, Joint Senate-House Foreign Affairs Subcommittee, Paris, France," September 9, 1947, box 468, folder 6; "Meeting of American Mission for Aid to Greece and Congressional Delegation," October 3, 1947, box 472, folder 4; Transcript, "Visit by Smith-Mundt Group to Italy," October 6, 1947, box 476, vol. 3, 13; "Visit by Smith-Mundt Group to Belgium," September 13, 1947, 5; "Visit by Smith-Mundt Group to Holland," September 14, 1947, box 476, vol. 1, Mundt Papers, 10.

30. Appendix II, "Information Concerning Norway," box 468, folder 7, Mundt Papers; Transcript, "Visit by Smith-Mundt Group to Norway," September 17, 1947, box 476, vol. 1, 13–14; Transcript, "Visit by Smith-Mundt Group to Germany," September 22, 1947, box 476, vol. 2, Mundt Papers, 38–39, 72–74.

economic cooperation. In a November speech to radio news editors in New York, Hickenlooper declared his support for the information programs and urged their expansion.[31] Also in November, Senator H. Alexander Smith met with officials from the Office of International Information (OII) to discuss action on the Smith-Mundt bill. (In fall 1947 the OIC was reorganized as the Office of International Information and Educational Exchange. The VOA was administered by the OII, which was a branch of this new office.) The New Jersey Republican indicated he was satisfied that the OII needed expansion and strengthening. Based on his travels, he considered the VOA an essential news source in Eastern Europe. Smith also said that the Senate members of the subcommittee wanted to bring the enabling bill to a vote as soon as possible and secure supplemental appropriations. Department officials suggested placing the OII's supplemental request into the Marshall Plan budget; Smith "thought the latter idea should be canvassed fully."[32]

The subcommittee's report on its trip demonstrated the connection made between the OII programs, especially the VOA, and the Marshall Plan. An outline for the report dwelled on the political uncertainty and the widespread economic disorganization that the subcommittee observed across Europe.[33] Issued January 30, 1948, the final report to the Senate made much of the stereotypes about the United States held by Europeans, and it described bitterly the motives behind Soviet information services: "[i]t cannot be emphasized too strongly that the Soviets and the Communists are today conducting aggressive psychological warfare against us in order thoroughly to discredit us and drive us out of Europe." To listen to the Soviets, the Marshall Plan was a desperate ploy to stave off depression in the United States, a plot to restore German military power, or blatant imperialism. The subcommittee advised that the information and cultural programs should "serve as the necessary corollary to the European recovery plan." In its present state, the USIS was "wholly inadequate," and the sub-

31. Hickenlooper to Dewey, October 22, 1947, box 41, folder "Smith-Mundt Committee October to December 1947"; November 14, 1947, box 9, folder "1947, Nov. 14," Bourke B. Hickenlooper Papers, Herbert Hoover Presidential Library, West Branch, Iowa.

32. Memorandum of meeting, November 13, 1947, box 121, folder "Smith-Mundt Investigating Committee," RG 59, RIIA, 1–2, 4–6; Scott Lucas, *Freedom's War: The American Crusade against the Soviet Union*, 41; Wagnleitner, *Coca-Colonization and the Cold War*, 55–56.

33. "Suggested Outline for Report on Smith-Mundt European Trip," box 476, vol. 1, Mundt Papers.

committee recommended numerous expansions, including initiation of VOA broadcasts for every European nation not yet targeted and increased coverage of the political conditions in each country.[34]

The Smith-Mundt subcommittee's enthusiastic endorsement of the State Department's information and cultural programs in conjunction with the Marshall Plan helped clinch passage of enabling legislation even before the report was printed. During a December 1947 executive session of the Senate's Foreign Relations Committee, Alexander Smith said that Robert Taft was going to put the Smith-Mundt bill on the calendar so that it could be passed in January.[35] When the bill came to the Senate floor, it met none of the protracted debate and opposition that had accompanied the failed attempt to approve the bill in July 1947. On January 16, 1948, the Senate passed the Smith-Mundt bill on a voice vote. The House accepted the Senate version three days later, and on January 27 President Truman signed into effect Public Law 402, *The United States Informational and Educational Exchange Act of 1948.*

The ease with which the VOA's authorization finally became law was deceptive. Considerable suspicions about the information program and personnel remained, even among supporters. Senator Henry Cabot Lodge, Jr., who endorsed the Smith-Mundt subcommittee's report, complained in December 1947 that the VOA "is run by a young man who doesn't know a damn thing about politics . . . I'll bet you that that fellow has no supervision at all." The Senator's brother, Representative John Davis Lodge, had traveled as part of the Smith-Mundt group; he too expressed concerns about personnel. Also in December, Senator Alexander Wiley (R–Wisc.), a member of the Foreign Relations Committee, wrote to Secretary of State Marshall expressing his worry that the OII might disseminate partisan propaganda. During a meeting with OII officials, Karl Mundt discussed finding a new assistant secretary of state for public affairs. Weary of clashes with members of Congress and frustrated with government work, William Benton had resigned in September 1947. Mundt "emphasized the fact that it was very important that there be a successor for Mr. Benton who would be acceptable to members of Congress." Otherwise, passage of the enabling

34. Senate Committee on Foreign Relations, *The United States Information Service in Europe,* 80th Cong., 2d sess., January 30, 1948, S.R. 855, 4–6, 11.

35. Transcript, Senate Committee on Foreign Relations Executive Session, December 18, 1947, box 2, folder 1, RG 46, Harry S. Truman Presidential Library, Independence, Mo., 51-52.

bill was jeopardized.[36] Such an "acceptable" person was U.S. Ambassador to Iran George V. Allen, who took over as assistant secretary of state for public affairs in 1948. Allen, who had begun his diplomatic career as a Foreign Service officer, had also worked as a journalist.

These concerns posed a challenge to the VOA that grew in the upcoming months and years. At last convinced that the U.S. government did, in fact, have good reasons to operate an international information service, conservatives continued to express doubts about how information was disseminated abroad, specifically, the ability and even desire of VOA officials to treat fully and objectively domestic political affairs. Herein lay the VOA's dilemma; it had two distinct audiences, each with different needs and expectations. In practical, workaday terms, informing foreign peoples about the United States and its policies generally meant presenting the U.S. government as a singular entity. In its news the VOA identified specific government officials, of course, and the agencies or branches that they represented, but the net intent and effect was to show government units acting in unison. Emphasis was placed on the international aspects of U.S. policies rather than on the details of their domestic origins. Telling foreign audiences about U.S. policies and their possible effects abroad was, after all, one of the tasks that the newly passed Smith-Mundt Act gave to the VOA. In laying out this task, however, the act also stipulated that the information disseminated abroad describe the actions of specific government agents such as Congress.[37] This instruction then defined the expectations of individual Republican members of Congress. As both participants in the policy-making processes and members of the opposition party, these legislators wanted to know whether or not the VOA was presenting a "full and fair" account of the dissent, brokering, and compromises between the Democratic administration and Republicans in Congress that ultimately produced U.S. policy—the very activities that involved and interested them. Because of the widespread impression that liberal partisans sat behind State Department policy desks and VOA microphones, Republicans were not so much concerned with the professional qualifica-

36. Ibid., December 16, 1947, 16; William Tyler to William Benton, November 7, 1947, box 7, folder "Congressional Misc.," RG 59, Records of the ASPA; Wiley to Marshall, December 10, 1947, in *Congressional Record,* 80th Cong., 1st sess., December 16, 1947, vol. 93, 11434–35; memorandum of conversation, October 14, 1947, box 117, folder "Special Material for Smith-Mundt Committees," RG 59, RIIA, 6.

37. *United States Information and Educational Exchange Act of 1948,* Public Law 402, 80th Cong., 2d sess. (January 27, 1948), 6.

tions of VOA employees, but rather with their personal political beliefs. Thus Lodge complained that the VOA chief knew nothing about politics, Mundt warned that the new assistant secretary of state for public affairs had better be acceptable to Congress, and Smith worried that the information programs would favor the Democrats in their respective programs. The solipsistic side of American political culture vis-à-vis foreign affairs revealed itself in such concerns: instructed to tell the world about America, State and VOA officials increasingly found their time and efforts directed toward telling members of Congress what the VOA told the world, or did not tell the world, about their political activities.

Chapter 3

Struggles over VOA Content, 1947–1949

The passage of the Smith-Mundt Act in January 1948 granted legislative standing to the VOA, but it did not establish clear guidelines for either the content or control of its programming. Two points proved troublesome. First, the act's mandate was overly broad, authorizing the dissemination of "information about the United States, its peoples, and policies promulgated by the Congress, the President, and the Secretary of State and other responsible officials of Government having to do with matters affecting foreign affairs."[1] It was impossible to report all the news that fit this list, yet each omitted or included news item was potentially damaging. Conservatives in Congress already suspected the VOA of slanting its broadcasts to the left—now, using the script review provision in the Smith-Mundt Act, they could look over VOA scripts in search of bias. Second, the act required the use of private media whenever possible, a stipulation anticipated in June 1947 by the Senate Appropriations Subcommittee, which set aside two-thirds of the VOA's budget to pay private broadcasters to produce scripts. With the majority of VOA programming in the hands of networks such as NBC and CBS, State Department officials struggled to maintain control of what was said on the air in the name of the U.S. government. They also wanted to refute Soviet propaganda about the United States, a move that seemed infeasible as long as the VOA did not produce its own programming. These problems drew NBC, CBS, members of Congress, and the State Department into numerous struggles between 1947 and 1949 to define and control VOA broadcasts.

1. *United States Information and Educational Exchange Act of 1948,* Public Law 402, 80th Cong., 2d sess. (January 27, 1948), 6.

I. Abandoning the Full and Fair Approach

Throughout 1947 information policy officials considered various methods of refuting attacks on the United States made by Soviet information services. A VOA programming evaluation officer had posed the challenge in March 1946: in order to avoid psychological warfare, the VOA needed to counter Soviet propaganda by presenting the American position in positive ways. Such advice reflected the prevailing "full and fair" approach in which the VOA ignored other nations' information activities and concentrated on providing factual, balanced news. The "full and fair" approach assumed that audiences would recognize the difference between facts and propaganda, that they would know whether or not they were being informed, influenced, or misled, thus making direct responses to other nations' claims unnecessary. During a planning session for VOA broadcasts to the Soviet Union the Secretary's Staff Committee noted that the Soviet people wanted accurate information about the United States; therefore, the broadcasts should contain straightforward, objective news and full texts of important statements on U.S. policy. Department officials also worried that rebuttals of propaganda might reduce the credibility of VOA programming and alienate audiences. "[W]e should avoid anything that will be construed as criticism of the Soviet government and its institutions or which will be received as anti-Soviet propaganda," stated guidance notes for the first broadcasts to the Soviet Union.[2]

At the same time State Department and VOA officials renewed commitment to the principle of "full and fair," Soviet information activities disturbed and frustrated them, leading to doubts about the approach's effectiveness. After telling Secretary of State Byrnes in February 1946 that the Soviet Union was aggressively expanding its international shortwave broadcasts, William Benton complained, "[t]o the Russians, propaganda is in fact 'psychological warfare' all the time, not merely during war." One month later OIC Director William T. Stone indicated that he wanted to redefine the general radio policy, which at the time banned VOA responses to attacks on the United States made by other governments.

---

2. Victor Hunt to William Stone, March 7, 1946, box 123, folder "Russia," RG 59, RIIA; Report of the Secretary's Staff Committee, "Project for Information Broadcasts in Russian to the Soviet Union," May 23, 1946, box 8, folder "German Radio 1946," RG 59, Records of the ASPA; "General Policy Considerations for Initial Russian Broadcasts," November 1946, box 5, folder "Voice of America," Charles W. Thayer Papers, Alphabetical Correspondence File, Truman Library, 1.

The U.S. Embassy in the Soviet Union advised in September 1946 that VOA broadcasts to the area needed to begin as soon as possible, with the goal of having the "greatest psychological influence on Soviet current thinking." Just before the broadcasts began on February 17, 1947, the State Department's Division of Research summarized foreign characterizations of the United States that emphasized industrial strife, racial conflict, and a relentless drive for world domination. The study concluded that the presence of negative images in countries bordering the Soviet Union increased in relation to the amount of Soviet control of those nations' affairs.[3]

In March 1947 William Benton suggested to Secretary Marshall and Ambassador to the Soviet Union Walter Bedell Smith that the strategy of simply explaining U.S. policy was not as effective as had been hoped. Benton suggested the use of direct rebuttals of Soviet propaganda, a move Marshall rejected. "Our sole aim in our overseas information program must be to present nothing but the truth, in a completely factual and unbiased manner," Marshall wrote Benton. Bedell Smith agreed with Benton, however, and urged Marshall to approve a harder line for the VOA. Shortly after the VOA began broadcasting to the Soviet Union, Bedell Smith cabled Marshall that the VOA was struggling to show that the United States was "highly-cultured" rather than neutralizing Soviet propaganda. In June the embassy warned that the Soviets deployed effectively the use of repeated half-truths and lies in order to malign the United States. This telegram prompted policy officials to seek a compromise. While reaffirmation of U.S. policy remained the guiding line, indirect refutation was encouraged. Rather than denying Soviet charges that domestic economic instability forced American imperialism, for example, the economic strength and stability of the United States was to be emphasized. In order to reject Soviet claims that monopolies controlled the U.S. economy, the VOA broadcast a piece on small-town banks and planned programming on antitrust laws.[4]

3. Benton to Byrnes, February 6, 1946, 811.42700(R)/2–646, RG 59, CDF; minutes of OIC staff meeting, March 11, 1946, box 119, first unmarked black binder, RG 59, RIIA; Moscow to Secretary of State, September 18, 1946, box 375, folder 3, Benton Papers; "Stereotyped Concepts about the United States Presented in Selected Foreign Countries," February 5, 1947, box 9, folder "1947–Stereotyped Concepts," Charles M. Hulten Papers, Voice of America File, Truman Library, iv, viii.

4. Benton to Marshall, March 7, 1947; Marshall to Benton, April 15, 1947; Moscow to Secretary of State, June 10, 1947, box 123, folder "Russia," RG 59, RIIA; Moscow to Secretary of State, March 1, 1947, 811.42700(R)/3–147, RG 59, CDF. Beginning in early

Given these tensions, it is not surprising that policy writers had difficulties formulating clear, precise aims for the VOA. Rejecting the current objectives as vague, Program Officer Victor Hunt offered these revisions in July 1946: develop overseas a complete understanding of U.S. life, explain that the United States desired freedom for all peoples, and declare American willingness for cultural cooperation. Six months later Hunt offered further revisions after bluntly stating that the Soviet Union had declared psychological war on the United States. Now needed were objectives that "take into account the facts of international life as they exist today," including emphasis on American military and economic strength, the nation's belief in democracy and social equality, and its commitment to international cooperation. Hunt was rephrasing rather than revising, a problem recognized in April 1947. Policy writers had worked for more than a year to define objectives, William Tyler wrote to William Stone, yet the results were "inconclusive and theoretical." "Yes," Stone penciled in the margin. Noting the current inability to counter attacks on the United States, Tyler proposed having the overseas libraries, films, and cultural exchanges continue the full and fair approach, while using radio and press to rebut anti-American propaganda through reiteration of policy aims and principles. Still, frustrations continued to mount. An official complained in December, "Nobody knows what propaganda is; nobody knows what cultural interchange is; nobody knows what effect information (either objective or highly colored) has on people—and this in spite of many surveys both academic and profane."[5]

Apparent in this discussion of program objectives was a belief that dedication to the facts and objectivity kept one's hands clean of propaganda, although some observers at the time recognized objectivity's slippery and elusive nature. When Undersecretary of State Dean Acheson

---

1947, direct attacks on the VOA constituted an important aspect of both Soviet domestic and foreign propaganda. See Alex Inkeles, "The Soviet Attack on the Voice of America: A Case Study in Propaganda Warfare"; Inkeles, "The Soviet Characterization of the Voice of America." For the policy compromise, see "OIC Policy with Respect to the Soviet Anti-American Propaganda Campaign," July 25, 1947, box 5, folder "Voice of America," Thayer Papers, Alphabetical Correspondence File; box 1, folder "General correspondence 1947"; Howland Sargeant to Robert Terrill, November 13, 1947, box 1, RG 59, Records of the ASPA.

5. Victor Hunt, July 11, 1946, and January 10, 1947, box 3, folder "PEB–Victor Hunt 1946"; Sax Bradford to Howland Sargeant, December 1, 1947, box 10, folder "Wm. Stone," RG 59, Records of the ASPA; Tyler to Stone, April 22, 1947, box 121, folder "Radio Advisory Committee on International Broadcasting," RG 59, RIIA.

defined information as "facts," Representative John Davis Lodge (R–Conn.) suggested that the very selection of facts could result in distortion.[6] For the most part, though, VOA policy officers believed that the full and fair approach was attainable. At the same time, they recognized its limitations in refuting Soviet descriptions of the United States. Government-sponsored truth about America was possible, but it alone could not refute the lies told abroad by the Soviet Union. An added approach was needed—directed truth, that is, factual rebuttals of Soviet (mis)characterizations of America. Because they believed that the Soviets forced this move, VOA policy writers were able to reconcile the new, aggressive and direct tone with their continuing commitment to truth and objectivity, which they thought was actually strengthened in the process: Soviet lies pushed the United States to tell the world the truth. Marshall's issuance of new policy in December showed this view. Reporting "the truth objectively and factually" continued as the basic principle of the information programs; however, "to present the policies and practice of the U.S. without reacting or referring to the charges brought to bear against us, is no longer enough." Approved were direct replies to Soviet charges with attribution to the sources of accusations.[7]

In late 1947 the newly formed National Security Council (NSC) joined the debate on information policy. At its second meeting the NSC discussed a paper on psychological warfare written by the State–Army–Navy–Air Force Coordinating Committee (SANACC). Marshall expressed concern that the use of psychological warfare would conflict with the "full and fair" policy of the VOA. Undersecretary of State Robert Lovett and CIA head Roscoe Hillenkoetter said the paper sought only to coordinate, under the direction of the Secretary of State, psychological activities with the foreign information program. The Secretaries of the Army, Defense, and Air Force (respectively Kenneth Royall, James Forrestal, and Stuart Symington) agreed that the State Department should assume responsibility for policy on these activities. The paper, SANACC 304/11, was referred to the NSC, which drafted a policy paper devoted to coordinating the government's information programs. NSC 4, delivered on December 9, 1947, and signed

6. Acheson defined propaganda as information with a purpose for the sender. For the exchange, see the House Committee on Foreign Affairs, *Hearings on H.R. 3342*, 80th Cong., 1st sess., May 1947, 20–21.

7. "U.S. Information Policy with Regard to Anti-American Propaganda," December 1, 1947, box 122, folder "Policy Guidance and Directions," RG 59, RIIA, 1.

by the president on December 18, began by describing in foreboding terms the motives of Soviet-sponsored anti-U.S. propaganda: "[t]he ultimate objective of this campaign is not merely to undermine the prestige of the U.S. and the effectiveness of its national policy but to weaken and divide world opinion to a point where effective opposition to Soviet designs is no longer attainable by political, economic, or military means."

The importance of this declaration is not easily underestimated. By linking Soviet information activities to the already established perception that the Soviet Union was spreading communism over the world, NSC 4 changed fundamentally the purpose of the VOA. Rebutting Soviet propaganda became far more important than telling the world about America. Giving short shrift to the full and fair approach, the paper stated that the United States had not yet effectively countered the incipient Soviet campaign. Accordingly, NSC 4 advised coordination of information and psychological activities under the Assistant Secretary of State for Public Affairs. To assist and advise, the Interdepartmental Coordinating Staff was set up, composed of the deputy director of the CIA and special assistants to the assistant secretaries of the Army, Navy, and Air Force. NSC 4 also issued a directive to the director of the CIA stating that covert psychological operations abroad were needed as a supplement to the information programs. George Marshall still disdained propaganda, but as this directive shows, his NSC colleagues evinced no such hesitation. In light of the view that Soviet propaganda served a world plan of domination, they believed the government had no choice but to adopt methods previously reserved for wartime.[8]

But the top secret meetings and decisions of the NSC were far removed from the VOA's studios. As long as private companies produced VOA broadcasts, intragovernmental debate on intent and content remained largely moot. Classified information could not be given to commercial personnel to aid in the writing of sensitive broadcasts, but by October 1947 NBC and CBS produced 75 percent of VOA broadcasts. State Department officials had resisted this stipulation and struggled throughout the summer and fall of 1947 to regain control of VOA broadcasts. In

---

8. "Minutes of the 2nd Meeting of the National Security Council," November 14, 1947, box 203, folder "Meeting 2," Harry S. Truman Papers, President's Secretary's Files, National Security Council Files (hereafter cited as NSC Files), 4–5; NSC 4, Coordination of Foreign Information Measures, December 9, 1947, and NSC 4-A, attached, box 203, folder "Meeting 4 December 17, 1947," NSC Files, 1–3. Lucas, *Freedom's War*, 47.

June Charles Bohlen had pointed out to Undersecretaries of State Robert Lovett and Dean Acheson that the State Department did not have adequate supervision over the broadcast companies, yet was liable for every word aired. Between June 20 and July 2, 1947, Secretary of State George Marshall appeared twice before the Senate Appropriations Subcommittee to ask that the State Department at least be given control over broadcasts to critical areas such as the Soviet Union, Eastern Europe, and the Far East, a request that subcommittee chair Joseph Ball (R–Minn.) granted. Funds for programming to these areas were limited to $470,000, however, which was "barely sufficient to maintain *minimum* programs of news and news analysis" (emphasis in original).[9]

In order to maintain as much control as possible over VOA broadcasts, the State Department limited contracts to NBC and CBS, raising concerns that the department would be accused of playing favorites. As it was, VOA officials had difficulties enough working with just the two networks. In October 1947 VOA Russian desk consultant Charles Thayer complained of the lack of coordination and advocated discontinuing all use of NBC and CBS. A State Department investigation of network productions turned up glaring problems. On October 7 CBS produced a fifty-five-line story on the formation of the Cominform (the Soviet-led reconstitution of the Third International), of which twenty lines detailed the favorable reaction of a British Communist, while the State Department was reported as having no comment. After the president approved NSC 4 in December, State Department officials considered methods to wrest control of script writing from the networks. Both NBC and CBS had recently refused to air scripts provided by the department. Thayer wanted to appeal to Congress, but William Stone disagreed, contending that members might well support the networks. In February 1948 Deputy Assistant Secretary of State Howland Sargeant told Undersecretary of State Robert Lovett that he was meeting with CBS and NBC representatives to discuss the recent problems. Sargeant pointed out that it would be difficult to evade the stipulation of

9. Howland Sargeant, "Proposed Method of Program Operation of the Voice of the United States of America," undated memorandum, box 126, folder "IBD New Program Plans," RG 59, RIIA; *Department of State Bulletin* 17 (October 12, 1947): 747–48. Bohlen to Lovett and Acheson, June 19, 1947, 811.42700(R)/6–1947, RG 59, CDF. On the shortage of funds, see George V. Allen, "Responsibility of Department of State and Private Broadcasting Companies for International Broadcasting," June 15, 1948, box 39, folder "State Department Correspondence 1948–49" [5 of 6], Truman Papers, White House Central File, Confidential Files, 6–8.

the Smith-Mundt Act requiring maximum use of private media.[10] That month, however, an unexpected controversy over VOA broadcasts allowed the department to discontinue use of NBC and CBS.

II. The "Know North America" Series

In February 1948 longtime VOA critic John Taber requested scripts of previously aired programs. The State Department sent Congressman Taber translations from a series called "Know North America," which was first broadcast to Latin America in June 1947 and then resumed in November. NBC writer Rene Borgia, a Venezuelan subject who had lived intermittently in the United States for twenty years, had written the scripts. The head of NBC's Spanish section approved the scripts for broadcast, and though the network forwarded the scripts to the State Department, no one in the VOA read them before airtime. According to OII officials, limited funds prevented the use of VOA personnel to review every program produced by NBC and CBS.[11] "Know North America" introduced Latin American audiences to the culture, history, and residents of the forty-eight states (the series did not include Canada and Mexico as part of North America) by describing the meandering journey of three male travelers. Two of the characters had never been to the United States; their companion served as tour guide. The episodes tried a light, humorous tone apparently intended to capture listeners' attention and help them envision the unique attributes of the American cities and regions visited by the travelers. The jokes were often tasteless or simply not funny, though, and the travelogue was rife with clichés and stereotypes. "Observing" Wyoming's Frontier Day celebration, the narrator exclaimed, "Look! What magnificent Indian girls!" "Feathered and naked," his companion added. In a different broadcast, the narrator declared Nevada's two biggest cities to be in competition: "In Las Vegas people get married and in Reno they get divorced." Other broadcasts claimed that land was free in Alabama and suggested that members of Congress left office as millionaires. In discussing American religion, the

---

10. Circular Telegram, September 4, 1947, 811.42700(R)/9–447; Mills to A.R.A., December 22, 1947, 811.42700(R)/12–2247; Sargeant to Lovett, February 6, 1948, 811.42700(R)2–648, RG 59, CDF; "Proposed Statement of Department Policy on International Broadcasting," October 13, 1947, box 5, folder "Voice of America," Thayer Papers; William Tyler to William Stone, November 4, 1947, box 128, folder "IBD NY Folder 1," RG 59, RIIA.

11. Allen, "Responsibility of Department of State," 15–16.

narrator referred to Brigham Young as a "primitive priest who didn't counsel virtue but imposed it" and declared that in Pennsylvania, Quakers "were and continue to be a social problem."[12]

Taber brought the series to the attention of his colleagues. When read aloud on the House and Senate floors, the "Know North America" scripts brought angry and repugnant responses. "Contemptible, damnable lies," declared Senator James O. Eastland (D–Miss.). Referring to the program on Alabama, Senator Homer Capehart (R–Ind.) remarked sarcastically, "I am certain that the people of Alabama . . . will appreciate that their money is being used to advertise them to the peoples throughout the world in such a light." Members of the Alabama delegation subsequently introduced a concurrent resolution to strike all VOA funds from the 1949 appropriations bill. Taber commented, "[O]ne could almost suspect the writers of this twaddle of a Machiavellian plot to ridicule the American people and present them to the rest of the world as morons and neurotics."[13]

Even before the uproar on the House and Senate floors, the House Committee on Expenditures in the Executive Departments began investigating the matter. Clare Hoffman chaired the committee as a whole; J. Edgar Chenowith (R–Colo.) headed the subcommittee on the State Department. Both men were obdurate critics of the State Department and the VOA, and the subcommittee attracted like-minded colleagues. In January 1947 Republican Fred Busbey had asked Hoffman to put him on the subcommittee so that he could help investigate the State Department. Since February 1947 Chenowith had maintained an ongoing investigation of the OIC, finding "gross waste and inefficiency" and "unqualified and questionable personnel." The subcommittee held hearings on "Know North America" from May 28 to June 3, 1948, calling sixteen witnesses. As the hearings opened, Chenowith told Assistant Secretary of State for Public Affairs George V. Allen that "[n]othing can be worse than what is going on now" and called for discontinuation of the VOA. Allen admitted that the VOA needed tighter supervision of scripts, but pointed out that NBC was to blame for the scripts in question. During a press conference at the White House that same day, President Truman

12. House Committee on Expenditures in the Executive Departments, *Investigation of the State Department Voice of America Broadcasts*, 80th Cong., 2d sess., June 15, 1948, H.R. 2350, 3–7.

13. *Congressional Record*, 80th Cong., 2d sess., April 27 and May 26, 1948, vol. 94, 6465, A2539.

observed "with a faint ironical smile" that Congress itself had dictated the VOA's use of private networks.[14]

But it was the VOA (and to a lesser degree, NBC) that took the blame for the broadcasts and negative publicity, not Congress. Chenowith's subcommittee questioned State Department and VOA officials about other scripts. A feature that lauded Paul Robeson's singing talent came under fire; the singer had recently refused to tell a Senate committee whether or not he was a communist. A program broadcast to the Soviet Union that suggested women should rinse their hair in beer created a bigger stir. "What kind of beer?" Chenowith asked Charles Thayer, now the acting chief of the VOA, who answered that beer rinses were "a legitimate way to keep hair set." The next morning a headline read, "'Voice' Advice of a Beer Rinse Draws Rebuke." The investigation even received international attention. According to the July 4, 1948, issue of the newspaper *Narodni List* (Zagreb, Yugoslavia), Chenowith's reprimand of Thayer for the Robeson and beer rinse broadcasts "proves better than anything else how deceitful, stupid and comical is the imperialistic Truman-Marshall propaganda."[15]

On June 15, 1948, Chenowith's subcommittee issued a scathing report. Although NBC was faulted for producing the "Know North America" series, the subcommittee deemed the State Department negligent for not

14. Busbey to Hoffman, January 17 and March 3, 1947; Chenowith to Hoffman, July 7, 1948, box 479, folder "Subcommittee on State Department," RG 233, file HR80A-F6.15. A State Department–sponsored exhibit, "Advancing American Art," which was shown overseas in 1946, drew the interest of Chenowith's subcommittee before "Know North America." Composed of paintings lent by U.S. corporations, the exhibit featured works by artists who were suspected communists. See Margaret Lynne Ausfeld and Virginia M. Mecklenburg, *Advancing American Art: Policy and Aesthetics in the State Department Exhibition, 1946-1948.* The Senate also called for an investigation of "Know North America." On May 27, 1948, Senator Homer Capehart (R–Ind.) introduced S.R. 245 to have the Interstate and Foreign Commerce Committee look into the broadcasts. The resolution was referred to a subcommittee of the Foreign Relations Committee, which held hearings June 1–4, 1948. Because the House Committee on Expenditures in the Executive Departments had already begun its hearings, the Senate subcommittee did not issue a report during the Eightieth Congress. Senate Foreign Relations Committee, *Executive Sessions of the Senate Foreign Relations Committee,* vol. 1, 80th Cong., 1st and 2d sess. For coverage of the House hearings, see "Chenowith Would Halt 'Voice' Programs," *New York Sun,* May 29, 1948; "Truman and Congress Rush 'Voice' Broadcast Inquiries," *New York Times,* May 28, 1948.

15. "'Voice' Advice of a Beer Rinse Draws Rebuke," *New York Herald Tribune,* June 4, 1948. The *Narodni List* article was translated by the U.S. Embassy, Belgrade, Yugoslavia, July 19, 1948, 811.42700(R)/7–1948, RG 59, CDF.

previewing the scripts. The report rejected outright Assistant Secretary of State for Public Affairs George V. Allen's claim that limited funds and under-staffing prevented proper supervision of privately produced scripts: "the Department should have known from day to day what type of material was being used in all broadcasts paid for with public money. Congress had the right to expect that degree of fidelity and efficiency." The report also criticized the "drivel" produced within the State Department, citing as an example the "beer rinse" broadcast. Promising to maintain oversight of the VOA for the next three months, the subcommittee made several recommendations. It advised that the Advisory Commission on Information mandated by the Smith-Mundt Act be appointed immediately. The subcommittee also suggested that all programming be written first in English or translated before airtime, and that language experts monitor broadcasts as they aired. The VOA studios in New York began immediately implementing these recommendations, but the pre-broadcast checks proved onerous, even impossible. As Allen commented privately, the checks were "like reading *The New York Times* everyday before sending it out to our libraries."[16]

For its part, the State Department placed most of the blame for "Know North America" on Congress and NBC. In a report to the president released the same day as the congressional findings Allen cited reduced budgets, the forced use of private networks, and difficulties working with NBC and CBS as the reasons why the controversial series made it on the air. Although the department should have had controls to catch the scripts, "under the limitations imposed by Congress a completely adequate system of pre-control could not have been established without sacrificing programs to the vital areas," that is, to the Soviet Union, Eastern Europe, and the Far East. Allen concluded his report by recommending that the State Department assume control over news, editorial roundups, and commentaries to all areas, leaving most features and entertainment to the networks, which would have to follow detailed guidelines provided by the VOA.[17]

Comparison of the "Know America" incident with the preceding NSC and State Department plans for information activities depicts two very different VOAs. The first was a crucial component of the developing counter-campaign against the perceived Soviet drive for world domination; the sec-

16. House Committee on Expenditures in the Executive Departments, *Investigation*, 9, 11–12, 15–16. Allen penciled the comment on a dispatch from the VOA studios in New York, June 18, 1948, box 8, folder "Know North America Series," RG 59, Records of the ASPA.

17. Allen, "Responsibility of Department of State," 16, 20–21.

ond, a bumbling outfit that paid NBC to defame the United States while it advised Russian women to wash their hair in beer. The first VOA soon overtook its negative alter-ego, for though the "Know North America" incident subjected the VOA to national, even global, ridicule, it solved the problem of cutting ties to the networks. With congressional approval, the VOA terminated its contracts with NBC and CBS as of October 1948. However, responsibility for its own programming did not give the VOA full control of content. Even before the agency took back its broadcasts, Republican members of Congress began looking over scripts. VOA officials were eager to avoid further controversy, but they also wanted to follow through on the recent top-level decisions to aggressively counter communist propaganda. Throughout 1948 and 1949, these pressures combined to produce muddled, sometimes contradictory broadcasts.

III. The Struggle for the Airwaves

An exchange in early 1948 between Ambassador to the Soviet Union. Walter Bedell Smith and Undersecretary of State Robert Lovett demonstrates the State Department's sensitivity to domestic interest in VOA broadcasts and the problems that arose when the VOA tried to avoid controversy. On January 9 the VOA broadcast to the Soviet Union a news item quoting Robert Taft's charge that President Truman's expansion of the New Deal was leading the United States toward totalitarianism. Using the terse language of the diplomatic cable, Bedell Smith explained that the broadcast gave "not only false picture U.S. politics but has sharp double edge. Among other things will lead Russian audience to belief VOUSA [VOA] organ of reactionaries. Advise careful VOUSA handling political statements during this campaign year. Some extreme and absurd statements made for political effect will give foreign listeners false impression American political scene and operation American democratic system."

Lovett wired back: "[R]ecognize validity criticism. However, you will readily understand that in view of scrutiny being given our scripts by the Congress it will be essential to report statements of influential committees on matters of legitimate interest . . . perhaps net effect over a long period of time will be to educate our European listeners in some of the peculiarities of the American political picture."[18] For the VOA, this essential reporting exceeded the normal journalistic standard of objectivity, of giving equal

18. Moscow to Secretary of State, Lovett to Moscow, January 10, 1948, 811.42700(R)/1–1048, RG 59, CDF.

coverage to opposing sides. Broadcasters and policy makers were placed in the difficult position of determining which issues were "matters of legitimate interest" to Congress, both as a singular legislative body and as a collection of committees and individuals with vastly differing notions of what was newsworthy. Since its inception the VOA had had a difficult relationship with conservative legislators, and as Lovett indicated, he did not want to worsen the VOA's standing. As Bedell Smith's complaint showed, however, avoiding controversy at home invited spreading confusion abroad, which undermined the VOA's original purpose—explaining U.S. policy and aims. The focus on domestic political news also hampered the VOA's revised purpose of directly rebutting foreign propaganda.

Analysis of the VOA's responses to congressional pressure on its broadcasts points to a domestic partisan struggle to fulfill specific political aims, both at home and abroad. The partisanship was twofold, pitting Republicans against Democrats and the legislative branch against the executive branch. With regard to VOA broadcasts, the struggle produced two competing narratives about national politics and international affairs circa 1948 and 1949. (As used here, "narratives" refer to involved parties' perceptions of domestic and foreign affairs, including notions about the near future.) The congressional Republicans' narrative projected the continued decline of New Deal liberalism, preponderate legislative control of foreign affairs, and continuing American commitment to the Chinese Nationalists. The VOA's narrative described the legislative and executive branches acting in unison to stop the spread of communism and explained that the government had done everything within its power to aid the Chinese Nationalists, but could do no more. From a practical standpoint, these disputes over the VOA's presentation might appear superfluous, a sort of shadow boxing lacking real punches. When congressional Republicans monitored the VOA's coverage of the Marshall Plan, for example, or pressured the VOA to expand its coverage of the Chinese Nationalists, they did not actually alter the massive aid plan or tangibly help Chiang Kai-shek's beleaguered army. When the VOA ceded to these pressures or preemptively avoided controversial subjects, it did not change State Department or presidential action. Yet both sides seemed to recognize that a certain *presentation* of an event could—or should—become to listeners the *reality* of the event.

Consider the VOA's coverage of Henry A. Wallace's 1948 presidential campaign. Wallace was vice president during Franklin Roosevelt's third term, but after a conspicuously cool endorsement from Roosevelt, delegates at the 1944 Democratic National Convention dropped him from the ticket in favor of Missouri's junior senator, Harry Truman. Wallace served as secretary of commerce from March 1945 until September 1946, when Truman dismissed him for delivering a speech critical of the administration's tough stance toward the Soviet Union. In December 1947 Wallace announced his candidacy for the presidency under the auspices of what was later named the Progressive party. Wallace's bid for office nettled the Truman administration by testing the allegiances of liberals, threatening to siphon votes away from the incumbent, and by drawing negative attention to the administration's foreign policy. Wallace opposed both the Truman Doctrine and the Marshall Plan, and in his platform he outlined an alternative to anticommunism, a foreign policy that placed the UN in charge of international aid and advocated a need-based dispersal of funds "without regard to the character of the politics and institutions of recipient nations."[19] For the VOA, Wallace posed a prickly challenge that pitted political exigencies against journalistic standards. Coverage of his campaign meant presenting audiences with blunt criticisms of the very policies that the Smith-Mundt Act required the VOA to report. Suppressed coverage, however, violated the principle of "full and fair" to which policy writers still clung, despite the recent decision to aggressively counter anti-American propaganda. To complicate matters even further, the VOA had run into trouble with congressional conservatives in April 1947 for broadcasting a favorable review of a book about the Wallace family (see chapter 2). News about Wallace's campaign might revive complaints that the VOA slanted its news to the left.

In January 1948 weekly guidance notes for the VOA tried to offset these contradictory pressures, stating that adequate coverage should be given to legitimate new developments without overemphasizing the prominence of the Wallace candidacy. The guidance asked that the phrase "third party" not be used to describe Wallace's campaign, at least until it attracted more supporters, and suggested that audiences be told about the various minor parties that usually sponsor candidates for the presidency.[20] In April VOA Chief Charles Thayer reviewed broadcasts aired between March 1 and March 23, counting references to Wallace or

19. Wallace is cited in Richard J. Walton, *Henry Wallace, Harry Truman, and the Cold War*, 185–86.

20. OIE Weekly Guidance #12, January 19, 1948, box 8, folder "OIE Guidance Notes 1–25," RG 59, Office of the Secretary of State Committee and Subject Files, 1943–1953.

his campaign. He found only six, and three of these were critical. Coverage of a March 18 speech delivered by Truman quoted the president as saying, "I do not want and I will not accept the political support of Henry Wallace and his communists," while the VOA's news roundup to the Far East and Eastern Europe carried a lengthy attack on Wallace by Senator Henry Cabot Lodge. Only one of the references mentioned Wallace's opposition to the administration's anticommunist policies.[21]

On May 18, 1948, Wallace's campaign received international attention when Josef Stalin responded to a speech Wallace had directed the previous week at the Soviet leader. Wallace had outlined a six-point proposal for ending the Cold War; Stalin called the plan a "concrete program for peaceful settlement of the differences between the U.S.S.R. and the United States." Whatever Stalin's sincerity, Wallace's campaign was developing prominence. Yet VOA guidance handed down two days after Stalin's response again stipulated avoidance of the phrase "third party." This careful handling of Wallace did not go unnoticed abroad. In a radio broadcast beamed in English to New York, a Soviet commentator questioned the VOA's conspicuous avoidance of Wallace's campaign.[22] In this instance, attempting a direct rebuttal to the Soviet charge (which was true) carried too many domestic political risks.

The Marshall Plan (officially known as the European Recovery Program, or ERP) also presented a distinct challenge to the VOA. In October 1947 a State Department Wireless Bulletin surmised that the aid program would pass in the spring, but only after Congress made changes, primarily reduction of the base amount from $20 billion to $12 billion for the program's four-year duration (a sagacious prediction: Congress passed the ERP in March 1948 and paid out $13 billion from 1948 through 1951). In the mean-

21. Thayer to Mucio Delgado, April 6, 1948, box 125, folder "Wallace Story," RG 59, RIIA. The VOA also tracked how much airtime was devoted individually to President Truman and GOP challenger Thomas Dewey. The OIC mentioned this tabulation in its report to the Senate subcommittee investigating the "Know North America" broadcasts. Lloyd Lehrbas to William Rogers, December 3, 1948, box 80, folder "Congressional Committee," RG 59, RIIA.

22. *New York Times*, May 18, 1948; Overnight Guidance #25, May 20, 1948, box 8, folder "OIE Weekly Guidance Notes 1–25," RG 59, Office of the Secretary of State Committee and Subject Files, 1943–1953. The Soviet broadcast was mentioned during hearings on the VOA's Senate Subcommittee of the Committee on Appropriations, *Departments of State, Justice, Commerce, and the Judiciary, Hearings before the Subcommittee of the Committee on Appropriations for 1949*, 80th Cong., 2d sess., March 1948, 195.

time, the bulletin advised presenting the proposed aid as "venture capital," an investment in Western Europe that would stymie communism. Most support in Congress for the Marshall Plan would stem from such security concerns, the bulletin continued, especially with regard to France and Italy. Despite this confidence that the aid would pass, the VOA was careful not to present the proposed Marshall Plan as a foregone conclusion or as an executive branch action. November guidance for the VOA outlined coverage of congressional committees' participation in order to make clear the legislative process involved in passage of the aid.[23] While brief mention of Congress's role was hardly extraordinary, it helped protect the VOA from charges that it slanted its news.

If VOA policy writers thought that members of Congress were interested in how the VOA reported the Marshall Plan, they were right. On December 7, 1947, the *Washington Post* reported that the VOA had prepared a broadcast that described American labor groups' support for the plan. After reading the article Clare Hoffman wrote to J. Edgar Chenowith, "It occurs to me that either the Subcommittee on Propaganda and Publicity or the State Department Subcommittee might wish to look into this matter."[24] Although neither subcommittee opened an investigation (the "Know North America" broadcasts soon preoccupied Chenowith's subcommittee), the letter showed conservatives' suspicion that the State Department was using the VOA to promote the Marshall Plan, as well as to emphasize the prominence of labor in American politics. After Congress approved the plan, guidance did instruct media to continue seeking material that showed organized labor's support for the aid package, but with more emphasis on European rather than American labor groups.[25] The careful wording of the instruction underscores the VOA's constant challenge in deciding what was newsworthy and objective. From an international point of view, the support of a large and powerful constituency (European labor) for the Marshall Plan clearly qualified as news. But from a domestic Republican point of

23. Wireless Bulletin #238, October 8, 1947, box 469, folder 2, Mundt Papers; Weekly Guidance Notes #6, November 11, 1947, and Weekly Guidance Notes #8, November 25, 1947, box 8, folder "OIE Guidance Notes 1–25," RG 59, Office of the Secretary of State Committee and Subject Files, 1943–1953.

24. Hoffman to Chenowith, December 8, 1947, box 479, folder "Subcommittee on State Department," RG 233, file HR80A-F6.15.

25. OIE Weekly Guidance #21, April 22, 1948, box 8, folder "OIE Weekly Guidance Notes, 1–25," RG 59, Office of the Secretary of State Committee and Subject Files, 1943–1953.

view, any coverage of American labor smacked of partisanship, as evidenced by Hoffman's response to the *Washington Post* article. Thus the VOA tried to balance its obligations as a news agency with its ever-precarious domestic situation.

In July 1948 New Hampshire Republican Styles Bridges requested copies of all VOA scripts mentioning the ERP for the period June 6–21, 1948. Bridges was a member of the Senate Appropriations Committee, which was then reviewing requests for aid to China and the ERP budget. Bridges also wanted to see the Far East Wireless Bulletins and VOA scripts covering the hearings on the China aid. The conservative senator, a supporter of the Chinese Nationalists, suspected that the VOA was giving favorable coverage to the ERP while deliberately glossing over Senate action on aid for Chiang Kai-shek and the Nationalists. Before submitting the scripts to Bridges a State Department official determined that all references to the ERP were strictly factual and without commentary.[26] Bridges's interest in VOA coverage of the Marshall Plan extended from an intensifying dispute between Congress's China lobby and the administration over the nation's Far East policy. Republicans and one Democrat with varying political and geographical backgrounds composed a pro-Chinese Nationalist bloc situated mostly in the Senate. Senator H. Alexander Smith and Representative Walter Judd each expressed personal interest in the fate of China, having lived there. Republican Senators Joseph Ball, Homer Ferguson (Mich.), Bridges, William Knowland (Calif.), and Kenneth Wherry worried that the administration's containment policies favored Europe at the expense of Asia. Senator Pat McCarran, a Nevada Democrat whose conservative views placed him far to the right of many Republicans, sought to advance his state's economic interests. As a leading producer of silver, Nevada stood to benefit from aid bills that supported China's silver-based currency. Each of these legislators distrusted the State Department's Far East desk, believing that it harbored communists and communist sympathizers.[27]

Changes in U.S. Far East policy set the State Department and the VOA on a collision course with the China bloc. In June 1946 a regional issues guide

26. William Hall to Styles Bridges, July 9, 1948, and George V. Allen to General Carter, July 15, 1948, box 79, folder "Senate Appropriations Committee," RG 59, RIIA.

27. As McCarran biographer and Nevada historian Jerome E. Edwards has pointed out, there was no significant difference between Nevada's Republican and Democratic parties during McCarran's political career. Both parties were conservative and traditionally emphasized state over national issues. Edwards provides numerous examples

for the OIC had appraised China's postwar situation and staked out a position for the VOA. The Nationalists were "authoritarian, race-proud and anti-capitalist," the guide read, warning also that "[t]hey will not be as imitative, capitalist, or liberal as the American-minded Chinese who were so important in the government at a decade ago." The Communists were also nationalistic, likely to follow the pattern of Soviet communism, but "within the limitations set by the temper of the population it rules." The guidance advised that the information programs "supplement the efforts of General Marshall, as long as they continue, to manipulate the power groups in order to achieve the first aim of internal unity." Chiang Kai-shek's adamant refusal to share power with Mao Tse-tung spiked the Marshall mission, however, and further frustrated the State Department officials responsible for Far East policy. By 1948 the Nationalists' corruption, unpopularity with the Chinese people, and chronic inability to stop Communist gains led to a top-level reevaluation of American support of Chiang Kai-shek. In March the NSC proposed that the United States provide only limited economic assistance to the Nationalists in order to prevent further disintegration of China's economy and to allow purchase of military supplies. NSC representatives of the military branches and the State Department all agreed that such aid would keep the United States from making an open-ended and risky commitment to propping up the Nationalists: "[t]he military responsibility for the survival of the National Government would be clearly placed upon Chinese shoulders." In September the State Department submitted policy papers to the NSC suggesting the likelihood of the Nationalists' defeat; by January 1949 Secretary of State Dean Acheson, Policy Planning Staff chief George Kennan, Undersecretary of State Dean Rusk, and East Asia adviser Walton Butterworth each wanted to cut off aid to the Nationalists.[28] In part to avoid backlash from Congress's China bloc,

---

of McCarran's defiance of his own party. In 1918 McCarran refused to support the Democratic candidate for governor; he often voted for Republican candidates; and he openly disagreed with Democratic foreign policy positions in the 1920s. See Edwards, *Pat McCarran: Political Boss of Nevada,* ix, 25, 31. On the China lobby, see William W. Stueck, *The Road to Confrontation: American Policy toward China and Korea, 1947–1950,* 16, 42–44; Robert M. Blum, *Drawing the Line: The Origin of the American Containment Policy in East Asia,* 19, 43; Nancy Bernkopf Tucker, *Patterns in the Dust: Chinese-American Relations and the Recognition Controversy, 1949–1950,* 162–67.

28. "Regional Issues Guide for China," June 5, 1946, drawer 19, Lawson File. For reconsideration of U.S. policy toward China, see "Draft Report of the NSC on the Position of the United States Regarding Short-Term Assistance to China," March 24, 1948, in Ernest R. May, *The Truman Administration and China, 1945–1949,* 87–91; Blum, *Drawing the Line,* 24–25; Warren I. Cohen, "Acheson, His Advisers, and China, 1949–1950."

however, this change was not made public until July 1949, when the State Department released its white paper on China.

But the VOA could not remain silent for nearly a year—it had a daily broadcast schedule. During the fall of 1948 VOA broadcasts tried to simultaneously downplay the Nationalists' dire situation and convince Chinese listeners that communism was not the solution to their nation's long-standing civil unrest. In reporting the withdrawal of Nationalist troops from Manchuria in October, the VOA was instructed to treat the matter briefly and factually, without comment, and to avoid giving the impression that the United States would stop supporting Chiang Kai-shek. Similar instructions applied to the potential evacuation of U.S. dependents from northern China. November guidance advised criticism of Soviet imperialism rather than of communism itself, which was labeled a negative approach. Because the Chinese people wanted peace, they would be willing to accept communism, further guidance observed. To counteract this trend, the guidance advised that media emphasize the subservience of Eastern European nations to the Soviet Union.[29]

Despite this cautious approach, VOA officials clearly anticipated the Nationalists' demise, and they began to take a bolder approach. In December VOA policy writers issued detailed guidance on reporting events in China. As long as Chiang was the legally recognized leader, the United States would continue to support him. The guidance also stated, "[b]y picking up comment critical of Chiang, however, we can later deny identification with, and complete all out psychological support of, the Chiang government." According to the guidance, it was important to "create a reservoir of credibility in our output to China in order to protect future operations in case the Communists come to power." A Communist takeover of China was strictly an off-the-air speculation, though. There was no indication that the State Department was even considering de facto recognition of a Communist regime, guidance in January 1949 cautioned. In April policy writers lifted the restrictions on editorial comment about the Nationalists and Communists, but gave explicit instructions: use only editorials from outside sources, eliminate or paraphrase extreme statements, skip any conjecture on what the pres-

29. Haldore Hanson to George Mann, October 27, 1948, box 91, folder "Kretzmann"; Overnight Guidance #19, December 7, 1948, box 89, folder "12/6–12/10/48"; Daily Guidance #1, November 1, 1948, box 89, folder "Thayer"; Overnight Guidance #10, November 15, 1948, box 89, folder "11/15–11/29/48," RG 59, RIIA.

ident or the State Department was thinking or planning with regard to China, and avoid the impression that U.S. public opinion was completely opposed to official policy. Guidance later that month outlined numerous points to emphasize in news and editorial comment, including the Nationalists' failure to make effective use of U.S. aid, the lack of unity among the Nationalists, their alienation from the Chinese people, and the United States' "demonstrated support [for democracy] in many areas, notably Western Europe." The guidance also listed points to avoid: references to American attempts to control events in China, the fate of Taiwan (then called Formosa), and the "implication that the setback in China is due to the failure of U.S. policy." In May guidance did all but state that a Communist takeover was imminent when it advised against giving the impression that the United States was particularly concerned about future relations with the Chinese Communists.[30]

Preparation for a Communist ascendancy also included limited or cautious reporting of the intensifying domestic political rancor over China. In January 1949 Styles Bridges suggested publicly that the State Department had opposed giving aid to China; guidance indicated that these comments "should not be picked up." (The same guidance then provided instructions for reporting Chinese press censorship). In February, fifty-one House Republicans asked the president to clarify U.S. policy. The letter was to "be handled briefly and factually in summary fashion without either minimizing or over-emphasizing its importance." Rather than dwell on the letter's description of setbacks, media were to use its positive statements. After Acheson met in executive session with Republican members of Congress, guidance prohibited any coverage beyond mention that the meeting took place and that the secretary of state had no comment. Media handled Acheson's March appearance before the Senate Foreign Relations Committee in a similar fashion.[31]

By spring 1949 the VOA had thus revealed in increments what the State Department had yet to state publicly: the Nationalists were fin-

30. Overnight Guidance #20, December 8, 1948, box 89, folder "12/6–12/10/48"; Overnight Guidance #55, January 28, 1949, box 89, folder "1/24–28" Overnight Guidance #102, April 6, 1949, box 89, folder "4/4–4/8"; Overnight Guidance #119, April 29, 1949, box 89, folder "4/25–4/29"; Overnight Guidance #123, May 5, 1949, box 89, folder "5/2–5/6," RG 59, RIIA.

31. Overnight Guidance #42, January 7, 1949, box 89, folder "Jan. 10–14"; Overnight Guidance #67, February 15, 1949, box 89; Daily Guidance notes, February 25, 1949, box 89, folder "Feb. 21–25"; Overnight Guidance #89, March 17, 1949, box 89, folder "March 14–18," RG 59, RIIA.

ished, and the U.S. government was planning for a Communist takeover. It was a risky move—Congress's China bloc was monitoring VOA coverage all the while. In March 1949 Representative Walter Judd requested scripts for broadcasts to China. According to a policy official, March's output revealed several potentially controversial items. For example, the VOA's Weekly Summary of Chinese News in the U.S. Press reported Chinese Communist news releases. A feature broadcast entitled "Small Happenings in the U.S.A." was also singled out; its description of an abundant economy could be criticized for alienating the Chinese, who suffered food shortages. Though Judd did not raise the anticipated complaints, problems arose with other members of the China bloc. In April the State Department's Wireless Bulletin in Shanghai was charged with ignoring Senator Pat McCarran's public criticism of Secretary of State Acheson. In January McCarran had proposed extension of $1.5 billion in aid to the Nationalists; in a letter to Senator Tom Connally (D–Tex.), which was made public, Acheson advised against the aid. On April 19, 1949, the conservative *Washington Daily News* reported that while the bulletin ran the full text of Acheson's April 15 letter, it said nothing about McCarran's April 16 response in which he accused Acheson of giving up on the Nationalists. Actually, the bulletin had requested a copy of McCarran's speech from his office on that day, but did not receive it until April 18. In lieu of the speech, the bulletin included summary of news service reports of McCarran's comments in its News Roundup section.[32]

That was not the understanding of Styles Bridges, however. At the May 1949 hearings on the State Department's budget for 1950 Bridges complained that the VOA had quoted Acheson as saying the Nationalists were finished while refusing to carry the comment of McCarran. Bridges asked whether or not the VOA was reporting the views of Congress as well as Acheson's and the State Department's.[33] In June 1949 Walter Judd requested a May 6 VOA script, "U.S. Comment on China." The broadcast described a preponderance of editorial opinion doubting the Nationalists' abilities to prevent a Communist takeover of China and questioning the Chinese people's support for the Nationalists. For example, the VOA

32. Martin Reynolds to Vestel Lott, March 25, 1949, box 72, folder "JO-JU"; McDermott to Allen, April 20, 1949, box 74, folder "McCarran," RG 59, RIIA; *Washington Daily News*, April 19, 1949.

33. Senate Subcommittee of the Committee on Appropriations, *Departments of State, Justice, Commerce, and the Judiciary, Hearings before the Subcommittee of the Committee on Appropriations for 1950*, 81st Cong., 1st sess., 1949, 186–87.

quoted *Christian Science Monitor* correspondent Gordon Walker, who said that the Nationalist government "seems to be wallowing about without leadership, finances or military power." Assistant Secretary of State for Public Affairs George V. Allen wrote to Walton Butterworth, "Judd may make a lot of noise about this script."[34]

Such broadcasts were not renegade; they followed the December guidance instructing the VOA to pick up outside comment critical of Chiang in order to maintain credibility with the Chinese people. To stay credible with the China bloc, however, the VOA needed to appear to support the Nationalists. As a result, some programming favored the Nationalists. In July 1949 the VOA devoted considerable attention to Chiang's summit meeting with Philippine President Elpidio Quirino to discuss setting up a Pacific security pact. The embassy in Tientsin questioned the pertinence of this coverage, noting Chiang's marginal political power and his unpopularity with the Chinese, whether Communists or not. Pointing out that Americans in Tientsin believed that the Nationalists were finished, the embassy advised, "VOA would serve more useful purpose if it devoted more time to direct refuting Communist lies at once while matters fresh in minds of Chinese."[35]

The issuance of the White Paper on China on July 30, 1949, finally backed the VOA's position by publicly articulating American aims in China. The White Paper all but stated that the United States expected an imminent Communist takeover of China, and it carefully documented the military and economic aid the United States had given the Nationalists since World War II. The White Paper also pointed out the corruption of the Nationalists and the ways in which they had alienated the Chinese populace. The VOA softened these statements by stressing American sympathy for the Chinese people, and it described bipartisan support for U.S. Far East policy.[36] The China bloc's reaction to the White Paper belied this claim. On August 22, 1949, Bridges, McCarran, and Knowland released their "Memorandum on the White Paper on U.S. Relations with China," which denounced the White Paper as a cover-up of the American desertion of China. Considering the China bloc's long-standing dissatisfaction with American policy in the Far East, the vehe-

34. Allen to Butterworth, June 17, 1949, 811.42700(R)/6–1749, RG 59, CDF.

35. Tientsin to Washington, July 15, 1949, 811.42700(R)/7–1549, RG 59, CDF.

36. Department of State, *United States Relations with China, with Special Reference to the Period 1944-1949*, iii–xvii, 390–409; Overnight Guidance #262, August 8, 1949, box 90, folder "August 1949," RG 59, RIIA.

ment reaction to the White Paper surely surprised few in the VOA. Those expecting the issue to fade, however, were wrong. Once the Chinese Communists took control of the mainland, attention shifted to the island of Taiwan, to which Chiang Kai-shek and his remaining forces retreated. The China bloc and other congressional Republicans thought the United States should help defend Taiwan against a Communist takeover, but throughout the fall of 1949 no official decision was made. Then in January 1950 Republicans discovered that the VOA had just announced that the United States would not help protect Taiwan. Once again, the VOA was caught in the middle of a fight over U.S. Far East policy, and it looked as if it slanted news to the administration's favor. The VOA faced other problems too, domestic and international, during the spring of 1950. The Soviets were jamming broadcasts, but the CIA and the Defense Department refused to provide help, and a previously obscure Republican charged the State Department with harboring communists.

Chapter 4

Will It Play in Peoria?
The Campaign of Truth, 1950

On April 20, 1950, President Truman announced the Campaign of Truth in a speech delivered before the American Society of Newspaper Editors. Truman accused "the Communists" of vilifying the free nations of the world with lies, half-truths, and shameless posturing. Although media in the free nations helped counter such invidious propaganda, countries behind the Iron Curtain did not enjoy freedom of the press. Because the VOA was often the only source of news for captive peoples, according to Truman, the Soviets were jamming it. The president called for a strengthening of the VOA's signal and a more aggressive tone, one that confronted the malicious propaganda head-on without resorting to Soviet tactics. Through the truth, the United States and the free world would refute lies and deliver positive messages about the American people and their nation's policies.[1] Counter-jamming and renewed dedication to the refutation of Soviet propaganda were not the only motives behind the Campaign of Truth, though. In January 1950, when the State Department began researching methods to overcome Soviet jamming, Truman's and the State Department's Far East policy makers came under fire in Congress. Against the wishes of the China bloc, Secretary of State Dean Acheson had decided, and the president had agreed, that the United States would not defend the Chinese Nationalists' stronghold of Taiwan (Formosa) against a Communist takeover. Congressional Republicans accused traitors on the State Department's Far East desk of conspiring against the Nationalists. The VOA entangled itself in the controversy because it revealed the policy before the administration did, and the ensuing negative attention prompted Truman and the State Department's Office of Public Affairs (OPA) to find ways to improve the VOA's domestic image and, more important, to

1. Harry S. Truman, "Going Forward with a Campaign of Truth."

justify the much-criticized decision about Taiwan. (The OPA, headed by the assistant secretary of state for Public Affairs, was the parent office for the Office of International Information, which administered the VOA. Public Affairs was also responsible for domestic public relations.) However, Senate hearings in March on Senator Joe McCarthy's (R–Wisc.) charges against the State Department blunted these efforts. That same month the CIA and the Defense Department rebuffed the State Department's efforts to enlist their help in stopping Soviet jamming of the VOA. Neither CIA nor Defense officials believed it was possible to fully overcome the jamming, and they were reluctant to divert their staff and resources to solving the VOA's transmission problems.

The Taiwan controversy, McCarthy's charges, and the State Department's failure to procure help for counter-jamming combined to give the Campaign of Truth an added purpose: reassertion of Truman's and the State Department's commitment to fighting communism. Circumstances during January to April 1950 presented Truman and the campaign's planners with an irresistible opportunity to both call for revitalization of the VOA—the original purpose—and to repair the president's and State Department's tattered images at home and abroad. In Truman's styling of the campaign, the "Truth" became a metaphor for not only the administration's answer to Soviet lies but also to McCarthy's falsehoods. Implicit in the campaign's presentation was the message that a president capable of and committed to telling the truth to foreigners surely told the truth to his own citizenry. To put it another way, the Campaign of Truth was supposed to play in Peoria as well as in Prague.

I. Trouble over Taiwan

With Mao Tse-tung's forces in control of China's mainland by the fall of 1949, the defense of the battered Nationalists' bastion on the island of Taiwan became a sensitive issue for both the administration and Congress. The Senate's China bloc, led by Republicans William Knowland (Calif.) and H. Alexander Smith (N.J.), demanded that the United States keep Taiwan out of the Chinese Communists' hands. Many administration officials also wanted to defend Taiwan; these included Secretary of Defense Louis Johnson, General Douglas MacArthur, and the Joint Chiefs of Staff (JCS). In October 1949 military representatives on the NSC drafted a policy paper stressing the island's strategic importance. Although in August 1949 the JCS had reported that the defense of Taiwan did not warrant overt U.S. military action, in December 1949 it advised that a modest program of military aid to prevent a Communist takeover of Taiwan was appropriate to U.S. national security. In early 1949 the State Department had also supported defending the island, even cautioning the NSC that U.S. troops might be required. By the fall of 1949, however, Secretary of State Dean Acheson and his Far East policy makers had decided that the U.S. defense of Taiwan, either through military intervention or aid to the Nationalists, would hamper efforts to drive a wedge between the People's Republic of China and the Soviet Union and would damage fragile American credibility in Southeast Asia. During the last week of December Acheson secured Truman's support for the State Department's position. On the morning of January 5, 1950, the president released a statement announcing that the United States would neither provide military aid to the Nationalists nor seek to establish military bases on Taiwan. To support this position the statement referred to the 1943 Cairo Declaration, which had promised the island to China.[2]

Truman was not the first to reveal the policy change, though. The VOA received guidance on Taiwan even before the decisive NSC meetings took place during the last week of 1949. On December 23, 1949, the policy planning staff for the Office of Public Affairs (OPA) issued Special Guidance #28 (SG 28). After pointing out that attention was fixed on Taiwan as the Nationalists withdrew from the Chinese mainland, SG 28 instructed that all material used should counter the "false impressions" that the island was of strategic importance to the United States. Specifically, the guidance required media to disclaim American responsibility for Taiwan, to explain that its loss would not hurt U.S. anticommunist goals, and to deny that Taiwan's defense would save the Nationalists. The guidance provided official background information for the VOA and the International Press and Publications Division, which produced pamphlets for the USIS libraries abroad. Hundreds of copies were also sent to other government agencies; an internal State Department investigation found that 350 copies of the guidance were distributed in Washington, New York, and abroad. Not surprisingly, the guidance's frank discussion of Taiwan did not stay confidential. General Douglas MacArthur's headquarters leaked news of the guidance to wire services in Tokyo, where it was picked up by the United Press (UP) on January 3, 1950. At that point the guidance's instructions became public knowledge, which was the intended outcome. According to

2. Blum, *Drawing the Line,* 168–70, 176, 180; John Lewis Gaddis, "Drawing Lines: The Defensive Perimeter Strategy in East Asia, 1947–1951."

Acheson, in the summer of 1949 General Albert Wedemeyer had proposed issuing a Public Affairs guidance considering the consequences of Taiwan's capture by the Chinese Communists. "On December 23 such a paper was sent out to (among a great many other recipients) General MacArthur's headquarters in Tokyo," Acheson wrote in his memoir.[3] Even Acheson was not prepared for the ensuing controversy, however, as MacArthur's leak directed attention away from Truman's statement and forced the State Department to adopt a defensive position.

On January 3, 1950, Senator Knowland read the UP wire report about SG 28. He immediately called Undersecretary of State James Webb and asked to see the guidance. Webb denied the request, citing security reasons. Knowland then made the same demand in writing to Acheson, who met privately with Knowland and H. Alexander Smith on the morning of January 5. Both Knowland and Smith had recently traveled to Taiwan and toured the Chinese Nationalists' bases there. According to Acheson's record of the conversation, he explained that the island was of neither military nor strategic importance to the United States, that the Cairo Declaration and Potsdam Conference promised it to China, and that threatening war over Taiwan vitiated American promises to support national self-determination. Acheson also assured Knowland that he would later show him SG 28. Both legislators remained skeptical. Knowland claimed that morale on Taiwan was good and its defense was necessary. Smith complained that the State Department should have consulted the Senate Foreign Relations Committee, and he warned that if the administration stood by its policy, bipartisan cooperation would cease.[4]

After the meeting, Knowland brought SG 28 to the attention of his colleagues. In a lengthy speech on the Senate floor Knowland asked pointed questions about the State Department's Far East desk, insinuating that Foreign Service officers John Paton Davies and John Stewart Service headed

3. Special Guidance #28, December 23, 1949. For the State Department investigation, see Howland Sargeant to Dean Acheson, March 6, 1950; Sargeant to Hulten, January 4, 1950, box 4, folder "Correspondence, Deputy Assistant Secretary of State for Public Affairs," Howland H. Sargeant Papers, Truman Library. For the MacArthur leak of SG 28, see Blum, *Drawing the Line,* 179; *Congressional Record,* 81st Cong., 2d sess., January 5, 1950, vol. 96, 79; Dean Acheson, *Present at the Creation: My Years in the State Department,* 350.

4. Knowland's letters and Webb's reply are reprinted in *Congressional Record,* 81st Cong., 2d sess., January 5, 1950, vol. 96, 79-85; memorandum of conversation, January 5, 1950, box 12, folder "China Policy 1950," RG 59, Records of the Officer of Congressional Relations.

a conspiracy to let Taiwan fall to the Chinese Communists. Knowland also suggested that Davies and Service wrote SG 28, and two days later he wrote to Acheson asking for the names of the guidance's drafters. On January 10 Acheson appeared before a closed session of the Senate Foreign Relations Committee, where Smith asked him if Davies and Service had drafted SG 28. Neither Davies nor Service were information policy writers; they had no hand in drafting the guidance. But Acheson refused to identify the actual writers, instead answering that he and acting Assistant Secretary of State for Public Affairs Howland Sargeant accepted full responsibility for the guidance. Although not a member of the Foreign Relations Committee, Knowland was present as an observer. In his January 17, 1950, reply to Knowland's January 7 letter, Acheson again declined to name the drafters of SG 28. Knowland subsequently complained of an "iron curtain" dropping between the State Department and Congress.[5]

Acheson attempted to reorient debate from the importance of Taiwan and China to the larger context of Far East policy, but his efforts intensified rather than ended the controversy sparked by SG 28. On January 12 Acheson spoke to the National Press Club and explained U.S. policy in the Far East. In what was commonly known as the "Perimeter Speech," Acheson sketched two strategic lines of defense in Asia. In the Pacific the United States would use military force, if necessary, to hold the line running from the Aleutian islands to Japan and on toward the Philippines. To contain communism on the mainland of Southeast Asia, the United States was willing to provide aid but not troops. Knowland dubbed the policy "appeasement by the installment plan." Debate on China ran long hours on the House and Senate floors, and Republicans asked whether or not the State Department had properly consulted the Pentagon and MacArthur. The accusation contained bitter irony for Acheson; MacArthur himself had proposed an Asian offshore defense line as early as March 1948. The narrow defeat of the Korean aid bill, which was to provide $150 million in economic assistance, demonstrated the gravity of the situation to Truman and the State Department. Rallied by the China bloc, the House voted against the bill 192–191 just one week after Acheson's National Press Club speech. (On February 9, 1950, the House did pass a revised bill authorizing $60 million in aid for Korea).[6]

---

5. *Congressional Record*, 81st Cong., 2d sess., January 5 and 23, 1950, vol. 96, 79–86, 161–62, 737; Blum, *Drawing the Line*, 182–83.
6. Gaddis, "Drawing Lines," 73–75; Blum, *Drawing the Line*, 183–85.

With regard to the VOA, the State Department initially delivered guidance that served Acheson's basic aim of placing Taiwan in context. Desks were instructed to report Truman's January 5 statement on Taiwan without emphasizing the island's status, which was only one part of American Far East policy. However, VOA broadcasts aired after January 6 shied away from this point. On January 10 guidance instructed the VOA to point out the rights of the Nationalists to retain China's UN Security Council Seat. Acheson's National Press Club speech gave the VOA another opportunity to reassert the perimeter strategy, but coverage was guarded and vague. Guidance instructed the VOA to comment on the dismemberment of the northern Chinese provinces and inform audiences in the Near and Far East that the United States was interested in the fate of peoples, not nations.[7] Part of Acheson's speech was broadcast in English to the Far East, but State Department officials carefully edited the tape before broadcast. Domestic media who were promised a recording waited three hours for the edited copy, a delay angrily protested by the National Association of Broadcasters. CBS newscaster Eric Sevareid complained, "[I]t was the most remarkable effort to protect a public official from himself that Washington has seen in years."[8]

For State Department officials, risking the ire of domestic broadcasters was better than providing Republicans with more grist for negative publicity. Indeed, instructions on China given after Acheson's speech seemed written for Republican rather than foreign audiences, as demonstrated by Special Guidance #31, "Recognition of Communist China," issued February 6. SG 31 stated that because of the forced closure and seizure of the U.S. Embassy in Peiping, recognition of the People's Republic of China was indefinitely delayed. Before making a decision, the secretary of state would consult with the appropriate committees of Congress. After noting that extension of the Communist regime's nearly total de facto control of the Chinese mainland to remaining territory would meet a standard requirement of recognition, SG 31 explained that the United States would still continue to regard the Nationalists as the legitimate government of

7. Overnight Guidance #365, January 6, 1950, box 90, folder "Jan 3–6"; Overnight Guidance #367, January 10, 1950, and Overnight Guidance #370, January 13, 1950, box 90, folder "Jan. 9–13," RG 59, RIIA.

8. House Subcommittee of the Committee on Appropriations, *Department of State Appropriation Bill for 1951, Hearings before the Subcommittee of the Committee on Appropriations,* 81st Cong., 2d sess., February 1950, 1066; "Radiomen Irate at Handling of Acheson's Talk," *New York Herald Tribune,* January 13, 1950.

China. Accordingly, the Nationalists would keep China's UN Security Council Seat. The guidance also made a nod toward missionary activities in China, a pet concern of Walter Judd and Senator Smith. Judd had served as a medical missionary in China, and Smith was a former Princeton history professor who had spent time in China through an academic exchange program. SG 31 instructed media to stress U.S. efforts to maintain private missionary, educational, and philanthropic activities. With reference to Taiwan, the guidance restricted any comment linking the island to the issue of recognition and prohibited speculation on what effects a Communist takeover would have on recognition. The guidance ended by instructing media to make it "clear that the U.S. neither has 'written off' China nor regards it as the entire Far Eastern problem."[9]

SG 31's restrictions on discussion of Taiwan and its emphasis on continuing support for the Nationalists had domestic justification. On February 6, 1950, Knowland requested all English scripts broadcast to the Far East for the preceding month. Just two days before Howland Sargeant had predicted that because of the guidance scandal, the department would have a tough time in its appearance before the Senate Appropriations Subcommittee. In March Sargeant ordered a careful analysis made of the scripts prior to the Senate hearings so that State Department officials could handle criticisms and answer questions.[10] Knowland apparently did not find anything objectionable in the scripts, but the VOA continued to play it safe. An April 5 broadcast to Canton described the efforts of twenty-five Christian organizations based in Hong Kong to deliver food to the mainland. Throughout April and May the VOA delivered steady reports on the status of the Nationalists and Chiang Kai-shek's activities. A broadcast over the Arabic desk on May 1 cited Chiang Kai-shek's verbal criticisms of the Chinese Communists, who were now routing the Nationalists.[11]

II. The "Static Curtain" and McCarthyism

As the State Department struggled to defuse the controversy over Taiwan, acting Assistant Secretary of State for Public Affairs Howland

9. Special Guidance #31, February 6, 1950, box 88, folder "Special Info Policy Guidances" vol. 2, RG 59, Miscellaneous Records of the Bureau of Public Affairs, Subject Files of the Policy Plans and Guidance Staff.

10. Sargeant to Hulten, March 3, 1950, box 4, folder "Correspondence, Deputy Assistant Secretary of State for Public Affairs," Sargeant Papers.

11. Voice of America Daily Broadcast Content Reports and Script Translations, 1950–1955, April 1950, boxes 1–2, RG 306, National Archives, College Park, Md. (hereafter cited as VOA Reports).

Sargeant and VOA engineers confronted Soviet jamming of broadcasts to the Soviet Union. The United States had protested the jamming when it began in early 1948, but the Soviet Minister of Foreign Affairs denied that his nation was interfering with any broadcasts. During the summer of 1949 the jamming increased and listeners in Moscow reported that they could not clearly hear the VOA, if at all. By January 1950 the CIA estimated VOA effectiveness at between just 15 to 20 percent. An observer in the Soviet Union reported in November 1949 that "the VOA is being so heavily jammed at present that most listeners have given it up as a bad job." Counter-jamming techniques such as clippers and concentrated transmissions were ineffective. To make matters worse, in February 1950 the VOA's chief engineer reported that the Soviets had taken active steps to modify and improve their already powerful jamming.[12]

CIA and State Department officials considered jamming of the VOA to be an outgrowth of Soviet expansionism. The CIA warned that "it has now become virtually certain that the Soviet Union intends to go its own way in the field of international radio communications as it has already done in other matters." Sargeant stated to CIA director Roscoe Hillenkoetter that the Soviets wanted to disrupt frequency transmissions all over the world and start a radio war. An unsigned State Department report declared that psychological warfare was one of the principal means by which the Soviets aimed to create and dominate a communist world.[13] By clearing VOA transmissions from the airwaves, jamming increased potential audiences for Radio Moscow and other communist broadcasts. These interpretations of Soviet jamming were consistent with NSC 4, which in December 1947 had warned that the Soviet Union was using propaganda to fulfill its international designs.

After taking office as assistant secretary of state for Public Affairs on February 12, 1950, Edward W. Barrett resolved to make counter-jamming a top priority. Barrett also wanted to redouble the OPA's efforts to convince the American public that the worldwide struggle against communism was at its most crucial point.[14] As he would soon discover, however, several

12. Central Intelligence Agency, "Historical Developments in the Jamming of the VOA by the USSR," January 20, 1950, box 257, folder "OSI Reports 1950," Harry S. Truman Papers, President's Secretary's Files, Intelligence File, Truman Library, 8–9; George Herrick to Lloyd Free, February 2, 1950, drawer 25, Lawson File.

13. CIA, "Historical Developments," 10; Sargeant to Hillenkoetter, February 3, 1950, box 5, folder "Jamming"; "USSR Psychological Capabilities," undated, unsigned memorandum, box 12, folder "Regaining the Psychological Initiative," RG 59, RIIA.

14. Lucas, Freedom's War, 81–83.

obstacles lay in his way. Barrett came to his post from *Newsweek* magazine, where he had served as editorial director for the last four years. During World War II he had headed the OWI's Overseas Operations; he was thus familiar with the VOA. In a March 6 memorandum, "Taking the Propaganda Offensive," Barrett told Undersecretary of State James Webb that the VOA needed to "[s]peed up the present program to throw additional transmitting equipment into the war of ideas in order to overcome Soviet jamming, etc." In a report given to Acheson three days later Barrett outlined specific steps his office was taking, including the drafting of a staff paper proposing ways of coordinating counter-jamming research and intelligence efforts among various government agencies. Barrett also asked that Truman direct the NSC to study the technical problems associated with Soviet jamming. Barrett concluded by suggesting that the president announce *"that he has determined to step up every means of getting understanding of our peaceful purposes through the Iron Curtain"* [emphasis in original].[15]

Truman was already interested in improving the VOA. In late February he asked Secretary of Defense Louis Johnson to broach the topic of the VOA with General David Sarnoff, president of the Radio Corporation of America (RCA). Sarnoff's involvement was desirable for several reasons. An expert on broadcasting, Sarnoff was in a position to provide needed guidance on counter-jamming methods. In light of the Taiwan controversy, the fame and prestige Sarnoff enjoyed as a successful businessman might bolster sagging support in Congress for the VOA. Furthermore, the general was an ardent supporter of government-operated international broadcasts. In 1943 Sarnoff had urged Secretary of State Cordell Hull to continue the VOA after the war, and as recently as January 2, 1950, Sarnoff had given a speech entitled "Problems of International Broadcasting; Proposals Made for Their Solution and the Establishment of the Principles of 'Freedom to Listen' and 'Freedom to Look.'" Sarnoff proposed that a committee made up of himself, Senators Brien McMahon (D–Conn.) and Ernest McFarland (D–Ariz.), Deputy Secretary of Defense Stephen Early, and Edward Barrett study ways to improve the VOA. On February 27 Johnson suggested to the president that he might make the committee's report the subject of a special address to the Congress, which "would assure the American people, as well as our allies and our friends abroad,

---

15. Barrett to Webb, March 6, 1950; Barrett to Acheson, March 9, 1950, *Foreign Relations of the United States* 1950, vol. 4, 274–76 (hereafter cited as *FRUS*).

that this country is doing everything possible in this important field."[16] Right after receiving Johnson's memorandum, Truman discussed "the exploitation of the Voice of America" with Sarnoff, who again proposed the committee. Truman gave this suggestion to Acheson, who forwarded it to Barrett. In his reply to Acheson, Barrett pointed out that Sarnoff's interest "touches directly a problem I have been giving high priority: how to gear up this Government for an all-out effort to penetrate the Iron Curtain with our ideas." Barrett explained that though Sarnoff's committee idea was worthy, its scope was limited, and more ambitious action would be useful, particularly a presidential directive making the matter a top priority. As indicated, Barrett had reiterated in his March 6 and 9 memoranda the need for Truman's involvement in order to secure interagency support for overcoming Soviet jamming. Barrett worried that Sarnoff's committee would actually hurt these efforts, and he was concerned that the committee would encroach upon the domain of the U.S. Advisory Commission on Information, set up by the 1948 Smith-Mundt Act. In the March 9 memorandum Barrett mentioned that a request from Truman to Sarnoff to head the proposed committee "will have to be handled carefully to avoid offending the existing committee headed by Mark Etheridge." Barrett brought the problem of overlap to the attention of Sarnoff, who countered that the Advisory Commission did not have the clout to secure the increase in appropriations that an improved VOA required.[17]

As these discussions were taking place, the State Department confronted the accusations of Senator Joe McCarthy. In a speech delivered in Wheeling, West Virginia, on February 9, 1950, the first-term senator charged the State Department with knowingly employing 205 communists. (Whether or not McCarthy actually stated that number is not known conclusively; he deviated from the printed copy of his speech, and a tape recording was erased shortly afterward). Within a few days McCarthy revised his numbers to eighty-one, then fifty-seven. The ensuing publicity surrounding the charges surprised McCarthy, who had trouble explaining his evidence and its sources. However inadequate his preparation to defend the charges, McCarthy's timing was good. The controversy over American Far East pol-

---

16. Johnson to Truman, February 27, 1950, box 140, folder "VOA," Truman Papers, President's Secretary's Files, General File; David Sarnoff, *Looking Ahead: The Papers of David Sarnoff*.

17. Truman to Acheson, March 1, 1950; Barrett to Acheson, March 2, 1950; Barrett to Acheson, March 9, 1950, *FRUS* 1950, vol. 4, 271–76; memorandum of conversation, March 10, 1950, box 12, folder "Regaining the Psychological Initiative," RG 59, RIIA.

icy still raged; the conviction of Alger Hiss for perjury was just weeks old. Furthermore, many congressional Republicans already had their eyes on the November elections, and they wanted to see a GOP majority in place when the Eighty-second Congress convened. When McCarthy faltered in backing up his charges, Republican Senators Homer Ferguson, Karl Mundt, and Kenneth Wherry lent support.[18]

The Office of Public Affairs was responsible for devising public strategies to convince the American public that the State Department's employees were loyal. Thus the newcomer Barrett confronted the challenge of revamping the VOA at the same time he led the department's efforts to refute McCarthy's charges. At a February 28 special Public Affairs staff meeting it was proposed that Barrett make discussion of ways to overcome problems resulting from McCarthy a regular topic at Acheson's daily 9:30 A.M. staff briefings. Just a few days later Barrett left the morning meeting and said, according to another Public Affairs official, "the Department and the Government must appear to have a positive program and must appear to be doing something. Can't just give impression 'we are sitting on our hands.'"[19] Obviously, Truman and Acheson were also concerned about the impact of McCarthy's charges. At their regular 12:30 P.M. meeting on March 6 Acheson told the president that "arrangements were well in hand for dealing with the McCarthy charges before the sub-committee of the Senate Committee on Foreign Relations." Acheson also briefed Truman on Barrett's memorandum "Taking the Propaganda Offensive." According to Acheson's notes, "[t]he President was much pleased and asked us to follow it up vigorously." Truman was soon leaving for a vacation in Key West, and Acheson indicated that Barrett's additional recommendations would be sent to the president as soon as they were ready. Truman and ranking congressional Democrats were confident that the Senate subcommittee hearings, which opened on March 8, would demonstrate the flimsiness of McCarthy's charges and dispel the negative publicity.[20]

18. For detailed accounts of the Wheeling speech and its aftermath, see Thomas C. Reeves, *The Life and Times of Joe McCarthy: A Biography*, 210–49.

19. Staff meeting agenda, February 28, 1950, box 7, folder "PA Staff Meetings"; J. W. S. to Francis Russell, March 3, 1950, folder "P-Policy Meetings, 1950–52," RG 59, Office of the Assistant Secretary of State for Public Affairs, Office of Public Affairs Subject Files (hereafter cited as OPA Subject Files).

20. Memorandum of conversation, March 6, 1950, box 66, folder "March 1950," Dean Acheson Papers, Truman Library; Reeves, *Life and Times of Joe McCarthy*, 242–43; Robert H. Ferrell, *Harry S. Truman: A Life*, 304–5.

They were wrong; the hearings failed to restore either public or congressional faith in the State Department. Senator Millard Tydings (D–Md.) opened the hearings by admonishing McCarthy that he intended to scrutinize his evidence and uncover his sources. This warning alienated Republican subcommittee members Bourke B. Hickenlooper and Henry Cabot Lodge, Jr. Throughout the hearings, both senators complained of Democratic partisanship, often refused to cooperate with the committee, and did not sign the committee report when it was released on July 17, 1950. Truman's initial refusal to release the loyalty files of persons on McCarthy's lists also hurt the subcommittee because it gave the appearance that the files contained incriminating evidence. On March 22 McCarthy held a press conference and demanded that the files for the eighty-one individuals be turned over to the Tydings committee for review. Tydings himself asked the president to do this in order to restore the committee's eroding credibility. Truman compromised by having FBI Director J. Edgar Hoover give the committee a summary of the file of Owen Lattimore, whom McCarthy had singled out as the State Department's greatest security risk. On May 4, 1950, the president finally allowed the committee to see seventy-one of the files. By that time, however, the Tydings committee had lost the opportunity to restore public confidence in the State Department.[21]

One week after the Tydings hearings began the OPA took aggressive measures to counter the domestic effects of McCarthyism. On March 16 Edward Barrett presented a public relations program to Undersecretary of State James Webb. Barrett first suggested that Acheson appear before the Tydings committee as the hearings drew to a close, "[i]f the atmosphere is right." In front of the committee, Acheson could point out the great harm done to the United States abroad by such hearings and assure the committee members that should the State Department find any communists or fellow travelers within its ranks, it would "clear them out pronto." Barrett also proposed that in the next six weeks the president should deliver a speech on American foreign policy and reassert his confidence in the State Department. Likewise, Acheson should speak at the annual meeting of the American Society of Newspaper Editors, scheduled for April. (This is where Truman delivered the Campaign of Truth speech). Finally, Barrett suggested that Acheson set aside time to meet with individual members of Congress. Barrett followed up on his own advice, meeting with key

21. Reeves, *Life and Times of Joe McCarthy*, 249, 263, 270, 284, 304.

Republican legislators. Their remarks were not encouraging. Karl Mundt told Barrett that "there still would be a good deal of smoke and doubt after the hearings were over." The Public Affairs staff echoed Mundt's prediction at its April 12 meeting, where it was suggested that the loyalty issue would continue to be a problem for at least a year.[22]

Assistant Secretary of State for Congressional Relations Jack McFall also worked hard to refute the charges against the State Department's loyalty. On March 22 McFall proposed to Undersecretary James Webb, who chaired a special strategy committee handling McCarthyism, that the department "supply carefully documented ammunition in speech form to friendly Senators." Subjects included "the obviously stale and pre-investigated character of Senator McCarthy's charges," and emphasis on the stringent screening and security procedures used in the State Department. McFall's office also maintained a twenty-five-page report dated March 23 that detailed individual senators' opposition to U.S. Far East policy, listing pertinent votes, speeches critical of the State Department, and summaries of chief concerns and favorite topics.[23]

While preparing defensive attacks on McCarthyism, Barrett also struggled to implement counter-jamming plans for the VOA. At a March 24, 1950, undersecretaries' meeting Barrett proposed a three-step program for handling jamming: the strengthening of VOA transmissions already in operation, the organization of a special staff group within the NSC to study the problem, and the establishment of a three-person technical advisory group composed of private citizens. Undersecretary of State Dean Rusk opposed using the NSC, arguing that the State Department had the basic authority and means to oversee interdepartmental study, but Barrett insisted. Because of the low priority given to research on jamming by other agencies, presidential direction based on a NSC recommendation was needed. Barrett's concern over the lack of help from other agencies was justified. That same day the State Department forwarded to the CIA a list of intelligence needs. In order to penetrate the jamming, the State Department

22. Barrett to Webb, March 16, 1950, drawer 24, Lawson File. Memorandum of conversation, March 25, 1950, box 60, folder "M-Z," RG 59, RIIA; record of meeting, April 12, 1950, box 7, folder "PA Staff Meetings," RG 59, OPA Subject Files.

23. McFall to Webb, March 22, 1950, box 7, folder "Numbered Memorandum," RG 59, Office of the Assistant Secretary of State for Public Affairs, Office of Public Affairs, Records Relating to the Department PR Working Group; "Senatorial Attitudes toward Far Eastern Policies," March 23, 1950, box 2, folder "Congressional Relations 1950," RG 59, OPA Subject Files.

required all available information on Soviet blocking techniques and equipment, as well as the latest technical research and recommendations. The information currently held by the State Department did "not appear to represent the complete body of data which has been available among the intelligence agencies." The letter reminded CIA director Roscoe Hillenkoetter that in July 1949 the CIA had taken on the responsibility of providing the State Department with specific technical data. Pending an NSC decision on the priority of VOA jamming in relation to other intelligence needs, the CIA was asked to collect, evaluate, and forward to the VOA pertinent technical information. The CIA had provided such data to the State Department in late August 1949, but the report was "completely inadequate for State's purposes." Subsequent correspondence with the CIA during the fall of 1949 showed little promise of improvement.[24]

The CIA's reluctance to help the State Department stemmed from the belief that the Soviets actually hurt themselves by jamming VOA broadcasts to the Soviet Union. Valuable radio equipment was diverted from other uses, and it was potentially helpful to the United States to have the Russian people know that their government went to great lengths to keep them from hearing the VOA. According to the CIA, "[t]hese advantages would continue even if no information could be transmitted." Furthermore, technical difficulties, the danger of initiating bitter "blow-by-blow retaliation," and high costs counted among the many disadvantages of continuing VOA broadcasts.[25] This response could hardly have been more dismissive. As far as the CIA was concerned, rather than playing a direct part in fighting the Cold War, the VOA was most useful as a decoy: as long as the Soviets considered the VOA to be a threat and jammed it, the actual content and reception of VOA broadcasts did not matter.

To make matters worse, an NSC analysis of VOA jamming needs also failed to give the State Department the support it sought. Dated April 4, 1950, NSC 66 reviewed the damaging effects of Soviet jamming, both on the VOA and international radio communications. Although jamming at that time was limited to the Soviet Union, its extension to broadcasts to the

24. Record of the Undersecretary's Meeting, March 24, 1950, *FRUS* 1950, vol. 4, 280–81. For the CIA's intransigence, see Special Assistant to the Secretary of State to Director of Central Intelligence, March 24, 1950, with Appendix 1 of the Report of the IAC Ad Hoc Committee on VOA Jamming, box 193, folder "Memorandum Approvals," Truman Papers, President's Secretary's Files, NSC Files; Frederick Oechsner to George V. Allen, November 4, 1949, drawer 25, Lawson File.

25. CIA, "Historical Developments," 10.

satellite countries was a distinct possibility. The report observed that many technical problems concerning counter-jamming could be solved by the Defense Department's Research and Development Board and the CIA's Foreign Broadcasting Information Bureau, but that efforts in support of the VOA had been insufficient due to the lack of priority for counter-jamming. After making this point, however, NSC 66 stopped short of ranking counter-jamming as an urgent task. Instead, it recommended that the NSC set up a special staff group of officials from the Federal Communications Commission, CIA, State, and Defense to determine jamming research needs. After receiving the group's report the NSC would then "establish the priorities adjustments required to provide support for the Voice of America in the fields of intelligence and of research and development." Not surprisingly, the CIA and the Defense Department continued to ignore the State Department. Just one day after NSC 66 was signed, the Defense representative on the interdepartmental Intelligence Advisory Committee (IAC), which had been formed in July 1949 to study jamming, stated for the record that "there was no method of overcoming Soviet jamming in the ultimate sense." On April 21 Hillenkoetter designated the CIA representative for the staff authorized by NSC 66, but he contended that the agency had been giving sufficient intelligence support to the VOA all along. Secretary of Defense Louis Johnson waited more than a month to reply to NSC 66 and bluntly stated that there was no need for the NSC to set up the proposed group because IAC was already working on the problem.[26]

III. McCarthyism and The Campaign of Truth

With the OPA's counter-jamming initiative stymied, domestic concerns—specifically McCarthyism—intertwined with planning for the Campaign of Truth, as demonstrated by Truman's handling of Senator William Benton's (D–Conn.) proposed Marshall Plan of Ideas. As former assistant secretary of state for Public Affairs, Benton was one of the State Department's and VOA's greatest allies in the Congress, though as a junior senator, his influence was limited. (Connecticut Governor Chester Bowles, Benton's former business partner, appointed Benton as senator on

26. NSC 66, "Support for the Voice of America in the Fields of Intelligence and of Research and Development," April 4, 1950, *FRUS* 1950, vol. 4, 288–90. For continuing problems with the CIA and Defense Department, see W. K. Scott to Anderson, April 5, 1950, box 5, folder "Jamming," RG 59, RIIA. Hillenkoetter to James Lay, April 21, 1950, and Louis Johnson to James Lay, May 10, 1950, box 193, folder "Memorandum Approvals," NSC Files.

December 17, 1949, to fill a vacant seat.) Benton deplored the attacks on the State Department, and he was one of McCarthy's earliest and most vocal critics in the Senate. Encouraged by his friend Robert Hutchins, president of the University of Chicago, Benton defended Acheson and the State Department in his first speech on the Senate floor on March 22, 1950. His remarks served as an introduction for the main purpose of his address, the "Marshall Plan of Ideas" (S.R. 243, 81st Cong., 2d sess.). S.R. 243 recommended a six-point program in the field of international information activities and exchange, including expansion of existing State Department activities and coordination of such activities between the noncommunist nations of the world.[27] Delivered just one month later, Truman's Campaign of Truth speech made these same two points.

Benton had consulted with Truman before making his speech, thus circumventing Barrett and the OPA.[28] On March 18 Benton sent a copy of S.R. 243 to Truman's staff in Key West, where the president was vacationing. The draft read, "[r]esolved, That the President is requested to cause to be initiated . . . an intensified program of information and exchange." Truman asked Benton to substitute "the United States" for "the President," and Benton complied.[29] The change in phrasing was significant because it left open the opportunity for Truman to make his own speech on the subject. As explained, Secretary of Defense Louis Johnson had suggested on February 27, 1950, that Truman give a speech before the Congress on the VOA, and Barrett had also proposed the speech idea in his March 9 and 16 memoranda regarding Sarnoff's proposal and the department's handling of McCarthyism, respectively.

Not long after Benton presented the Marshall Plan of Ideas to the Senate, plans for Truman's speech took shape. On April 12 White House speechwriter George Elsey informed an NSC member that the president was

27. Hyman, *The Lives of William Benton*, 428–29, 453–58.
28. Benton's action presented Barrett with a dilemma. Benton's support in the Senate for the information and educational program was badly needed, yet like Sarnoff's proposed high-profile committee, S.R. 243 offered no real help in securing interagency support for counter-jamming of the VOA. On March 30, 1950, Charles Hulten, the general manager of the Office of International Information and Cultural Affairs, wrote Benton that his proposal was being considered; however, the State Department was in the process of devising its own plan for an expanded program, and whether or not the two could be combined remained to be determined. Box 43, folder "Campaign of Truth," RG 59, RIIA.
29. Benton to David Niles, March 20, 1950, box 113, folder "Benton, William, US Senate," Truman Papers, President's Secretary's Files, General File.

giving a speech in a week on American propaganda. According to Deputy Undersecretary Max W. Bishop's account of the conversation, Elsey told the NSC member that there was no connection between the speech and NSC 66, despite apparent similarities. The speech had been decided on some time ago, and "this subject is a 'favorite theme' of the President's." Considering NSC 66's focus on counter-jamming, Elsey's claim suggested that Truman did not regard the speech as just a part of the program to overcome Soviet jamming. Edward Barrett, who headed efforts to stop Soviet jamming, played only a small part in writing the speech, further indicating that procuring support for the VOA's counter-jamming needs was not the only aim of the speech.[30]

Was the president simply giving an address on "a favorite theme," or did the domestic political problems incurred by McCarthyism motivate him as well? Also on April 12, Senator Tydings sent a memorandum to the president suggesting strategies on "how to reestablish the White House and the Truman Administration as the foe of Communism at home as well as abroad." According to Tydings, although the public largely supported foreign policies such as the Marshall Plan and NATO, they were worried that the administration was overlooking the threat of communism within the United States. Republicans in Congress exploited the issue of communist infiltration of the State Department in order to weaken support for the administration's domestic program. Tydings proposed that Truman give a speech that did the following: "[Explain to] the people you are the implacable foe of Communism, what you have done and are doing to eradicate it and hold it in check at home and abroad; that you are doing everything in your power to keep the government above any known Communistic influences."[31]

Though it is difficult to measure how seriously or carefully Truman considered Tydings's memorandum, the advice echoed the concerns and suggestions that Edward Barrett, Louis Johnson, friendly senators, and the White House staff had given the president throughout the spring.

---

30. Max Bishop to Dean Rusk, April 12, 1950, box 45, folder "VOA NSC 66," RG 59, Records of the Policy Planning Staff Relating to State Department Participation in NSC. According to Barrett, he submitted materials concerning the Campaign of Truth to Elsey and his colleagues, who then wrote the American Society of Newspaper Editors speech. Barrett was then asked to read over the draft. Oral History Interview, Edward W. Barrett, July 9, 1974, Truman Library, 71.

31. Tydings to Truman, April 12, 1950, box 1268, folder "Subcommittee on Loyalty of State Department," Truman Papers, White House Official File.

Furthermore, Truman's inner circle openly discussed the idea of using the Campaign of Truth to contain the damage caused by McCarthy. The subject of the VOA came up during a meeting between Truman, Acheson, and Senate Foreign Relations Committee chair Tom Connally held just one week after the declaration of the Campaign of Truth. The three men agreed that consultation with Senate Republicans such as Styles Bridges, Alexander Wiley, and Henry Cabot Lodge might help restore bipartisanship in foreign policy. Then Acheson asked Connally if he thought "it would be helpful in getting the McCarthy charges off the front page if a subcommittee, on which Senators Smith and Lodge might be present, would take up the Benton Resolution and get outstanding figures to testify." Connally was pessimistic: "he thought the McCarthy charges were so sensational that they would continue to occupy the front page, and that while he hoped that the Voice of America, strengthened and improved, would be useful he had doubts as to whether it would reach the right people."[32] This discussion was consistent with Truman and Acheson's handling of the VOA since February. Together, the Sarnoff committee, the White House's handling of Barrett's March proposals on improving the VOA, the ineffectual NSC 66, and Truman's revision of Benton's "Marshall Plan of Ideas" indicate that the president and Acheson considered the strengthening of the VOA to be a solution to a persistent domestic political problem as well as to the problem of getting information about the country's foreign policy to audiences abroad.

The link between McCarthyism and the Campaign of Truth is strengthened further by comparing Truman's American Society of Newspaper Editors speech with NSC 68, which Paul Nitze, head of the State Department's Policy Planning Staff, wrote between February and April 1950. Though the Campaign of Truth speech and NSC 68 were drafted independently, the language used in both is strikingly similar. In ominous terms, NSC 68 described the immediate need of the United States to challenge Soviet communism on all fronts. NSC 68 stated that the Soviet "assault on free institutions is world-wide now," also warning that "[a]t the ideological or psychological level, in the struggle for men's minds, the conflict is worldwide." Nitze recommended that the United States "organize and enlist the energies and resources of the free world in a positive program for peace which will frustrate the Kremlin design for world domination." In his speech Truman echoed these words: "[T]he cause of free-

32. Memorandum of conversation, April 27, 1950, box 66, folder "April 1950," Acheson Papers, 2.

dom is being challenged throughout the world today by the forces of imperialistic communism. This is a struggle, above all else, for the minds of men. Propaganda is one of the most powerful weapons the Communists have in this struggle." Truman concluded by calling on the State Department to coordinate its information activities with the other free nations of the world "in a sustained, intensified program to promote the cause of freedom against the propaganda of slavery."[33]

Both Truman's speech and NSC 68 reflect the siege mentality that overtook the administration in late 1949 and early 1950. Both the CIA and the OPA believed that Soviet jamming of the VOA showed the inexorable expansionism of the Soviet Union. In late 1949 Truman and senior officials in the State Department grew increasingly dubious of George Kennan's contention that the United States could safely concentrate on economic rather than military applications of containment. As a result, the creator of containment and the strongest advocate of its flexible implementation found his influence dwindling.[34] Indeed, Nitze had replaced Kennan as head of the Policy Planning Staff. Senior officials' commitment to all-out containment during early 1950 contrasted sharply with GOP charges that the Truman administration was soft on communism. Of course, the public and congressional Republicans were not privy to top secret documents that showed the administration's concerns and plans. Perhaps ironically, when Truman signed NSC 68 later that year, he ordered it kept secret because he worried that its dire predictions would frighten the American public. Truman directed *"that this report be handled with special security precautions in accordance with the President's desire that no publicity be given this report or its contents without his approval"* [emphasis in original]. NSC 68 thus presented the administration with a dilemma: it displayed unwavering resolve to fight communism, yet its existence could not be revealed directly. Whether or not Truman himself accepted NSC 68 in toto is almost irrelevant. As historian Ernest May has observed, "[i]n face of a united bureaucracy warning that the world risked enslavement, a president already under attack from the right could not afford simply to do nothing."[35]

33. NSC 68, "United States Objectives and Programs for National Security," April 14, 1950, in Ernest R. May, ed., *American Cold War Strategy: Interpreting NSC 68*, 28, 31, 79. For the president's speech, see Truman, "Going Forward," 669, 672.

34. John Lewis Gaddis, *Strategies of Containment: A Critical Appraisal of Postwar American National Security Policy*, 83–84.

35. May, *American Cold War Strategy*, 14.

In this sense, the Campaign of Truth speech served as a filter through which the administration could safely articulate its concerns about Soviet expansionism and prove its resolve to stop it. By presenting the Soviet threat in terms of a worldwide ideological challenge, Truman and his advisers cleansed NSC 68 of its extreme tone without removing its imperatives. The battle for people's minds signified the real battle, but safely so: words were not warheads. Throughout his speech Truman suggested that if given the "plain, simple, unvarnished truth," oppressed peoples of the world would choose democracy over communism. The Campaign of Truth speech also provided an opportunity to counterattack the right, though the president was careful not to mention any names. In his opening remarks on April 20 Truman lauded the editors present for presenting objectively the facts readers needed in order to form their own opinions. Then the president took a swipe at Republicans: "[F]oreign policy is not a matter for partisan presentation. The facts about Europe or Asia should not be twisted to conform to one side or the other of a political dispute. Twisting the facts might change the course of an election at home, but it would certainly damage our country's program abroad." After stressing the vital role a free press plays in determining what a nation should do, Truman added, "[T]here is too much nonsense about striped trousers in foreign affairs. Far more influence is exerted by the baggy pants of the managing editor."[36]

Truman spoke not just to the nation's newspaper editors; he also addressed McCarthy himself. That same day the Wisconsin senator addressed the American Society of Newspaper Editors. In a lengthy speech McCarthy defended his charges against the State Department, emphasizing that liberals in the Roosevelt and Truman administrations provided the channel through which communists were subverting the government. Though the speech essentially reiterated what he had said publicly all spring, the State Department took it seriously. The next day a Public Affairs official wrote to Undersecretary James Webb that McCarthy had made a "distinct impression." His audience's applause was extended, and the State Department came out looking bad. The department was ready for McCarthy's redux, though. On the last day of the ASNE convention Secretary of State Dean Acheson delivered a case-by-case defense of

36. Truman, "Going Forward," 669. For a similar interpretation of the links between the Campaign of Truth and NSC 68, see Walter L. Hixson, *Parting the Curtain: Propaganda, Culture, and the Cold War, 1945–1961*, 14–15.

State Department officials. Just two days before, Barrett had submitted a report, "Current Opinion about the State Department," to Acheson's office. The report noted that four out of ten press and radio commentators and six out of ten citizens believed that the State Department may have had disloyal employees. There was another reason for Acheson's speech as well. After reading a draft of NSC 68 in early April, Barrett had suggested to the secretary that the government needed to raise public awareness about the problems described and to show that steps were being taken to solve them. In his address Acheson acted on Barrett's proposal by warning that the Soviet Union threatened not only the United States but also "the civilization in which we live and to the whole physical environment in which that civilization can exist."[37] Like the president, Acheson was rebutting McCarthy while assuring the public that the administration was capable of meeting the Soviet threat.

But as Senator Connally had predicted at his April 27 meeting with Truman and Dean Acheson, publicity for an improved VOA did not budge McCarthy from the headlines. True to the fears of Barrett and the others in the OPA, members of Congress and the American public continued to believe that the State Department had disloyal employees. The Tydings committee continued its investigation through July; it too failed to restore the State Department's sullied image. These disappointments aside, the OPA was able to concentrate on securing supplemental appropriations from Congress to pay for the VOA's expansion and worldwide counterjamming equipment. As officials prepared in June for these budget hearings, communist North Korea's invasion of the Republic of Korea abruptly added a new priority. Both NSC 68 and the Campaign of Truth had warned that the Soviet Union and its communist allies were bent on world domination; the invasion seemed to show this ominous prediction coming true. Now the VOA became part of the U.S. war effort to turn back communist aggression on the Korean peninsula.

37. McCarthy speech before the American Society of Newspaper Editors, April 20, 1950, box 17, folder "Disloyalty Investigation, McCarthy, Joseph," Hickenlooper Papers, Foreign Relations Subseries, 12–14; Lloyd Lehrbas to James Webb, April 21, 1950, drawer 23; Barrett to Battle, April 20, 1950, drawer 22, Lawson File; *Department of State Bulletin* 22 (May 1, 1950): 672; Barrett to Acheson, April 6, 1950, *FRUS* 1950 vol. 1, 225–26; Nancy E. Bernhard, "Clearer than Truth: Public Affairs Television and the State Department's Domestic Information Campaigns, 1947–1952," 561–63.

Chapter 5

Conflict Becomes Consensus
The VOA and the Korean War

North Korea's invasion of South Korea in June 1950 overshadowed plans to implement the Campaign of Truth. Yet the war also invigorated the VOA, giving it new purpose. During July, as the North Korean army routed South Korean defense forces and hastily assembled UN troops, the VOA consciously sought to sustain morale and rally worldwide support for the U.S.-led UN counterattack. Soon this aim expanded to include the attempted demoralization of North Korean soldiers and civilians. In late October, when Chinese intervention crushed hopes of quick and total victory, the VOA renewed these efforts and took on the task of convincing the Chinese people and government that the UN invasion of North Korea (Democratic People's Republic of Korea) did not threaten them. Soviet characterizations of U.S. actions also led to programming seeking to prove the facts as understood by VOA officials—that the Soviets were responsible for the war, and that the United States and United Nations fought on the one true side of liberation and democracy.

At home the VOA faced a far different challenge. For congressional Republicans, the battle to define the truth about the Korean War was twofold—the United States versus the Soviet Union, and the administration versus the minority party. Republicans interpreted the VOA's delay in blaming the Soviet Union for the attack on South Korea (Republic of Korea) as a ploy to conceal the Democrats' long-running "appeasement" of communists, which they believed had encouraged the invasion. This reasoning prompted scrutiny of VOA scripts during the summer and fall of 1950 as various Republican members of Congress tried to show that the VOA was whitewashing Democratic failures and flaws. In early 1951 Senate debate on the president's power to send additional U.S. troops to Europe increased the friction between the administration and Republicans, as did the furor greeting Truman's recall of General Douglas

MacArthur in April. These events disrupted the VOA's efforts to build worldwide support for U.S. action in Korea and rebut communist propaganda, for they conveyed an image of domestic political turbulence and an unpopular war. Consequently, VOA officials decided to downplay Republican dissent in order to present to the world an image of a nation and government united in the fight against communist aggression.

I. Korea on the Airwaves

On the night of June 25, 1950, the VOA's English Program to Europe interrupted its regularly scheduled feature to report that North Korean troops had crossed the Thirty-eighth parallel, entering South Korea.[1] Within the next twenty-four hours President Truman quickly made two crucial decisions: the Soviet Union had ordered and was sponsoring the invasion, and the United States would help defend South Korea. The former decision was practically instinctive. In the hours following the North Korean attack the State Department's Office of Intelligence Research drafted a report that stated the invasion must have been "a Soviet move" because Moscow had complete control over North Korea. This evaluation was not second-guessed. Worried that other Soviet-initiated invasions were imminent, Secretary of State Dean Acheson warned American embassies and consulates on June 26 about the possibility of such attacks, especially in Germany. Acheson's fear, shared by top military and diplomatic officials, created a problem for the VOA, particularly with regard to the new Campaign of Truth.[2] To blame the Soviet Union for the attack reflected the truth as perceived by administration officials, but ran the risk of provoking the Soviets.

The VOA thus tried to convey blame without explicitly stating that the Soviet Union had instigated the attack on South Korea. On June 26, 1950, Overnight Guidance instructed that "unofficial comment placing blame

1. English Program Schedule to Europe, June 25, 1950, box 4, folder "June 10 to July 3 1950," RG 306, VOA Reports.

2. "Intelligence Estimate," June 25, 1950; Secretary of State to Certain Diplomatic and Consular Officers, June 26, 1950; Memorandum of conversation, Truman et al., June 26, 1950, *FRUS* 1950, vol. 7, 148-54, 166, 178. For forty years scholars in the West supported the belief that Stalin had orchestrated the North Korean attack. See, for example, Adam Ulam, *The Communists: The Story of Power and Lost Illusions, 1948–1991,* 81–82. The opening of Soviet archives in the early 1990s, however, revealed evidence that the initiative for the invasion came from North Korean leader Kim Il Sung, who persistently sought Stalin's approval to reunify the peninsula. See Kathryn Weathersby, "New Findings on the Korean War."

on Moscow" could be used as long as the source was made clear, but "avoid impression that this is official line." The next day, this policy was changed with the approval of Undersecretary of State Dean Rusk and George Kennan. "No RPT [repeat] no good purpose can now be served, and much harm may be done, by explicitly associating USSR with responsibility for development this situation. Purpose SHLD [should] be to let facts of recent days speak for themselves." An internal review of June coverage of the hostilities in Korea concluded that the VOA did not directly identify the Soviet Union as the aggressor. In the first half of July, however, VOA writers began using a variety of thinly coded phrases and news items to blame the Soviets. The French desk referred to "the forces of those who encourage them [North Korean forces]," while Czech news pointed out that the North Koreans were using Soviet-made war materiel. The VOA's Mandarin-language broadcasts warned China, "[a]s the Soviets exposed their hand in Poland, so have they done so in Korea." Guidance for the second week of July prohibited charging the Soviet Union with *"initiating"* hostility, yet encouraged the use of comment to "directly or by implication assign the Soviet Union moral responsibility for the Korean conflict" (emphasis in original). Nearly a month after the invasion the VOA still drew only indirect connections between the Soviet Union and the invasion of South Korea. Guidance on July 19 called for "extended exploitation" of Truman's address to Congress, pointing out that the speech did not specifically blame the Soviets but rather assigned "moral responsibility," the phrase already approved for broadcast.[3]

The VOA's oblique way of blaming the Soviets for the invasion reflected uncertainties about the world situation, but ironically, this caution caused political troubles at home. Congressional Republicans blamed North Korean aggression on years of soft appeasement policy in the Far East. The day after the invasion Styles Bridges asked, "Mr. President, will we continue appeasement?" and stated that the United States had given away Manchuria and allowed Poland to fall to communism. Senator William Knowland complained that the Far East had long been given lower prior-

3. Overnight Guidance #484, June 26, 1950, box 90, folder "June 1950"; OII Monthly Content Report, July 12, 1950, box 109, folder "OII Monthly Content Reports," RG 59, RIIA; telegram, June 27, 1950, 511.00/6–2750, RG 59, CDF; French script, July 3, 1950; Czech script, July 7, 1950; "The Stream of Abuse," July 11, 1950, boxes 4–5, RG 306, VOA Reports; Weekly Guidance #14, July 6, 1950; Weekly Guidance #16, July 19, 1950, box 4, folder "Weekly Guidance," RG 59, RIIA.

ity than Europe and the Middle East for support against communism. After Truman addressed Congress on July 19, 1950, Senate Minority Leader Kenneth Wherry promised that Congress would cooperate with the mobilization of American troops, but he blamed the crisis in Korea on years of giving into the Soviets. The same day Representative George Dondero (R–Mich.) said, "[w]e are reaping the whirlwind from the conferences at Yalta, Tehran, and Potsdam by the Roosevelt and Truman administrations." Republicans agreeing with Wherry and Dondero included, among others, Representatives Arthur Miller, Paul Shafer, Lawrence Smith, Noah Mason, and Walter Judd, and Senators George Malone and Robert Taft.[4] Already predisposed to believing that the VOA slanted its news to the administration's favor, Republicans suspected that the VOA was whitewashing Democratic appeasement in Korea.

For example, the VOA's coverage of the Senate investigation of McCarthy's charges came under scrutiny. As North Korean forces advanced deep into South Korean territory, the Tydings committee wrapped up its hearings amid rancorous partisanship. McCarthy claimed eighty-one State Department files had been "raped" to remove incriminating evidence, a charge that Tydings indignantly denied. In its final report released on July 17 the committee excoriated McCarthy for making false charges and perpetuating a vast hoax. Republican committee member Henry Cabot Lodge filed a separate minority report, while his colleague Bourke B. Hickenlooper declined to sign either report. Two days after the release of the Tydings report John Taber requested VOA scripts for July 18. Styles Bridges also asked for scripts, and copies of VOA output to the Far East for July 17–19 were sent to both men. Subordinates assured Assistant Secretary of State Edward Barrett that the Tydings Majority report was "covered 'adequately' in the scripts." Taber did not agree. In a July 27 letter to Secretary of State Acheson he criticized news of the hearings and suggested that the department use the McCarran security rider (which permitted the dismissal of federal employees without following standard civil service procedures) to clean up the VOA. Edward Barrett, who drafted a four-page reply to Taber, defended the VOA's coverage of the Tydings Report, which "underscored the fact that a really free nation does not choke

4. *Congressional Record*, 81st Cong., 2d sess., June 26 and July 19, 1950, vol. 96, 9154–55, 9158, 10643; radio address, July 19, 1950, box 18, folder "Radio NBC 7–19–50," Kenneth Wherry Papers, Nebraska State Historical Society, Lincoln; Theoharis, *The Yalta Myths*, 98; Ronald J. Caridi, *The Korean War and American Politics: The Republican Party as a Case Study*, 39–44.

off political discussion and dispute."[5] For Barrett, this showed the essential difference between the Soviet Union and the United States. The Soviets suppressed embarrassing news; Americans did not.

Barrett's spirited defense was misdirected; he and Taber were talking past one another. Barrett conceived of the VOA's duty and challenges in international terms—that was his job, after all. As assistant secretary of state for Public Affairs, Barrett was responsible for telling the world about American policies and people, and he took his task seriously. Just like his predecessors George V. Allen and William Benton, Barrett found the VOA's work complicated by the lies told about the United States by the Soviet Union in its international information programs. Taber, however, defined the VOA's international task using domestic terms. As far as he was concerned, what the Soviet Union said about McCarthy (and the effects on American prestige abroad) was less important than what the VOA said about McCarthy, or other Republicans' actions, for that matter. The VOA was part of the State Department under the control of a Democratic president; could the VOA be trusted to tell the truth about unpopular and damaging revelations about either? Taber thought not. Reviews of scripts were thus necessary to keep the VOA from discrediting Republicans and promoting the administration.

Political differences between the VOA and the United States' Eastern European communities further undermined the VOA's standing with congressional Republicans. Some Eastern Europeans living in the United States wanted the VOA to promote nationalist and separatist agendas for their respective home countries. In order to coerce the VOA they sent accusations of communism within the VOA to members of Congress. In February 1950 Senator H. Alexander Smith (R–N.J.) received a letter from *Slovak Amerike* editor John Sciranka claiming that certain VOA employees were disloyal. Smith gave the letter to Barrett, who turned the matter over to the State Department's security unit for investigation. (A Slovakian nationalist, Sciranka would within a year appear before Senator Pat McCarran's Internal Security Subcommittee. See chapter 6.) In late August

---

5. "Tydings Asserts F.B.I. Cleared State Dept. Files," *New York Herald Tribune*, June 22, 1950; "McCarthy Is Held Refuted on Files," *New York Times*, June 25, 1950; Reeves, *Life and Times of Joe McCarthy*, 304. For Taber's interest, see Mitchell to Barrett, July 27, 1950, box 60, folder "A-G," RG 59, RIIA; Taber to Acheson, July 27, 1950; Barrett to Taber, August 2, 1950, box 65, folder "Foreign Relations—Voice of America," George M. Elsey Papers, Truman Administration Subject File, Truman Library.

1950 Senator Homer Ferguson (R–Mich.) forwarded a constituent letter to the VOA that charged Russian and Ukraine desk employee Alexander Barmine with being a Soviet agent. The letter writer demanded that the VOA take Ukrainian broadcasts off the Russian desk and set up a separate section. Throughout 1950 and 1951 Slovakian separatist groups made similar accusations against Czech Desk Chief Karel Sheldon, sending their complaints to Representatives John Rooney (D–N.Y.) and Karl Stefan (R–Nebr.), the latter of whom was born in Bohemia. In a draft letter for Stefan and Rooney, Barrett said the charges against Sheldon were not uncommon given the rivalries dividing America's Eastern Europeans communities. "No matter what we do or say on the Voice of America, we can anticipate that one or more of the relatively important factions will be engaged in filing complaints about the Voice's work."[6] By taking their complaints to members of Congress, these factions contributed to the perception that the VOA was soft on communism.

The VOA's treatment of the war in Korea attracted the most Republican attention. During August 1950 requests for scripts about Korea or news broadcast to the Far East inundated VOA offices. Staff in New York and Washington reported being "greatly strained by constant Congressional requests for scripts, recordings and information of all kinds." George Dondero asked for original and translated scripts for all daily broadcasts to Germany, the Soviet Union, Poland, and Austria from May 1 through mid-August, a package that would have exceeded twenty thousand pages. Instead, Dondero was sent scripts from each month. In order to meet the high demand, VOA chief Foy Kohler suggested that the VOA turn its scripts over to the Library of Congress's Legislative Reference Service, which could then make the necessary translations and provide them to interested members of Congress. Barrett rejected the idea because he did not want legislators to see scripts that he did not first review. An incident that occurred in July showed why. When Kenneth Wherry requested scripts to Korea for July 23–27, Barrett ordered the script for one

6. Smith to Barrett, February 21, 1950; Barrett to Smith, March 10, 1950, box 76, folder "Smith, H. Alexander (Sen.) New Jersey 1950"; Sargeant to Barrett, August 5, 1950, box 75, folder "Rooney"; Hulten to Wilber, September 23, 1950, box 60, folder "M-Z," RG 59, RIIA; August 28, 1950, 511.004/8–2850, RG 59, CDF; Barrett to Acheson, "Background Statement," March 27, 1951, drawer 22, Lawson File, 2–7; "Summary of Karel Sheldon Case," undated, box 4, folder "Phone Notes HHS," RG 59, Records of the Assistant Secretary of State for Public Affairs, Edward Barrett 1950–1951 (hereafter cited as Barrett Files).

broadcast held back—it had fifteen minutes of commentary on a Harvard University experiment in which pigeons were being trained to play Ping-Pong. According to a Public Affairs official, Barrett was extremely upset that such programs were being aired. Whatever Barrett's personal appraisal of the script, his decision to withhold it from Wherry violated the Smith-Mundt Act, which stipulated that any radio script "on request, . . . shall be made available to Members of Congress."[7]

On September 1, 1950, an administrative assistant for William Knowland called the VOA's New York offices and requested all news scripts for August 28–31, indicating that the material was needed as quickly as possible. Policy writers in New York surmised that Knowland was interested in the VOA's coverage of Douglas MacArthur's August 26 statement to the Veterans of Foreign Wars. The general had emphasized the importance of keeping Taiwan in Chiang Kai-shek's hands. After reviewing the scripts, policy writers assured Barrett that Knowland's request could be met without fear of "serious repercussions," and Barrett sent the scripts on September 7. The VOA had reported MacArthur's statement, making it clear that it represented personal opinion, not official U.S. policy, and Knowland's office made nothing further of the matter, at least with regard to the VOA.[8]

The struggle to convince congressional Republicans that the VOA's programming was nonpartisan distracted VOA officials from their main goal:

7. "USIE Progress and Problems," August 25, 1950, box 192, folder "Reports USIE Advisory Commission"; Scott to Anderson, September 8, 1950, box 59, folder "Scripts," RG 59, RIIA; memorandum to Dondero, August 28, 1950, 511.004/8–1450; Kohler to Barrett, August 10, 1950, 511.004/8–1050; November 20, 1950, 511.004/11–2050, RG 59, CDF. For Barrett's violation of the Smith-Mundt Act, see *United States Information and Educational Exchange Act of 1948*, Public Law 402, 80th Cong., 2d sess. (January 27, 1948), 10. By October 1950 a compromise between Kohler's and Barrett's positions was struck. The department forwarded monthly samplings of VOA scripts to the Library of Congress, where interested legislators could read them. This way, control over the content open to review lay with the VOA. William Player to Barrett, October 26, 1950, box 76, folder "Smith, H. Alexander (Sen.) New Jersey 1950," RG 59, RIIA.

8. William Manchester, *American Caesar: Douglas MacArthur 1880–1964*, 568; Sulkin to Player, September 1, 1950; Barrett to Knowland, September 7, 1950, box 60, folder "H–L," RG 59, RIIA; Player to Barrett, September 7, 1950, 511.004/9–750, RG 59, CDF; "'Voice' Has Its Troubles," *New York Herald Tribune*, September 3, 1950. In early October, however, Knowland complained publicly about a magazine article distributed in the USIE libraries overseas. Knowland accused the authors of promoting an agenda of appeasement because they suggested that the United States might be able to have a working relationship with the Chinese Communists. Unsigned notes, October 7, 1950, box 60, folder "Knowland," RG 59, RIIA.

to aid the U.S.-led counterattack on North Korea. A Special Guidance issued five days after the invasion stated that media should build confidence in the free world's decision to carry out the UN resolution to defend the Republic of Korea.[9] Other guidance instructed the VOA to boost the morale of South Korean forces by summarizing American press accounts of their bravery. In late July the failure to halt the North Korean march toward Pusan was given a positive spin: say that we are trading space for time, weekly guidance advised. VOA output also sought to undermine North Korean fighting resolve by describing worldwide support for the UN and predicting certain victory. When the Soviet Union characterized U.S. action as a racial war against Asians, the VOA struck back by immediately broadcasting the news that troops from Thailand and the Philippines were joining the UN forces in Korea. By September 15 a complete plan for rallying the South and demoralizing the North was in place. The plan even outlined postwar information program aims, though the success of General Douglas MacArthur's risky landing at Inchon—taking place on September 15—was obviously not yet apparent.[10]

Hopes for a quick and decisive victory were soon dashed. Truman's decision to allow MacArthur's forces to cross the thirty-eighth parallel prompted Chinese intervention in late October. As U.S. forces approached the Yalu River, the border between China and North Korea, Chinese troops poured into a wide gap between the two rapidly advancing flanks. MacArthur had chosen to ignore reports of Chinese military activity; as a result, American and UN forces were ill-prepared for this counter-invasion from the north.[11] The rapid gains of the preceding weeks vanished as the U.S. military reeled in its longest retreat ever, back to and beyond the Thirty-eighth parallel. Lost too in the retreat was the widespread belief that the conflict was nearing an end. This bitter setback intensified the prevailing desire to use the VOA to maintain morale and, in order to rebut communist characterizations of U.S. aims, to justify U.S. involvement on democratic and peaceful grounds. After pointing out that the Chinese may have entered the war out of fear that U.S. forces intended to cross the Yalu

9. Special Information Policy Guidance on Korea #8, 511.00/6–305, RG 59, CDF.

10. Overnight Guidance #503, July 21, 1950, box 90, folder "June"; Weekly Information Policy Guidance #17, July 26, 1950, box 4, folder "Weekly Guidances"; "Summary of Psychological Warfare Activities—Korea," July 29, 1950; "Country Paper for Korea," September 15, 1950, box 18, folder "Korea," RG 59, RIIA; "'Voice' Denies U.S. Is 'Fighting Asia,'" *New York Post*, August 20, 1950.

11. Manchester, *American Caesar*, 600–601.

River, Edward Barrett expressed the opinion that "the Russians have prob- ably encouraged these fears by falsified 'intelligence' reports and the like." At the same time, Barrett continued, the Chinese were using propaganda to make the United States out as an aggressor. Accordingly, Barrett and the other members of the Interdepartmental Coordinating Staff, which bal- anced the information and psychological warfare activities of the military and State Department, recommended that the VOA and other media spare no effort to "get the true facts across to the Chinese Government and peo- ple." Guidance issued right after this meeting instructed the VOA and other media to use any official U.S. government statements indicating that the United States and United Nations were not threatening Chinese terri- tory or interests, but rather were trying to help the Korean people create an independent nation for themselves.[12]

II. Transformation of Dissent and Partisanship

The domestic and foreign pressures bearing on its programming created a dilemma for the VOA. In light of the attention congressional Republicans were giving the agency, the rift between the minority party and the execu- tive branch could not be ignored without risking backlash. But if the VOA did not make clear official U.S. policy, it failed its stated mission. Moreover, the war in Korea brought morale concerns into the equation. Coverage of domestic dissent undermined efforts to build worldwide support for the U.S.-led troops in Korea. The solution? The VOA transformed conflict into consensus, that is, it consistently presented Republican dissent as a normal product of the nation's democratic system. On the surface, such handling seems ordinary. Political debate and disagreement often does produce con- sensus (or compromise), and the right to dissent is a hallmark of American democracy. In its coverage, however, the VOA put the cart before the horse. Rather than show minority party dissent as a step toward agreement or as a genuine difference of opinion, the VOA presented consensus as a done deal and dissent as ex post facto haggling, a sort of minor negotiation about details. In this handling, the VOA stripped dissent of its substance and turned it into an image, a symbol that enriched the VOA's narrative about the efficacy and superiority of American democracy, but which did not dis- rupt efforts to convince foreign audiences that Republican members of

12. "Re: Chinese in Korea," Edward Barrett notes, November 7, 1950, box 4, folder "FE, EUR 1951," RG 59, Barrett Files; Special Information Policy Guidance on Korea #27, November 7, 1950, box 47, folder "FE—Regional Bureau Far East," RG 59, RIIA.

Congress supported fully the administration's prosecution of the war. VOA officials justified this style of reporting on other grounds too. Often vitriolic and ad hominem, Republican criticism of the president and administration officials seemed less like authentic political dissent than election-year mudslinging, thus warranting its re-presentation.[13]

Concerns about the coverage of partisanship surfaced before war broke out on the Korean peninsula. In November 1949 Republican John Foster Dulles faced Democrat Herbert Lehman in a special election in New York to fill a vacant U.S. Senate seat. As an off-year political event the race received national attention, and VOA officials deemed it worthy of coverage. They expressed concern, however, that foreign audiences might interpret campaign rhetoric as evidence that Republicans and Democrats could no longer work together on foreign policy. Accordingly, policy writers decided to present the election's outcome in positive terms no matter who won: "If Dulles wins, it may be pointed out that he is an outstanding architect of bi-partisan foreign policy. If Lehman wins, it should be made clear that voters have supported Administration." Lehman won, but events during January and February 1950—the Taiwan controversy, the conviction of Alger Hiss for perjury, McCarthy's charges—increased the desire to maintain an image of domestic bipartisanship. In March Kenneth Wherry publicly demanded the resignation of Secretary of State Dean Acheson, dubbing him "the idol of left-wing, appease-Russia agitators." A few days later VOA guidance stated that "election year attacks" on foreign policies and the officials responsible for them should be connected to the public discussion that is expected in a democracy. The guidance added, "[s]tories should not indicate US confusion at this time when strength and purpose are needed."[14]

Weekly Policy Information Guidances, introduced in April 1950, reiterated the need to present strength and purpose. As explained by a prototype sent to missions abroad, the purpose of weekly guidance was to provide themes that the VOA and other media should nurture to serve U.S. interests. The most important theme "should be solid evidence of basic strength, unity, purpose of non-Soviet world," and the guidance cited as

13. For a discussion of how the VOA and other media defined and presented democracy to audiences abroad, see Laura A. Belmonte, "Defining Democracy: Images of Politics in U.S. Propaganda, 1945–1959."

14. Overnight Guidance #326, November 8, 1949, box 90, folder "11/7–11/11"; Overnight Guidance #420, March 27, 1950, box 90, folder "March 1950," RG 59, RIIA; Nebraska Republican Founders Day speech, cited in press release, March 21, 1950, box 21, folder "Res. 118," Wherry Papers.

useful examples several Republican statements supporting the administration's conduct of foreign policy. Developing this theme further, guidance in early June instructed the VOA to cover the recent statements of the president and Secretary of State Acheson that the United States would use its moral and material strength to maintain its goals of peace and freedom in the world.[15]

After war broke out in Korea the VOA's presentation of political unity became more pronounced than in the spring. In mid-July the Senate Appropriations Committee cut Point IV funds to $10 million. The Point IV program, which provided scientific and technological aid for underdeveloped nations, sought to halt the spread of communism, and the administration had lobbied for full funding. The Senate's budget reduction suggested that Congress might not be as acquiescent in fulfilling the administration's foreign policy requests as it had been in the past. This worried VOA policy writers. Guidance called the budget reduction "psychologically embarrassing" and instructed the VOA to air only brief news items about Point IV until further developments. In August guidance stated that in order to avoid discouragement abroad, "US Congressional and political debate should be put into perspective" by presenting minority party statements as part of the democratic process of developing a unified position. The guidance further stated that outside commentary on the end of bipartisanship should be countered with evidence of unity. Guidance on Taiwan instructed that the current heated debate should be balanced by emphasizing Truman's position. In early October the VOA broadcast a feature entitled "Congressional Accomplishments" that lauded Congress's rapid and unanimous approval of UN actions in Korea. The feature also called the Congress the true government of the people, commenting that "the bi-partisan foreign policy of Congress which was fully reflected in the activities of the past session, once again shows that under a democratic system," freedom was defended.[16]

The November midterm elections, scheduled just over a week after the Chinese entered the war on the side of North Korea, challenged greatly the presentation of bipartisanship. Days before the election, guidance

15. 511.00/4–750; Weekly Guidance #10, June 8, 1950, 511.00/6–850, RG 59, CDF.

16. Weekly Guidance #15, July 13, 1950, 511.00/7–1350, RG 59, CDF; Weekly Guidance #20, August 17, 1950; Weekly Guidance #22, August 30, 1950, box 4, folder "Weekly Guidances," RG 59, RIIA; "Congressional Accomplishments," October 3, 1950, box 7, RG 306, VOA Reports.

explained that some campaigns gave the impression abroad of widespread partisan disagreement on foreign policy. Accordingly, the VOA was to emphasize all evidence showing continued bipartisanship. The election's outcome suggested that continuing such emphasis might be difficult. Republicans gained twenty-eight seats in the House, five in the Senate; notable defeated Democrats included Senators Scott Lucas (Ill.) and Millard Tydings (Md.). Nevertheless, after the election the leading theme for VOA output was the "Continuity of US Foreign Policy," drafted in order to ease fears abroad that the new Congress would disrupt or reverse standing policies. Accordingly, the VOA solicited statements from key congressional Republicans. On November 10 Senator Wherry made a statement for a VOA broadcast in which he promised that Republicans would cooperate with the president, but he added that "people around the world should know that in the United States foreign policy is made by the people through their representatives in our government." Wherry's comment seemed to be a veiled attack on the State Department, especially Dean Acheson, no favorite of conservative Republicans. As the war situation worsened the criticism of Acheson grew louder, prompting Truman to defend him during a December press conference. While the VOA's Turkish desk reported that Truman refused to dismiss his embattled Secretary of State, a thirty-six-page news script broadcast to the Soviet Union made no mention of the issue. As the VOA prepared to cover Truman's State of the Union address in early January 1951, guidance reiterated the importance of projecting harmony: "Every effort should be made to keep speech above and outside context of current debate on foreign policy."[17]

The "current debate" to which the guidance referred was the incipient struggle over the president's power to send troops overseas. Introduced by Wherry on January 8, 1951, S.R. 8 declared that the president should send no American ground troops to Western Europe for the purposes of NATO until Congress drafted a policy on the matter. S.R. 8 echoed the concerns of Robert Taft, who had attacked the administration's foreign policy in a lengthy Senate speech just three days before Truman's State of the Union address. Taft warned that the United States should undertake no further

17. Overnight Guidance #324, November 4, 1950, box 90, folder "Oct. 31–Nov. 4"; "Continuity of US Foreign Policy," November 1950, box 109, folder "OII Monthly Content Report"; Overnight Guidance #622, January 8, 1951, box 91, folder "January 8–12, 1951," RG 59, RIIA; statement, November 10, 1950, box 18, folder "Radio Recording—Voice of America," Wherry Papers; Turkish Desk Schedule, December 19, 1950, Russian news script, box 10, RG 306, VOA Reports.

military obligations for the duration of the Korean War, and he proposed a "pay-as-you-go" budget for fighting communism. Taft's speech and the Wherry Resolution sparked acrimonious debate over the president's constitutional powers. In private and public statements Wherry made it clear that for him, the struggle was first a constitutional issue and second a matter of foreign policy.[18] VOA guidance on the Troops to Europe debate, however, forbade discussion or comment on questions relating to Congress's authority to prevent the dispatch of American forces. The VOA took this line throughout its coverage of S.R. 8. In April guidance advised that "[t]o cushion impact acrimonious debates and manifest uncertainties on some foreign policy issues, particularly troops for Europe, we must redouble our efforts to make clear to Foreign audiences that present differences are over means, not ends."[19]

For VOA officials, containing the damage S.R. 8 inflicted on the appearance of domestic political harmony was a top priority. A February report entitled "Combatting the Crisis of Confidence" warned that many nations' support for the United States was dwindling. Restoration of confidence depended on demonstrating that an effective working relationship existed between Congress and the executive branch, especially the State Department. Because such a relationship was currently lacking, "the Executive Branch often finds itself at the mercy of an inadequately informed and irresponsibly led Congressional majority, whose fears and passions deeply color, when they do not control, the development of foreign policy." The report reflected the view of domestic Public Affairs chief Francis Russell, who in late December had described a Republican strategy to undermine the confidence of the American public, implement an isolationist foreign policy, and set up a junta in Congress to dictate policy to the administration. In order to protect the president from congressional criticisms, regular consultation with members of Congress who were not on the Foreign Relations or Affairs Committees was proposed. The goal was not necessarily to solicit policy suggestions and criticisms, though. If the consultation offer was refused, the "President will have gained the

18. *Congressional Quarterly Almanac*, vol. 7, 220–21; Wherry to Darryl Zanuck, January 18, 1951, in Marvin E. Stromer, *The Making of a Political Leader: Kenneth S. Wherry and the U.S. Senate*, 130; Wherry to Arthur Vandenberg, January 31, 1951, box 12, folder "1951"; press release, April 4, 1951, box 13, folder "S. Res. 8," Wherry Papers.

19. Overnight Guidance #651, February 15, 1951, box 91, folder "February 12–17 1951," RG 59, RIIA; Weekly Guidance #53, April 4, 1951, 511.00/4–451, RG 59, CDF.

advantage that goes with making a definite effort and placing the responsibility for failure where it belongs."[20]

To further develop the appearance of domestic political harmony, the VOA placed members of Congress behind its microphones. In December 1950 Assistant Secretary of State for Congressional Relations Jack McFall advised Edward Barrett that the use of legislators on VOA broadcasts not only introduced U.S. officials to audiences abroad but also familiarized the congressional participants with the information program. McFall pointed out that "a balance in selecting bipartisan candidates" was maintained.[21] To provide evidence of this balance, the VOA's Program Operations Branch included in its 1951 semi-annual report a list of all members of Congress who appeared on air, their political affiliations, and the subjects of their broadcasts. From January to June 1951 a roughly equal number of Democrats and Republicans participated in VOA broadcasts; however, 21 percent of these appearances were made by outspoken Republican critics of the administration.[22]

President Truman's recall of MacArthur in April 1951 greatly strained the VOA's efforts to gloss over the friction between congressional Republicans and the administration without appearing to exclude the former from broadcasts. Republicans took great interest in the VOA's coverage of the firing. While the VOA made sure to consistently include Republicans' reactions to the firing in its broadcasts, it downplayed the existence of conflict between Republicans and the administration over Far East policy. Tension between the president and the commander of U.S. forces in Korea had reached a breaking point during the last week of March, when the Joint Chiefs of Staff informed MacArthur that Truman was preparing a cease-fire proposal. MacArthur, who had been lobbying to enlarge the scope of the war, promptly issued a preemptive statement threatening all-out war on China. The action was grossly insubordinate as

20. "Combatting the Crisis of Confidence," February 1, 1951, box 17, folder "Miscellaneous," 5–5A; McWilliams to Acheson, January 30, 1951, box 81, folder "Misc.," RG 59, RIIA; Cross reference sheet to December 28, 1950, memorandum, Russell to Sargeant, box 6, folder "Memoranda—President and White House 1948–52," RG 59, OPA Subject Files.

21. McFall to Barrett, December 27, 1950, box 81, folder "Misc.," RG 59, RIIA, 6.

22. Of 164 appearances from January to June 1951, 35, or 21 percent, were made by Republicans who frequently criticized the administration. These figures were tabulated from the Program Operations Branch, "Semi-Annual Report, January 1, 1951—July 1, 1951," Subject File Cabinet 8, drawer "R," folder "Radio Studies and Reports," United States Information Agency Historical Collection.

well as damaging to the American bargaining position with China. Truman chose not to fire MacArthur, though, instead reprimanding him for violating an order to clear all public statements with the White House. The VOA took a cautious line on the episode, banning all references to MacArthur's failure to clear his statement and the existence of differences between the State Department and the General. On April 5, 1951, Representative Joe Martin (R–Mass.) added to the controversy surrounding MacArthur by reading on the House floor a letter the general had sent him three days before his statement on China. "There is no substitute for victory," MacArthur wrote, stating that the Chinese Nationalists on Taiwan should join the U.S. forces in Korea and warning that Europe would fall to communism if the war in Asia was lost.[23]

Truman relieved MacArthur of his command late in the evening of April 10. During the preceding five days, VOA officials—like the rest of the nation—did not know whether or not Truman was going to recall MacArthur. Guidance was decidedly vague, instructing the VOA to neither overplay nor underplay the MacArthur-Martin correspondence. Indeed, the studios in New York were initially ordered to clear all output on MacArthur with Washington before broadcast. Policy writers in New York complained that this was impossible, so approval by telephone was permitted instead. Coverage relied heavily on editorial roundups and congressional reaction, especially from prominent Republican critics of the administration. On April 9 the Hungarian desk aired commentary from Senators Homer Ferguson, Styles Bridges, William Knowland, and Robert Taft.[24]

News of the firing followed the pattern of presenting consensus. After reporting Truman's reasons for recalling MacArthur, the Czech desk indicated that Ferguson, Knowland, Taft, Kenneth Wherry, and Bourke Hickenlooper were criticizing the president's decision. The broadcast then used the firing to praise the free world system: MacArthur had violated his obligation to carry out the will of the people. Guidance issued that day banned speculation that the firing would "produce deep cleavages on basic issues in US public opinion and Congress." For the next week the VOA reported mixed details of MacArthur's return to the United States,

23. David McCullough, *Truman*, 835–38; Special Overnight Guidance, March 24, 1951, box 91, folder "March 19–23 1951," RG 59, RIIA.

24. Overnight Guidance #688, April 9, 1951, box 91, folder "April 9–13 1951," RG 59, RIIA; Joseph Phillips to Edwin Kretzmann, April 11, 1951, 511.00/4–1151, RG 59, CDF; daily broadcast schedule, April 9, 1951, box 16, RG 306, VOA Reports.

domestic and international reactions to his recall, and assurances that UN aims in Korea would not change. On April 16 Karl Mundt's office requested copies of all VOA scripts relating to MacArthur's dismissal. According to Mundt's administrative assistant Bob McCaughey, the senator had received numerous complaints from members of Congress and newspaper reporters over the VOA's treatment of the recall. Officials promised to send McCaughey the material but informed him that they would not be able to provide Central News File material on the firing—John Taber already had it. Freshmen Senators Everett Dirksen (R–Ill.) and Richard Nixon (R–Calif.) also requested scripts, and they were not alone. In an internal report covering the week ending April 21 the VOA indicated that it had "reproduced major stories of MacArthur coverage to meet heavy Congressional demand." A newspaper article on the VOA heightened interest in its reporting. "Voice Pipes Truman Line on MacArthur," read the headline for a Scripps-Howard story carried by the *New York World-Telegram and Sun* on April 23. The piece accused the VOA of selecting domestic press commentary slanted to Truman's favor in its broadcasts to the Far East. The *World-Telegram and Sun* quickly retracted the claim, however, citing errors in editing made by a commercial Japanese news service that had transcribed the broadcasts. During these hectic days the VOA continued to cover Republicans' reaction to MacArthur's recall. Dirksen's opinions aired in the program "American Viewpoints" on April 22–24; other VOA programming used the comments of Senators William Jenner (R–Ind.) and William Knowland.[25]

However, guidance on MacArthur's address to Congress on April 19 demonstrates the desire to mute the growing controversy. The speech itself created a minor behind-the-scenes crisis. Initially it was decided to carry the

25. Czech news script, April 11, 1951, 12; daily broadcast schedules and news scripts for Turkish, Bulgarian, Serbo-Croat, Rumanian, Russian, and Slovenian desks, April 12–20, 1951, boxes 16–17, RG 306, VOA Reports; Weekly Guidance #54, April 11, 1951, 511.00/4–1151, RG 59, CDF. For Republicans' requests for scripts, see Special Commentary #464 "The MacArthur Contribution," April 11, 1951, box 41, folder 2881, Everett McKinley Dirksen Papers, Everett McKinley Dirksen Congressional Center, Pekin, Ill.; M. B. Vandenberg to Howland Sargeant, April 16, 1951, box 59, folder "Scripts"; Barrett to Dirksen, April 23, 1951, box 60, folder "Congressional"; Lott to Oechsner, April 25, 1951, box 74, folder "N-O-P"; "USIE Progress and Problems Report," April 21, 1951, box 95, folder "USIE Progress and Problems Reports," RG 59, RIIA, 3. For the VOA's continuing coverage of MacArthur's dismissal, see *New York World-Telegram and Sun*, April 23 and 24, 1951; Barrett to Dirksen, May 5, 1951, box 69, folder "DA-DZ," RG 59, RIIA.

speech live over the VOA, but at noon on April 18 the White House reversed the order. Meetings and conversations held that evening and the next morning produced a compromise between Public Affairs officials and White House Press Secretary Joe Short: if no advance copy of MacArthur's speech could be found, it would be carried live. Employees manning the VOA transmitter in Munich were not raised to confirm the hook-up needed for live coverage until members of Congress began applauding MacArthur's entrance. With regard to MacArthur's statements, media were instructed to observe that on three points, the general and the administration agreed: every effort must be expended to meet a two-front threat, there must be no appeasement of aggressors, and "Formosa [Taiwan] must not be 'surrendered' to the Chinese Communists."[26] Considering Truman's public statements that the United States would not use troops or military aid to prevent a communist takeover of Taiwan, the latter claim must have struck attentive listeners as disingenuous, if not openly contradictory.

The VOA's efforts to project domestic unity continued through the spring, as seen in coverage of the Senate investigation of U.S. foreign and military policies in the Far East. Meeting together, the Committee on Foreign Relations and the Committee on Armed Services convened hearings on May 3, 1951. Republicans' questioning of MacArthur, the first witness, clearly sought to discredit the China policies of Truman and the State Department. Senator Alexander Wiley (R–Wisc.) asked MacArthur if anyone other than members of Congress had consulted him about George C. Marshall's mission to China in 1946. MacArthur said no. Hickenlooper queried MacArthur if it was possible to retake China from the Communists, while Knowland asked the general if he had ever stated that Taiwan held no strategic value to the United States.[27] Despite this partisanship, the VOA reported that "the Senatorial inquiry . . . proved that no difference exists in the basic points of American policy, and that, despite the debate which resulted from the recall of General MacArthur, the country continues determinedly its plan for the preservation of peace." This statement aired on May 14, but policy makers had reached their conclu-

26. D'Alessandro to Puhan, April 25, 1951, 711.21/6–2051; Memorandum of conversation, Edward Barrett and Joe Short, April 19, 1951, 511.00/4–1951, RG 59, CDF. For the VOA's coverage of MacArthur's speech, see Overnight Guidance #696, April 19, 1951, box 91, folder "April 16–20 1951," RG 59, RIIA.

27. Senate, Committee on Armed Services and Committee on Foreign Relations, *Military Situation in the Far East, Hearings before the Committee on Armed Services and Committee on Foreign Relations*, 82d Cong., 1st sess., pt. 1, May 1951, 31, 56, 122–23.

sions about the hearings more than a week before. On May 2, the day before the hearings began, Weekly Guidance instructed the VOA to emphasize the basic agreement by Republicans and the administration to stop communist agression, and to explain that any debate was over means, not ends. A month later a VOA policy writer ordered changes in a script entitled "Moscow's Strange Silence on MacArthur Hearings." In part, the script read, "[t]he testimony proves quite conclusively that there were wide differences of opinion between General MacArthur and the highest officials of the U.S. government." The policy writer suggested that the script emphasize peace rather than the hearings' partisan side.[28]

As the VOA continued recasting dissent as consensus, congressional Republicans kept requesting scripts. In May Dirksen asked for a sampling of VOA broadcasts covering the last six months; he received 166 scripts. In June Knowland asked for scripts, program announcements, and evidence of public reaction to the VOA. Policy writers did not soon forget this attention to broadcasts aired during the spring of 1951. In November they established a procedure for submitting policy guidances to congressional committee investigators. In order to prevent the investigators from searching freely through back files, selected guidances were to be shown as "*good typical examples*" [emphasis in original]. Overnight Guidance #696, dated April 19, 1951, was one such example. The guidance, which focused on MacArthur's speech to Congress upon his recall, provided a strange mix of points. While it observed that MacArthur contradicted policies established by the president and other top officials, it also stated that "Formosa must not be 'surrendered' to the Chinese communists." This echoed MacArthur's position at the same time that it contradicted Truman and Acheson's policy. Should congressional Republicans look for signs of slanting, however, this guidance offered counter-evidence.[29]

The VOA's coverage of the war in Korea, the November 1950 elections, S.R. 8, and the recall of MacArthur reveals a conscious effort to convey an image of bipartisanship and political harmony to audiences overseas.

28. Greek news script, May 14, 1951, box 18, RG 306, VOA Reports, 5; Weekly Guidance #57, May 2, 1951, 511.00/5–251, RG 59, CDF; EE/P Joseph Kolarek to Joe Phillips, June 14, 1951, box 5, folder "VOA MacArthur," RG 59, Miscellaneous Records of the Bureau of Public Affairs, Records Relating to World-Wide Program Objectives.

29. Sargeant to Dirksen, May 26, 1951, box 60, folder "A-G"; Albert Pickerell to Nancy Henderson, June 14, 1951, box 72, folder, "KN-KU to 7/51"; Frederick Oechsner to Stevens, November 8, 1951, box 87, folder "G-Misc."; Overnight Guidance #696, April 19, 1951, box 91, folder "April 16–20," RG 59, RIIA.

This projection of domestic consensus and the emphasis on ends rather than means was not entirely inaccurate. In the sense that Republicans agreed *generally* with the anticommunist goals of the Truman administration, yes, consensus existed. But consensus defined so vaguely provided few clues to foreign listeners as to the United States' specific actions concerning Korea or to the dispatch of additional troops to NATO. Moreover, the presentation of Republican dissent as natural but nondisruptive "conflict resolution" glossed over a persistent problem afflicting the conduct of foreign affairs during the Cold War: partisan battle for control of the political power and channels needed to achieve both international anticommunist goals and domestic policies. Congressional Republicans simultaneously voted to support the U.S. initiative to defend South Korea and blamed the Roosevelt and Truman administrations for helping cause the invasion. At the same time Republicans supported NATO, Wherry and Taft organized resistance to Truman's efforts to send additional troops without first securing Senate approval.

The interest displayed in VOA scripts after MacArthur's recall in April 1951 demonstrates continuing suspicion that liberal partisans in the VOA were suppressing dissent and slanting broadcasts to the administration's favor. The irony of these suspicions is that they were half-right. VOA officials were repackaging domestic dissent, though in their opinions not necessarily to promote the administration. Rather, their aim was to sustain international morale and support for the UN action in Korea. Whatever the intentions of State Department policy makers, the VOA's projection of domestic harmony and its minimization of Republican dissent highlights the essential vagueness of its broadcasts. In order to sustain the appearance of consensus, the VOA reiterated broadly defined end goals of the United States, continually glossing over the debate on means.

Chapter 6

Everything but the Truth
The VOA's Expansion Troubles, 1950–1952

The VOA's domestic troubles during the Korean War were not limited to controversies over its coverage of the conflict. Between 1950 and 1952 the VOA experienced a variety of disruptions, external interference, and internal problems as it tried to implement the Campaign of Truth. Long past were the battles over whether or not the VOA should be on the air, but agreement over the VOA's anticommunist purpose did not make its fulfillment any easier. Ballooning budgets and overly ambitious goals caused the agency to expand too rapidly, leading to administrative problems, ill-spent funds, and poorly developed projects. Mindful of these problems, Congress's Appropriations Committees rebuffed requests to increase the VOA's budget. In the summer of 1951 charges that liberals dominated the VOA resurfaced after Nevada's conservative Senator Pat McCarran probed the backgrounds of the agency's writers and broadcasters. The VOA also had difficulties in its own home, the State Department. VOA policy officers struggled constantly to secure reliable policy guidance for broadcasts, finding their efforts blunted by officials who considered the radio agency to be of little importance or even a nuisance. Meanwhile, the VOA was joined on the airwaves by Radio Free Europe (RFE) and Radio Liberation (RL), broadcasting to Eastern Europe and the Soviet Union, respectively. Ostensibly, private foundations administered RFE and RL; however, the CIA secretly provided substantial financial and intelligence support to both stations. The creation of RFE and RL further demonstrated the increasing importance given to propaganda within the United States' rapidly expanding Cold War offensive; it also revealed growing impatience with the VOA's limitations. Rather than concentrating on broadcasting abroad its version of the truth, the VOA continued to be distracted by domestic difficulties between 1950 and 1952.

I. Paying for the Truth

After President Truman proposed the Campaign of Truth in April 1950, State Department officials drafted a strategy to win congressional approval of an $89 million budget to fund the campaign. Assistant Secretary of State for Public Affairs Edward Barrett indicated that the continued support of the president was needed to secure congressional action during the remaining months of the Eighty-first Congress. Undersecretary of State James Webb explained the urgency of the campaign to James Lay, the executive secretary of the NSC, and asked for the council's endorsement. Just two days before the invasion of South Korea Webb also asked the president to give the Campaign of Truth budget his strongest support when he next met with congressional leaders.[1] On July 13, 1950, Truman forwarded to the House an $89 million supplemental budget request, of which $41 million was slated for construction of VOA transmitters and counter-jamming equipment, an amount that by itself exceeded by $5 million the entire State Department budget request for fiscal year 1951.

Hearings on the supplemental budget were held July 17–26, 1950. The war in Korea provided an obvious context for the request, both for members of Congress and State Department officials. In his opening statement, Secretary of State Acheson stated that Soviet propaganda about the war in Korea made implementation of the Campaign of Truth even more imperative than when it was announced in April. Barrett made a similar point before a Senate committee. Congressman Karl Stefan suggested that since construction of the VOA's counter-jamming facilities would take two years, the State Department needed to review the "entire situation as it is related to the present conditions and the present crisis."[2]

In late August the House Appropriations Subcommittee approved $62.7 million of the original request, also authorizing the use of $15.2 million in counterpart funds collected abroad by the Economic Cooperation Administration (ECA). None of the cuts were applied to the VOA's funds.

1. Barrett to Undersecretary James Webb, May 10, 1950, 511.004\5–1050, RG 59, CDF; Webb to Lay, May 26, 1950; note 1 to memorandum, James Webb to the President, June 23, 1950, *FRUS 1950*, vol. 4, 311–14.

2. House Subcommittee of the Committee on Appropriations, *Supplemental Appropriation Bill for 1951, Hearings before the Subcommittee of the Committee on Appropriations*, 81st Cong., 2d sess., July 1950, 2, 56; Senate Committee on Foreign Relations, *Hearings on S.R. 243, Expanded International Information Program*, 81st Cong., 2d sess., July 5–7, 1950, 107.

In a publicly released letter, Truman urged the Senate to restore the funds cut by the House: "[a]t a time when the Kremlin is sparing no effort to spread the most flagrant lies about this country and our allies, we must forge ahead with this great and affirmative campaign." Though the Senate increased the two amounts to $77.9 million and $19.6 million respectively, the House prevailed in the conference report. The final budget allotted $63.9 million for the information program and an additional $15.2 million in ECA funds.[3] Still, the two amounts combined represented nearly 90 percent of the original and unprecedented request of $89 million. The Campaign of Truth was ready to move ahead.

Yet the funds came with an additional price: intensified scrutiny of expenditures. Just as the war in Korea helped win approval of funds for the Campaign of Truth, it also prompted widespread concern in Congress over the administration's fiscal policies, especially after the entry of China into the war smashed hopes of imminent victory. During 1951 tax hikes, resource shortages, and the threat of inflation spurred opposition in Congress to increases in foreign aid programs. For example, during the summer Congress trimmed more than $1 billion from an $8.5 billion omnibus economic and military aid package that included funds aimed at expanding the ECA. Then in the fall Congress disbanded the ECA altogether, replacing it with the Mutual Security Agency (MSA), a new organization intended to be independent of the State Department.[4]

The VOA was also a target for budget cuts during 1951. For the 1952 information program budget the State Department requested more than $1.1 billion, to which was added a $97.5 million supplemental request for the construction of new VOA transmitters, the so-called "Ring Plan." The plan was the VOA's primary counter-jamming initiative, calling for the construction of fourteen high-power radio transmitters to surround the Iron Curtain and overpower Soviet jamming. Congress had already granted $41 million for the Ring Plan in the September 1950 Campaign of Truth budget, but after the NSC urged the plan's expansion, on March 2, 1951, the president asked Congress for an additional $97.5 million for the project.[5] The extraordinary request—which the Budget Bureau had reduced from an ini-

3. Editorial note, FRUS 1950, vol. 4, 316–17; "President Pleads for 'Truth' Funds," New York Times, August 31, 1950.

4. Michael Hogan provides a full account of the administration's efforts to maintain the ECA against congressional opposition. See The Marshall Plan: America, Britain, and the Reconstruction of Western Europe, 1947–1952, 380–92.

5. Robert Pirsein, "Voice of America," 175–78.

tial figure of $111 million—led members of the House's and Senate's Appropriations Committees to question whether or not the VOA was capable of properly spending so much money. When drastic cuts appeared likely, even Truman backed away from supporting the controversial $97.5 million supplemental VOA request.

At the March 1951 hearings, members of the House Appropriations Subcommittee on the State Department greeted the VOA's regular 1952 budget and the Ring Plan supplemental request with hostility, suspicion, even disgust. After examining the budgets for privately contracted research projects on the VOA, Karl Stefan suggested that it resembled the WPA, a New Deal relief agency. For the next several hours Stefan and other committee members continually questioned the use of funds and the cost of various projects; very few inquiries related to the VOA's support of the war efforts in Korea. When State Department officials could not clearly explain how much progress had been made on the construction of radio facilities, Chairman John Rooney (D–N.Y.) stated that it was unacceptable that such questions could not be answered. Clearly, committee members suspected that the VOA was wasting the funds Congress had already allotted it. Indeed, two months before the hearings, Rooney had ordered a team of investigators to examine the VOA's operations in preparation for the appropriations hearings.[6]

Such concerns were not unwarranted. As the hearings were taking place, the VOA and the OII were undergoing expansion at a dizzying pace. At the beginning of 1950 the VOA had broadcast in twenty-three languages; by September 1951 forty-six languages were on the air. Personnel ranks swelled to meet the increased production and engineering needs. Between July 1950 and September 1951 the VOA added nine hundred new staff members, bringing the total employees to nearly two thousand.[7] Efforts to fill these positions began even before Congress appropriated funds to pay salaries; in August 1950 the OII's general manager authorized recruitment of up to 50 percent of the new personnel positions requested in the Campaign of Truth supplemental budget, although it had not yet been approved. Recruiters fanned out across the United States, visiting cities to

6. House Subcommittee of the Committee on Appropriations, *Department of State Appropriation Bill for 1952, Hearings before the Subcommittee of the Committee on Appropriations,* 82d Cong., 1st sess., March 8, 1951, 705–833; Edward Barrett, "Background Statement," undated, box 5, folder "The Secretary 1951," RG 59, Barrett Files; box 24, folder "House Investigating Group," RG 59, RIIA.

7. Acting Secretary of State to the Executive of the National Security Council, May 26, 1950, *FRUS 1950,* vol. 4, 311–12; Pirsein, "Voice of America," 200–202, 211.

conduct interviews, while embassies abroad also recruited new employees. In May 1951 Barrett admitted in a report distributed to members of Congress that the program as a whole "expanded more rapidly than [was] consistent with maximum efficiency." Commenting directly on the VOA, two years later Barrett noted that there was such a mood of urgency to expand the VOA in 1950 that many tasks were done faster than should have been the case.[8]

The Ring Plan's domestic side also suffered problems. The project called for six high-power shortwave stations to be built in the United States; these stations were to feed the VOA's signals to the fourteen overseas stations. Procurement of sites for the U.S. stations took longer than expected, delaying construction.[9] However, slow progress on the Ring Plan was not entirely the VOA's fault. Outside pressure to influence the choice of contractors interfered with the completion of the feeder station in California. Bids for that project were received in December 1950; VOA officials planned to award the contract during the last week of February 1951. Final action was not taken until two months later, though. On February 19, 1951, California Senator William Knowland called Ben Brown, the acting assistant secretary of state for Congressional Relations, to make inquiries on behalf of a California company, Union Diesel Engine. Union's bid was the lowest by fifty-two thousand dollars, but because it contained contingencies and exceptions, VOA officials did not consider it reliable. On February 24 Knowland requested that Ben Brown meet with representatives of Union Diesel, which he did three days later. After learning that it was not going to receive the contract, Union Diesel or Knowland apparently asked the Senate's Small Business Committee to investigate possible discrimination by the VOA in its selection process. When no wrongdoing was found, the contract was awarded in April 1951 to the next lowest bidder.[10]

8. "Facts Regarding Questions Raised Concerning the Expanded Campaign of Truth," May 9, 1951, box 219, folder 3, Mundt Papers, 2, 41–43; Barrett to Carl Marcy, June 15, 1953, Foreign Relations Committee Report, 1953–1954, folder "Information Agency Correspondence," RG 46, file SEN 83A-F7, National Archives, Washington, D.C.

9. "Ring Plan," undated, box 1, folder "040 State Department"; "Status of Major Radio Facilities Projects, June 30, 1951, box 3, folder "040 State Department," Harry S. Truman Papers, Psychological Strategy Board Files, Truman Library (hereafter cited as PSB Files).

10. United States Advisory Commission on Information, Subcommittee of the Radio Advisory Committee, "A Report on the Planning and Administration of the Radio Facilities Program of the Voice of America," June 22, 1951, 511.004/7–651, 5; Ben Brown, February 27, 1951, 511.004/2–2751, RG 59, CDF; William Player to Barrett, February 19, 1951, box 56, folder "IBD," RG 59, RIIA.

In order to refute the spendthrift reputation the VOA had with the Appropriations Committees, particularly John Rooney, Edward Barrett compiled a detailed list of complaints and drafted responses. Accusations included luncheons that cost nine dollars per person and the failure to follow exactly the literal words of the House Appropriations Committee Report. In his draft report to Acheson, Barrett cited a hotel maître d' on the actual cost of the lunches, but as the assistant secretary of state knew, establishing the actual cost of catering bills was not going to save the VOA's budget from cuts.[11] After meeting with Barrett, White House aide George Elsey indicated that Rooney was "going to do his best to knock out all new [VOA] facilities." Elsey suggested that the president ask the Speaker of the House and other influential congressional Democrats to impress upon Rooney the importance of the VOA funds. Reports coming from the Hill indicated that the subcommittee was planning to substantially reduce the $97.5 million request.[12]

Truman and Secretary of State Acheson worried, however, that efforts to procure the full VOA facilities request might jeopardize regular State Department appropriations, which were scheduled for hearings being held right after action on the VOA budget. During an April 5 meeting with Acheson the president "was extremely doubtful" that a successful floor fight could be mounted to restore the cut. Truman did issue a public statement that day opposing the rumored cut, but it had no effect.[13] On April 6 the House Subcommittee slashed the supplemental facilities request to $9.5 million, a 90 percent cut. In its report the subcommittee cited improper planning, poor management, and unjustified delays as the reasons for the tremendous cut. Furthermore, many sites for the Ring Plan's transmitters

11. Barrett had the report drafted in order to answer charges made by John Rooney "in conversations aside of the Appropriations Committee on the floor of Congress," as reported by Marlow to Compton, May 23, 1952, box 87, folder "Comments on Questions Raised Concerning the Campaign of Truth," RG 59, RIIA; Barrett to Acheson, "Comments on Charges That Have Been Made against the Campaign of Truth," March 29, 1951, box 5, folder "The Secretary 1951," RG 59, Barrett Files. On May 9, 1951, the final report was released as "Facts Regarding Questions Raised Concerning the Expanded Campaign of Truth" and distributed to members of Congress. Box 219, folder 3, Mundt Papers.

12. Elsey, meeting notes, March 24, 1951; Elsey to Truman, April 3, 1951, box 65, folder "Foreign Relations—Voice of America," Elsey Papers; Editorial note, *FRUS 1951*, vol. 1, 919.

13. Memorandum of conversation, April 5, 1951, box 68, folder "April 1951," Dean Acheson Papers, Truman Library; *Public Papers of the Presidents: Harry S. Truman, 1951*, 218.

had not yet been chosen, resulting in vague cost estimates. "The Committee fully believes in a strong, effective Voice of America," the report stated, but because of these problems, it could not support implementation of the Ring Plan for the time being. John Taber, ranking Republican on the House Appropriations Committee, supported the cut, suggesting that communist sympathizers within the VOA were "trying to keep [it] from amounting to anything."[14]

After the Senate declined to restore the Ring Plan supplemental budget, a sympathetic legislator offered a behind-the-scenes explanation of the Appropriation Subcommittees' hostility. Representative John Vorys (R–Ohio) confided to a department official that he had "checked around and had gotten the impression that the Senate presentation did not go over so well." Vorys also indicated that at the House hearings in March Karl Stefan and John Rooney believed that Barrett and OII General Manager Charles Hulten had acted antagonistically, that they had "a chip on their shoulder" [sic]. Rooney in particular seemed to dislike Hulten. In August 1950 Rooney told Barrett that he thought Hulten was a poor administrator and should be fired. Barrett defended Hulten by reviewing his qualifications and experience, but the New York congressman continued to call for his dismissal, indicating that Hulten had "messed up the New York building business, for example." This problem resulted partially from a misunderstanding about finding additional office space for the VOA in New York City. During questioning about a budget request for buying a building, Hulten had said that $3 million would cover costs, not realizing that the structure recommended by the government's Public Building Services did not meet adequately the VOA's space needs. As Barrett learned, Rooney's dislike for Public Affairs officials was not limited to Hulten. In a memorandum for his files, Barrett stated that Rooney often treated him brusquely, even telling him, "you've made a complete mess of the operation." In light of Rooney's antagonism and his position as chairman of the House Appropriations Subcommittee on the State Department, Barrett concluded, "I fear anything might happen to the Department's appropriation request for the Campaign of Truth."[15]

14. House Subcommittee of the Committee on Appropriations, *Third Supplemental Appropriation Bill, 1951*, 82d Cong., 1st sess., April 6, 1951, 7–8; "'Voice' Seeking Restoration of 90% Fund Cut," *New York Herald Tribune*, April 9, 1951.

15. Barnard to Barrett, May 7, 1951, box 78, folder "Congressional"; "Statement Regarding Purchase of Building in New York City," box 44, folder "New York Building," RG 59, RIIA; "Background Statement," box 5, folder "The Secretary 1951," RG 59, Barrett Files, 1–7.

Three months after the harsh decision regarding the Ring Plan's supplemental budget, the House Appropriations Subcommittee delivered its report on the 1952 regular budget, reducing by $30 million the original $1.1 billion request for all the information and cultural programs. Efforts to persuade the Senate Appropriations Subcommittee to restore funds were unsuccessful. As was the case at the House hearings, the war in Korea and the VOA's part received scant attention. Ranking Democrats Pat McCarran and Kenneth McKellar instead focused questioning and testimony on line-item estimates, the current use of funds, and the VOA's effectiveness. McKellar asked if just one Russian had ever been questioned about listening to the VOA. Later in the hearings McKellar told Edward Barrett, "I do not think you know a thing in the world about what you are doing. You are playing haphazard with the American people's money, and it is perfectly outrageous." Not surprisingly, the Appropriations Subcommittee made more cuts when it released its report in August. The House had recommended $85 million; the Senate approved $63 million, which represented a total reduction of $52 million from the original regular 1952 budget request.[16]

II. Defending the Messengers

While Senator McKellar openly derided Edward Barrett at the hearings on the 1952 budget, his colleague Pat McCarran caused far more serious problems for the VOA's operations. Three months before the hearings took place McCarran launched a detailed investigation of the VOA and OII. The motives and results of this probe help explain the Senate Appropriations Subcommittee's added reductions in the 1952 budget, yet the consequences of the investigation extended beyond the program's budget woes. During the summer of 1951 McCarran's work prompted congressional Republicans to look into the backgrounds of VOA freelance writers. Once again, accusations that liberals dominated the VOA rang out on the House and Senate floors and filled columns in newspapers and magazines.

16. Although hearings on the 1952 budget were held before hearings on the supplemental budget, the House first took action on the latter. House Subcommittee of the Committee on Appropriations, *State, Justice, Commerce, and the Judiciary Appropriation Bill, Fiscal Year 1952*, 82d Cong., 1st sess., July 10, 1951, 6-8. For McCarran's and McKellar's complaints, see Senate Subcommittee of the Committee on Appropriations, *Departments of State, Justice, Commerce, and the Judiciary Appropriation Bill, Hearings before the Subcommittee of the Committee on Appropriations for 1952*, 82d Cong. 1st sess., July 1951, 1810-11, 1877. For the final budget, see Senate Committee on Appropriations, *Departments of State, Justice, Commerce, and the Judiciary Appropriation Bill, 1952*, 82d Cong., 1st sess., August 21, 1951, 10.

Pat McCarran was a Democrat, but his affiliation with the party of Franklin Roosevelt and Harry Truman was a function of Nevada politics rather than political principles. McCarran was a prominent member of the China bloc and an outspoken critic of Truman's Far East policies. A close ally of Joe McCarthy's, McCarran sponsored the Internal Security Act of 1950 and chaired the Senate Internal Security Subcommittee. He also chaired the Senate Appropriations Subcommittee on the State Department, and it was in this capacity that he investigated the administrative functions of the VOA and OII. On March 30, 1951, just days before the House slashed the VOA's $97.5 million facilities budget request, McCarran requested detailed information on media policy channels, organizational charts, job descriptions, and summaries of all current research and construction projects. McCarran also wanted to know what steps were taken to secure clearance for "particular sensitive broadcasts" [sic].[17] After requesting twenty copies of the report so that it could be distributed to each member of his subcommittee, McCarran asked that the material be delivered within two weeks.

McCarran seemed to have several motives for the investigation. Like members of the House Appropriations Subcommittee on the State Department, McCarran believed that the OII wasted money and operated inefficiently. According to a Department official, a McCarran aide indicated that the investigation would focus on the employment of overpaid policy formulators, the shortage of working-level staff, the expense of VOA equipment, and an insufficiently anticommunist tone. Because McCarran often asked the OII to take on friends or constituents, the investigation might also have been an attempt to expedite or increase the hires. In February an applicant referred by McCarran was approved for hire pending security clearance; Edward Barrett had spoken personally with McCarran about the applicant. In June Barrett informed McCarran that two more referrals were being placed in the State Department's bi-national centers in Latin America, although as Barrett observed delicately, both women needed to learn Spanish before leaving. Finally, McCarran might have had punitive aims. In January 1951 he wrote to Barrett asking that Fallon, Nevada, be given favorable consideration for the location of a new VOA transmitter, but it was constructed elsewhere.[18]

17. McCarran memorandum, March 30, 1951, box 74, folder "McCarran," RG 59, RIIA.
18. William Player, memorandum for the files, February 13, 1951; Edward Barrett to McCarran, June 26, 1951, box 60, folder "M-Z"; Sitrick to Oechsner, April 16, 1951; Bill McMenamin to Leo Pinkus, undated, box 74, folder "McCarran, Pat," RG 59, RIIA;

The OII delivered all the material requested by McCarran by April 14, the deadline set by the senator, though the Appropriations Subcommittee hearings were not scheduled until July. In an unusual move, McCarran convened the Internal Security Subcommittee, which he also chaired, along with the Appropriations Subcommittee on the State Department, declaring that the $1.1 billion budget requested for 1952 activities warranted the participation of the Appropriations Subcommittee members. McCarran stated that the purpose was not necessarily to find communists within the VOA but to identify communist sympathizers. As this joint hearing was taking place, investigators for the Internal Security Subcommittee began interviewing VOA employees in New York City. The subcommittee was particularly interested in three staffers: Czech Desk Chief Karel Sheldon (who Slovakian separatists had complained was a communist in fall 1950; see chapter 5), Czech Desk writer and announcer Vojtech Andic, and Radio Information Specialist Leslie Logan. According to a witness interviewed by the subcommittee, these three were "closely associated with and influenced by" three known communists. The witness, John Sciranka, stated further that these communists provided script material used by the three VOA staffers. (Sciranka had already complained about supposedly disloyal VOA employees to Senator H. Alexander Smith.) McCarran's distinction between communists and sympathizers impugned suspected liberal partisans without having to prove they were actually communists. As the *Washington Daily News* described the hearings, "McCarran Interested in Slant, Not Reds."[19] If communists were able to use VOA employees as mouthpieces for communist propaganda, as claimed by the Internal Security Subcommittee's witness, how could the VOA be anticommunist? McCarran's tactic thus dramatically increased the burden of proof placed on suspected subversives. In addition to proving that they were not communists, they also had to demonstrate that their friends, acquaintances, and coworkers were not communists, either. In 1950 McCarthy had charged the State Department with knowingly employing communists; in 1951

McCarran to Barrett, January 5, 1951, 511.004/1–551, RG 59, CDF. Nevada's junior senator, Republican George Malone, also lobbied for a transmitter to be located in Nevada. Three times (April 3, July 25, and October 26, 1950), he made inquiries to OII officials. Box 73, folder "MA," RG 59, RIIA.

19. "Reds Slanting 'Voice,' Senate Groups Hear," *Washington Post*, July 10, 1951. For the New York investigation, see Win King to Dick Arens, July 13, 1951, box 325, folder "VOA 1951–52," RG 46, Records of the Senate Internal Security Subcommittee. "More Mystery Witnesses Called in 'Voice' Probe," *Washington Daily News*, July 10, 1951.

McCarran charged the VOA with employing communist sympathizers or dupes.

The hearings held by the Internal Security Subcommittee added to Republicans' complaints that the VOA was overtly liberal, using only left-leaning commentators on the airwaves. During April and May congressional Republicans had scrutinized the VOA's coverage of MacArthur's recall, looking for coverage favorable to the president. Throughout the summer of 1951 interest in the VOA's supposed political slant continued. McCarran himself raised the issue in June, when he charged that VOA commentator Raymond Swing had been listed during WWII as a sponsor for the National Council of American-Soviet Friendship. The council was now listed on the attorney general's list of communist front organizations. As Swing explained to Edward Barrett, he had withdrawn his name after the war, but the council continued to list it, even after he threatened legal action. Swing's defense did nothing to abate the controversy surrounding himself. In late June Representative Lawrence Smith (R–Wisc.) characterized Swing as "the outstanding apologist for the blunders made at Yalta."[20]

The political leanings of other VOA writers and commentators soon came under fire. John Taber had been requesting a steady supply of VOA scripts; in July he and Homer Ferguson each requested an itemized list of all freelance writers used by the VOA and how much they were paid. After receiving the list Ferguson made further inquiries into the backgrounds of individual writers, as did Taber. House Appropriations Committee employee Robert Lee also reviewed and took copies of several VOA scripts to Taber. A former FBI agent, Lee was responsible for drawing up the list of 108 present or potential State Department employees that McCarthy had used to substantiate his charges in 1950. Lee selected three VOA interviews with Socialist Norman Thomas; in one Thomas stated, "I and all Socialists would oppose any effort to reinstate Chiang in China." Lee also told a VOA official about an experiment recently conducted by several senators. Twenty individuals with conservative backgrounds had applied for jobs with the information programs; according to Lee, not one was hired. Meanwhile, Representative Kenneth Keating (R–N.Y.) complained that the government was using its international propaganda techniques on the American people, citing an article from *U.S. News and World Report* that accused the State Department of devising "a clear plan of propaganda to be laid down by

20. *New York Journal American*, June 9, 1951; Swing to Barrett, June 9, 1951, 511.004/6–1251, RG 59, CDF; *Congressional Record*, 82d Cong., 1st sess., June 29, 1951, vol. 97, A4770.

Voice of America and State Department employees around the world." In late July Karl Mundt told another official that his colleagues were complaining to him about the VOA's use of commentators considered liberal. Mundt added that he believed there was reason for the complaints.[21]

Just a few days after the conversation with Mundt the chief of the VOA, Foy Kohler, was instructed to draw up a list of all freelance or temporary writers or broadcasters who could be labeled conservative. The task was not as simple as the request implied. As Kohler pointed out, the VOA used language specialists who transcended the labels of liberal or conservative: "By and large again these language technicians are militantly antisoviet; many among them are DP's [displaced persons] and defectors." The labels of "conservative" or "liberal" were also difficult to apply to writers hired to adapt works of fiction for features. Most of these individuals were fledgling writers with few publications. How was the VOA supposed to determine their political views? Finally, the VOA had used the speeches or articles of conservatives such as Anne O'Hare McCormick and Dwight Eisenhower, but because these individuals offered their services gratis, they did not appear on the VOA's purchase order lists. The controversy over the political views of VOA writers and broadcasters also spilled over into the International Press Division (INP), which distributed pamphlets and magazines at the USIS libraries abroad. A former freelance writer for the INP published three critical articles in the *Denver Post* about the State Department information programs. In mid-August a list was put together of right-leaning writers whose publications had been used. "[C]ertainly a fine conservative bunch," commented Thurman Barnard, who headed efforts to demonstrate the information programs' balance between conservative and liberal.[22]

21. Taber to Barrett, July 11, 1951, 511.00/7–1151; Barrett to Ferguson, August 3, 1951, 511.00/8–351; Ferguson to Humelsine, August 23, 1951, 511.00/8–2351, RG 59, CDF; Memorandum of conversation, Barrett and John Rooney, July 10, 1951; Mary Vandenberg to Frederick Oechsner, July 23, 1951, box 4, folder "1951 Congressional Relations," RG 59, Barrett Files. For Lee's part in McCarthy's charges, see Reeves, *Life and Times of Joe McCarthy*, 227–28. For suspicions about the liberal bias, see Sulkin to Hulten, July 5, 1951, box 59, folder "Scripts"; Memorandum of conversation, Mundt and Jesse MacKnight, July 27, 1951, box 60, folder "M-Z," RG 59, RIIA; "The Government Spends Millions to Influence Public Opinion," *U.S. News and World Report*, no date or issue given, in *Congressional Record*, 82d Cong., 1st sess., June 4, 1951, vol. 97, A4059.

22. Barnard to Kohler, August 2, 1951; "Leading Political Themes on VOA during July," Kohler to Barnard, August 9, 1951, box 56, folder "IBD"; Joseph Sitrick to Barrett, August 7, 1951, box 87, folder "D-Misc."; Thurman Barnard to Frederick Oechsner, August 14, 1951, box 87, folder "Free Lance Writers," RG 59, RIIA.

Also in August, Barrett ordered complaints about the VOA to be culled from the *Congressional Record* in anticipation of final action on the 1952 budget. Representative Clarence Brown (R–Ohio) called the VOA an appeaser for waiting seven months to blame the Soviet Union for the invasion of South Korea, and he proposed cutting funds to a bare minimum until the proper people were brought in to operate the VOA. During the past months thirty-one members of Congress had criticized the VOA, all of them Republicans except Representative Eugene Cox, a conservative Southern Democrat. Complaints included ineffectiveness of VOA broadcasts, misuse of funds, and overlap with other government information programs. Many of the attacks clearly sought to discredit the State Department. A recurring claim: the VOA could never be the true voice of America as long as the State Department managed it. The VOA's problems stemmed from the State Department's policies, charged Representative Alvin O'Konski (R–Wisc.), while Cox called for an overhaul of the State Department.[23] Such charges against the VOA's administration and the State Department were hardly new. In spring 1947 congressional Republicans had said similar things during debate on the VOA's appropriations and the Smith-Mundt bill.

Broadcasts made by Raymond Swing revealed the VOA's precarious position vis-à-vis domestic politics and its vulnerability as a target for attacks on liberalism. After the charges about a leftist slant Barrett asked policy writer Oren Stephens to review Swing's broadcasts, all of which were commentaries. On October 11, 1951, Stephens reported that except for a "few unfortunately worded sentences," the scripts were fine, that is, uncontroversial. Stephens did not say that about Swing Commentary #64, "A Look at the 82nd Congress," which aired on October 22. According to Swing, the Congress failed to improve the conditions of the nation: "It considered no social legislation, it took no action on civil rights. It passed only a minor modification of the Taft-Hartley Labor law." Stephens penciled in the margins of the script, "Is this bad?" adding, "How the GOP press missed this, I can't imagine."[24] The issue was not simply whether or not the VOA balanced out such liberal commentary (which was clearly distin-

23. Joseph Sitrick to Edward Barrett, August 1, 1951, box 60, folder "Congressional," RG 59, RIIA.

24. Stephens to Barrett, October 11, 1951, box 5, folder "Raymond Gram Swing File"; Raymond Swing Commentary #64, "A Look at the 82nd Congress," October 22, 1951, box 5, folder "VOA 1952," RG 59, Miscellaneous Records of the Bureau of Public Affairs, Records Relating to World-Wide Program Objectives.

guished from news) with conservative opinions, as the keepers of such lists seemed to hope. Rather, the issue concerned the VOA's existence as a symbol of liberalism, as evidenced by the ongoing Republican attack on the VOA. In the logic used by these Republicans, the VOA was liberal because the State Department was liberal, because the entire executive branch was liberal. In other words, the VOA was a symptom of a larger disease. Given this approach, attempts to show that the VOA did use conservatives or that Swing's broadcasts represented commentary were unlikely to mollify Republican critics.

III. Looking for Guidance

With its 1952 budget requests slashed and its writers and broadcasters under attack, the VOA faced still more domestic troubles during 1950 and 1951. Rather than originating in Congress, these problems arose within the State Department. In order to report news about official U.S. policy, the VOA required up-to-date, specific guidance, a need made even more pressing by its daily broadcast schedule. The process by which the VOA received policy, however, was fraught with several long-standing obstacles and hitches. These included delays in drafting and delivering official policy or responses to current events, policy makers' indifference to the VOA's guidance needs, and inefficient policy delivery channels. Dating back to the State Department's 1945 takeover of the VOA, these problems had become so great by 1951 that they regularly disrupted VOA operations. In May policy writer Joe Phillips counted between thirty to thirty-five persons involved in the final editorial checks on just one weekly guidance.[25]

For as long as the VOA had been on the air, it faced delays between the occurrence of events and the drafting of an official response or policy. To a certain extent such delays were unavoidable—policy on every possible global development simply did not exist. In early 1946 a policy officer observed that when he had worked for the OWI, directives could not cover all situations that arose, leading to improvisation about "the presumed intention or spirit of the national policy in the domain under consideration." When Greece experienced revolts in January 1946, VOA broadcasters in New York waited impatiently for guidance from Washington, only to receive a terse statement from the Near East political desk that offered

25. Memorandum of conversation, Joe Phillips, May 3, 1951, box 100, folder "Misc. Memos," RG 59, Miscellaneous Records of the Bureau of Public Affairs, Subject Files of the Policy Plans and Guidance Staff.

few clues on the likely U.S. response.[26] How could policy makers provide guidance they had not yet written? This inevitable lag-time presented the VOA with a difficult dilemma. If the VOA failed to provide accurate, breaking news about important world events and the U.S. government's action, foreign listeners would simply stop tuning into the VOA and turn their dials to the BBC or other shortwave stations. If, however, the VOA guessed wrongly about the likely U.S. response, they risked alienating not only foreign listeners but also the president, the secretary of state, members of Congress, and a host of other officials involved in the policy-making process.

To make the situation worse, the VOA continually experienced problems in procuring policy already written or established. In 1946 an OIC official pointed out that relations with Poland hinged on U.S. policy toward Germany, yet for guidance he had only two outdated speeches delivered by the secretary of state. A year later the OIC's general manager complained about "our lack of policy articulation." Overnight guidance in December 1948 offered the following qualification about the close of a UN conference held in Paris: "We are trying to get policy guidance." With regard to ongoing planning for the Atlantic Pact, the same guidance explained, "[w]e will attempt to get policy briefing." In May 1950 participants in a progress and problems meeting indicated that the VOA needed to have quotable, attributable text from department officials in order to make clear U.S. policy, a request that suggests they were not receiving such items. Sometimes the need for material was so great that desperate VOA writers turned to outside news sources for information. Two days after the North Korean invasion of South Korea the VOA studios in New York waited on background information needed for a story being broadcast to the Far East. When policy desks in Washington failed to send the material, the broadcasters picked it up from an ABC newscast. This practice was not uncommon, especially during crisis situations. "Sometimes we would turn on a radio, or see what was on television to find out what the hell was going on," the former chief of the central news file recalled about his years with the VOA.[27]

26. William Tyler to E. Bellquist, January 7, 1946, "Memorandum on an Overseas Information Service," box 122, folder "Basic Information Policy 1945"; K. L. London to Victor Hunt, January 24, 1946, box 42, folder "Radio (IBD) Greece," RG 59, RIIA.

27. K. L. London to Maurice Rice, January 6, 1946, box 42, folder "Poland"; Overnight Guidance #22, December 10, 1948, box 90, folder "12/6–12/10/48" "USIE Progress and Problems," May 12, 1950, box 192, folder "Reports USIE Advisory Commission," RG 59, RIIA; William Stone to William Tyler, August 2, 1947, Drawer 19, Lawson File. On the

These policy procurement difficulties had several sources, including vague explanations of U.S. aims and how the information program fit into these goals. "U.S. foreign policy can be implemented satisfactorily only if we know what it is," an official observed in June 1948. The next month domestic public affairs director Francis Russell pointed out a contradiction between the statements of Assistant Secretary of State George V. Allen and Charles Bohlen. To his staff, Allen said that the promotion of democracy was a main goal of U.S. foreign policy; in an off-the-record talk to State Department officials, Bohlen said it was not. As Russell explained, the problem was not just about who was right, Allen or Bohlen, but also involved deciding what the department should say about spreading democracy overseas. Two years later confusion persisted on how the information programs should describe American aims. An internal review of the policy procedure uncovered several problems, including inadequate guidance on objectives in individual countries and areas of the world.[28] In June 1950, just before the invasion of South Korea, a policy writer outlined the purposes of the information program: tell the world that the United States has a coherent foreign policy that upholds peace and safeguards freedom. Days later another policy writer asked a colleague to review the third draft of a related paper that also stressed the United States' commitment to maintaining world peace and protecting freedom against the Soviet threat. The reviewer commented that the paper did not provide the specific direction needed by field officers and regional output desks. "How far are we willing to go in representing these objectives in the case of the dependent peoples and the French of North Africa, for example?" the reviewer asked.[29] For VOA writers, vagueness made writing news difficult—how were they to convert such broad and sweeping statements of policy into usable, specific news items?

Inefficient methods of passing policy along, which dated back to the State Department's takeover of the VOA, also accounted for the difficulties in procuring guidance. Minutes of a meeting held in December 1945 indicated

---

use of outside news sources, see Foy Kohler, June 28, 1950, box 1, folder "IBD General Corr. 1950," RG 59, Records of the ASPA; interview by the author with Barry Zorthian, November 7, 1995, Arlington, Va.

28. G. A. Mann to Howland Sargeant, June 3, 1948, box 3, folder "P/POL"; Leon Crutcher, "Policy Guidance of OII Media Operations," May 1, 1950, box 94, folder "OII/D," RG 59, RIIA; Francis Russell to George Allen, July 12, 1948, box 2, folder "Democracy as an Objective in American Foreign Policy," RG 59, Office of the Assistant Secretary of State for Public Affairs, Office of Public Affairs Subject Files.

29. Shep Jones to Walter Schwinn, June 12, 1950, 511.00/6–1250, RG 59, CDF.

that weekly directives were being delayed eight to nine days while the necessary approval signatures were acquired. Obviously, directives lost their pertinence when they arrived after the week had ended. Reduction in the number of approvals only partially expedited policy transmission. An April 1947 overview of the process showed just how complicated was the route by which guidance arrived in the hands of VOA writers: after guidances were written, the policy coordinator in Washington sent them to the Policy Information desk at the VOA's studios in New York City, which converted the guidance into outlines of the daily radio output, known as Daily Guidance Notes. Before the Policy Information desk passed the notes on to the radio desks, however, the policy coordinator in Washington had to approve them. To understand how foreign audiences reacted to broadcasts, the VOA relied on telegrams to and from U.S. embassies, yet such cables were first routed through Washington. In order to reduce this delivery delay, Assistant Secretary of State for Public Affairs George V. Allen asked in September 1948 for an automatic relay between Washington and New York. The deputy undersecretary of state for administration denied the request because it took away controls over what the VOA sent to the field. Other attempts to expedite the transmission of guidance and advice failed too. By May 1949 guidance still made five separate stops before arriving on the desks of VOA writers.[30]

Clearly the VOA's location in New York impeded efficient policy delivery. Numerous delays and violations of procedure resulted from miscommunications between personnel in New York and Washington. For example, VOA staff in Washington were often asked to clear telegrams for delivery to the field on behalf of the VOA's New York offices. As a Washington-based employee pointed out, "Naturally, we cannot clear cables on behalf of [VOA-New York] if we do not know [its] position." Other problems included overuse of telephone contact, which created delays. Just as attempts to streamline the delivery of policy failed, so too did attempts to tighten contact between Washington and New York. Beginning in November 1950 Edward Barrett sent a member of the Washington-based Information Policy Planning Staff to New York for a weekly meeting about policy, while a New York-based VOA official came

---

30. Box 119, first unmarked black binder; Victor Hunt to William Stone, April 28, 1947, box 125, folder "Misc. 1947–48," RG 59, RIIA; Allen to Robert Lovett, September 30, 1948; Humelsine to Allen, December 21, 1948, 811.42700(R)/12–2148, RG 59, CDF; F. Fischer to Walton Butterworth, May 6, 1949, box 3, folder "POS/POL," RG 59, Records of the ASPA.

to Washington. But in January 1951 the VOA's New York offices asked former President Herbert Hoover to appear on a broadcast before securing the approval of the Information Policy Planning Staff, which rejected the idea. An embarrassing situation was avoided when Hoover declined the invitation.[31] As the incident showed, coordination between the VOA's two main offices was not improving.

The creation of the Psychological Strategy Board (PSB) in April 1951 posed yet another obstacle to VOA policy channels. Composed of representatives from the CIA and the State and Defense Departments, the PSB was ostensibly responsible for guiding all executive agency psychological operations.[32] PSB members disagreed, however, over the precise definition of their duties. Just three weeks after their first meeting, the CIA staff member stated that the PSB should maintain "surveillance" over all psychological operations, while State, Defense, and JSC staff members thought that the PSB should carry out planning and coordination activities as defined by NSC 59/1 and 10/2. The PSB's confused mission resulted in spotty contact with lower-level State Department officials. According to the CIA representative on the PSB, Board Director Gordon Gray's contact with Undersecretary of State James Webb was not relayed to "the lower echelons."[33]

The greatest source of the VOA's policy procurement difficulties, though, was the indifference, even animus, that many State Department officials had for the VOA and other information and cultural programs, which resulted in neglect or half-hearted support. Department personnel from Foreign Service officers in the field up to the secretariat level did not believe that media operations belonged in the State Department, or even should be done at all, and shunning of the VOA and other media units began once the department took over their operation. In October 1946 two

---

31. Morton Glatzer to Foy Kohler, January 30, 1950, box 193, folder "Inter-Office Memos—New York & Washington"; "USIE Progress and Problems," October 6, 1950, box 192, folder "Reports USIE Advisory Commission"; Barrett to Hulten, November 20, 1950, box 55, folder "Public Affairs"; Anthony Miccoci to Hulten, January 2, 1951, box 47, folder "EUR-Regional Bureau," RG 59, RIIA.

32. Harry S. Truman, "Directive Establishing the Psychological Strategy Board," June 20, 1951, *Public Papers of the Presidents, Harry S. Truman, 1951,* 341–42.

33. "Report on Work of PSB Staff," Joseph Phillips to Barrett and James Webb, August 9, 1951, box 3, folder "040 State Department"; Charles Norberg to John Sherman, October 12, 1951, box 13, folder 091.411, PSB Files; Scott Lucas, "Campaigns of Truth: The Psychological Strategy Board and American Ideology, 1951–1953," 288–90; Lucas, *Freedom's War*, 131–32.

OIC officials complained separately that the information program received little support from the embassies. One month later Assistant Secretary of State for Public Affairs William Benton asked Secretary of State James Byrnes for a public proclamation of support for the VOA in order to head off its elimination by the Republican-controlled Eightieth Congress. Byrnes refused to make such a statement. The State Department, particularly the political desks, do not "treat the information arm of its foreign policy with the trust and confidence due to any of the specialized agencies of the Department," complained a VOA policy writer. In April 1949 a Foreign Service officer informed George Kennan of low morale and disgust among the VOA's New York employees, who did not believe that the department supported their endeavors.[34]

Mistakes by the VOA made worse its ostracism. As a result of both policy procurement difficulties and lapses in pre-broadcast controls, the VOA sometimes made erroneous statements about official U.S. policy. In a May 1951 broadcast the VOA suggested that communist peace feelers were genuine, a direct contradiction of Acheson's own public statements. "Neither VOA executives nor State Department policy experts make a final check of any broadcast before it is transmitted," noted *Pathfinder* magazine. Later that year an internal investigation of the New York studios discovered that many broadcasts aired without even regional desk clearance from Washington.[35] The VOA thus found itself in a vicious circle. Policy makers consistently refused to provide the VOA with timely guidance, which led to mistakes, which in turn reaffirmed the belief that the VOA did not belong in the State Department.

During 1951 Edward Barrett tried in vain to tighten the ties between the information program and State Department policy makers, including the

34. Jesse MacKnight to William Stone, October 18, 1946, box 8, folder "A S/S Foreign Affairs Chronological File 146, Oct.," Jesse MacKnight Papers, Truman Library; Maurice Rice to William Stone, October 25, 1946, box 42, folder "Correspondence Misc.—Russia," RG 59, RIIA. For Byrnes's lack of support, see Benton to Byrnes, November 7, 1946, and Byrnes to Benton, November 11, 1946, box 4, folder "Secretary Byrnes 1946," RG 59, Records of the ASPA. Edwin Kretzmann to William Stone, undated, box 4, folder "P/POL," RG 59, RIIA; John Davies, Jr., to George Kennan, April 11, 1949, box 45, folder "Davies, John P., 1947–49," RG 59, Records of the Policy Planning Staff, 1947–1953.

35. As reported by Barrett in a letter to Acheson, June 8, 1951, box 5, folder "The Secretary 1951," RG 59, Barrett Files; John Gerrity, "What's Wrong with the Voice of America," *Pathfinder*, May 16, 1951, 17; Pirro-Shea report, September 10, 1951, 511.004/11–351, RG 59, CDF.

man at the top, Dean Acheson. In February Barrett wrote to Undersecretary of State James Webb that a top information official needed to be in regular touch with the secretary and kept apprised of major issues. Regarding efforts to bring Barrett into regular contact with Acheson, Howland Sargeant commented that "you [Barrett] have done a good job so far as it is possible under the present Secretary and under the present system." Sargeant added that Barrett had "wisely resisted" efforts to limit his top-level contact. As suggested by these comments, the secretary was not fond of the international information program. Karl Mundt's former administrative assistant put it bluntly: Acheson "could [not] of cared less." Although he publically supported the VOA, Acheson worked around it within the confines of the State Department. As undersecretary of state in April 1947 he and George Kennan, the head of the Policy Planning staff, agreed to exclude an OPA representative from that body. Years later U.S. Advisory Commission member Mark Etheridge remarked that Acheson had twice ignored his suggestion that the assistant secretary of state for Public Affairs be placed on the Policy Planning staff.[36] Without support from the top the VOA stood little chance of fully integrating itself into the State Department's operations and solving its policy guidance problems.

IV. Crowding the Airwaves: Radio Free Europe and Radio Liberation

As the VOA worked to win congressional approval of its Campaign of Truth budget in July 1950, a tiny portable 7.5 kilowatt transmitter in Lampertheim, West Germany, beamed into Czechoslovakia a half-hour radio program mixing news and political analysis. Within a few weeks the same transmitter delivered similar programs into Romania, Poland, Hungary, and Bulgaria. These broadcasts inaugurated Radio Free Europe (RFE), a station that put émigrés and refugees from Eastern Europe on the air so that they could promote democracy and encourage resistance to Soviet-directed rule within their former homelands. Though its beginnings were modest, by December 1952 RFE was airing 218 hours of programming each day, produced in and aired from twenty-two studios situated in

36. Barrett to Webb, February 1, 1951, box 5, folder "U-Undersecretary 1951," RG 59, Barrett Files; Sargeant to Barrett, September 7, 1951, box 4, folder "Correspondence, Deputy Assistant Secretary of State," Sargeant Papers; Robert McCaughey, interview by the author, tape recording, Madison, S.D., June 19, 1995; Carlton Savage, Executive Secretariat of the PPS, April 24, 1947, box 10, folder "Information Policy," RG 59, RIIA; Oral History Interview, Mark Etheridge, June 4, 1974, Truman Library, 47.

its Munich headquarters. A relay station in Portugal and a collection of short- and medium-wave transmitters broadcast the programs into Czechoslovakia, Poland, Hungary, Romania, and Bulgaria. By 1953 a staff of more than seventeen hundred, most of whom were former citizens of these Eastern European nations, worked for RFE.[37]

On the surface, the story behind RFE's creation appeared to demonstrate that the United States' resolve to conquer communism and spread democracy was not limited to government action. In early 1949 State Department officials mulled over ways to handle émigrés and refugees from Eastern Europe, many of whom were former political leaders and government officials. The department's sympathies clearly lay with these strident anticommunists now residing in the United States; however, diplomatic business had to be conducted with the representatives of the communist governments. George Kennan and Dean Acheson agreed that the creation of a private, nonprofit entity to aid the refugees was the best course of action, and they asked former U.S. Ambassador to Japan Joseph C. Grew to plan such an organization. Grew turned to his friend DeWitt C. Poole, also a veteran of the Foreign Service, and their collaboration produced the National Committee for a Free Europe (NCFE) in June 1949. The pedigree of the NCFE was impressive, counting among its members Sullivan and Cromwell attorney Allen Dulles, who helped draft the papers of incorporation and served as the NCFE's first president; *Time-Life* publisher Henry Luce; future President Dwight D. Eisenhower; and Adolph Berle, diplomat and adviser to Franklin Roosevelt. As explained by Grew at a press conference, the purpose of the NCFE was not to provide charity for the émigrés and refugees but rather to help them find adequate employment and nurture a democratic leadership cadre. International broadcasting was a logical choice to accomplish both of these goals, and plans to set up a radio station began a month after the NCFE's incorporation. NCFE member Frank Altschul, a banker, chaired the subcommittee on radio; in turn, he asked former Office of Strategic Services officer Robert E. Lang, now working as an advertising director, to study ways to begin broadcasting.[38]

While these plans were underway the NCFE also organized the Crusade for Freedom, a series of rallies and parades held across the country begin-

---

37. Sig Mickelson, *America's Other Voice: The Story of Radio Free Europe and Radio Liberty*, 30–33; Robert Holt, *Radio Free Europe*, 14–15; Hixson, *Parting the Curtain*, 63.

38. Holt, *Radio Free Europe*, 9–12; Hixson, *Parting the Curtain*, 59; Mickelson, *America's Other Voice*, 14; Lucas, *Freedom's War*, 67–69; Michael Nelson, *War of the Black Heavens: The Battles of Western Broadcasting in the Cold War*, 39–45.

ning in 1950. The centerpiece of the crusade was the Freedom Bell, a copy of the Liberty Bell in Philadelphia's Independence Hall. Americans turning out for the Crusade for Freedom in their hometowns were asked to give so-called freedom dollars to help keep the voice of free Europe on the air; between 1950 and 1952 these donations totaled several hundred thousand dollars. To support the Crusade of Freedom and RFE, the Advertising Council came up with public service announcements that appeared in print, radio, and later television.[39] The NCFE and the Crusade for Freedom thus made for powerful anticommunist propaganda. While prominent Americans gave their time and talents to the NCFE, average Americans donated their hard-earned money, one dollar at a time, to help Eastern Europeans who had been uprooted from their homes by Soviet communism. All three groups, of course, were bound together by a common goal: to ultimately destroy communism and spread democracy.

But this, the official explanation of RFE's origins, elided significant details relating to the extent of the U.S. government's role in setting up and funding RFE. The State Department was not the only involved executive branch agency; the CIA also helped plan and maintain RFE's operations. Soon after its creation in 1947 the CIA had begun carrying out covert political activities abroad. For example, through its Special Procedures Group the CIA worked to prevent a communist victory in Italy's 1948 elections by secretly funding the campaigns of Christian Democrat candidates. In June 1948 the Special Procedures Group was renamed the Office of Special Projects (OSP), but both names conveyed the open-ended definition of the outfit's responsibilities. The OSP was an office well hidden within an agency already reluctant to disclose the nature of its work. Policy directives from the State and Defense Departments ostensibly provided links to the rest of the national security structure, but in practice the OSP was accountable only to the director of the CIA. After yet another name change—the OSP was renamed the Office of Policy Coordination (OPC)—this secretive office joined State Department officials in planning ways to utilize émigrés and refugees from Eastern Europe. The new director of the OPC, Frank Wisner, was a former OSS officer who, after the OSS's liquidation in 1945, served as a deputy to the assistant secretary of state for Occupied Territories. Through both his OSS and State Department work, Wisner recognized that displaced Eastern Europeans could perform valuable func-

---

39. Mickelson, *America's Other Voice*, 51–55; Hixson, *Parting the Curtain*, 59–60; Nelson, *War of the Black Heavens*, 46–49.

tions in the United States' multifaceted struggle to stop communism. Rather than simply finding gainful employment for the refugees, Wisner wanted to actively use them to help free their homelands from the control of Soviet communism through broadcasting and psychological warfare. Under his leadership the OPC became directly involved in the planning for radio broadcasts to Eastern Europe, aided by two million dollars of leftover Special Procedures Group money and a shortwave radio transmitter.[40] The formation of the NCFE implied that the U.S. government was relinquishing oversight of the émigrés and refugees to capable private hands, but behind the scenes, government involvement was actually increasing in a highly secretive fashion. When the NCFE and its purposes were announced in June 1949, no mention was made of Wisner's and the OPC's part. In the years to come the CIA served as a surrogate, secret parent to RFE, funneling to it millions of dollars that paid salaries and equipment costs. Without this money, RFE could not have remained on the air, yet the connection to the CIA was not publicly revealed until 1967, though thousands of government officials, journalists, and persons familiar with RFE knew of the CIA's support.[41]

The effort to conceal the CIA/RFE connection stemmed from several sources. First and foremost, secrecy was de rigueur, and rare was the CIA or NSC official who questioned the need to reveal as little as possible about the CIA's functions. Of course, no intelligence operation can perform effectively without subterfuge and secrecy, but governmental bodies that had some oversight control, such as Congress's Appropriations, Armed Services, and Foreign Relations/Affairs Committees, emboldened the CIA to answer only to itself by approving budgets without detailed examinations. Within the national security structure, the NSC, JCS, Defense and State Departments, and the president himself often made it clear that they were more interested in results rather than the methods used. Second, maintaining a public appearance that RFE was privately funded and administered was necessary from a propaganda standpoint. To reveal that the Crusade for Freedom did not, on its own, support RFE might cast aspersions on America's dedication to liberating Eastern Europe from

40. Mickelson, *America's Other Voice*, 11–17; Lawrence C. Soley, *Radio Warfare: OSS and CIA Subversive Propaganda*, 221–22; Richard H. Cummings, "Covert Broadcasting during the Cold War."

41. Stacey Cone, "Presuming a Right to Deceive: Radio Free Europe, Radio Liberty, the CIA, and the News Media."

Soviet communism. In the CIA's view it was more effective to let the world think that private American citizens generously donated their own money to the cause of freedom. (This argument conveniently overlooked the basic fact that through their tax dollars private American citizens were still generously paying for RFE—they just did not know it.) Third, revelation of the RFE/CIA connection was likely to lead members of Congress and the American public to a very pertinent question: since the VOA was already the U.S. government's voice to the world, why was RFE needed? The question could also be turned around; why then was the VOA needed?

Without revealing the true nature of RFE, its directors nonetheless provided an answer to both halves of the question. General Lucius Clay, who directed the postwar occupation of Germany for the United States, joined the NCFE in December 1949 and was an ardent supporter of putting RFE on the air. As he explained, "[w]hen I left Germany, I came home with a very firm conviction that we needed in addition to the Voice of America a different, broader voice—a voice of the free people—a radio which would speak to each country behind the Iron Curtain in its own language." (Clay apparently overlooked the fact that the VOA was already broadcasting behind the Iron Curtain in the languages spoken there.) Two months before RFE aired its first broadcast Frank Altschul declared that the VOA could not engage in aggressive psychological warfare, but that the RFE, since it was a private entity, could. C. D. Jackson, president of the NCFE and later Dwight D. Eisenhower's adviser on propaganda, expressed a like-minded opinion in September 1951. "We can play tricks, we can denounce, we can take chances, we can act fast, all things that an official propaganda agency cannot do." Such statements reveal just how energetically government officials responsible for propaganda had rejected the "full and fair" approach articulated for the VOA in the fall of 1945. In November 1947 Secretary of State Marshall had suggested at an NSC meeting that a paper relating to propaganda programs (SANACC 304/11) change the phrase "psychological warfare" in its title, but as demonstrated by ensuing NSC policy papers on the subject, Marshall's squeamishness represented a minority point of view.[42] By the summer of 1950, when RFE aired its first broadcast, the perception that the Soviet Union

42. Clay is quoted in Holt, *Radio Free Europe*, 15. For Altschul's view, see Hixson, *Parting the Curtain*, 59; Mickelson, *America's Other Voice*, 26. Jackson is quoted in Cone, "Presuming a Right to Deceive," note 29. "Minutes of the 2nd Meeting of the National Security Council," November 14, 1947, box 203, folder "Meeting 2," NSC Files, 4.

sought world domination and was using psychological warfare to that end, the Campaign of Truth, and the war on the Korean peninsula had combined to bring a full embrace of propaganda in both overt and covert forms. By concealing the partnership between the CIA and NCFE, Radio Free Europe enjoyed, as Clay, Altschul, and Jackson made clear in their respective statements, much more flexibility than the VOA.

Impatience with the VOA and its limitations developed concurrently with both the introduction of RFE and the willingness to step up U.S. propaganda efforts. In July 1948, one year before planning began for RFE, the State Department considered putting émigrés and refugees from Eastern Europe and the Soviet Union behind VOA microphones. Out of concern that these political refugees were resented in their homelands, Marshall rejected the idea, and from Moscow, U.S. Ambassador Walter Bedell Smith agreed. "[U]se of any Soviet refugee on VOUSA [VOA] would not only be ineffectual but would undoubtedly excite resentment and ridicule against our broadcasts," Smith cabled.[43] (Smith's concurrence is striking; in October 1950, he would assume directorship of the CIA, thus presiding over RFE and its legion of refugee broadcasters.) Use of Eastern Europeans by the VOA also risked confusing listeners, who might interpret the refugees' statements as official U.S. policy. However, the decision to not use Eastern European or Soviet nationals on the VOA was not permanent. Language skills and familiarity with target audiences made them ideal employees, though the Smith-Mundt Act's restrictions—FBI background checks and the employment of aliens only when a qualified citizen could not be found—still applied.

Nevertheless, the VOA's obligation to report U.S. policy resulted in constant difficulties in dealing with refugees and émigrés. In 1950 Eastern Europeans dissatisfied with the VOA told Republican members of Congress that communists had infiltrated various language desks (see chapter 5). In July 1951 Senator H. Alexander Smith (R–N.J.) forwarded to Assistant Secretary of State for Public Affairs Edward Barrett a copy of the *Ukrainian Bulletin* that contained an article critical of VOA broadcasts to the Ukraine. As Barrett observed in his reply, the problem "is not what the VOA broadcasts [say], but what the Government's policy is with respect to the Ukrainian independence movement. The Voice of America must reflect US foreign policy; it does not make it." The content of news output on the

43. The Secretary of State to Certain Diplomatic Missions, July 16, 1948; Ambassador in the Soviet Union to the Secretary of State, July 22, 1948, *FRUS* 1948, vol. 4, 425–26.

VOA's Eastern European and Soviet desks was often hotly disputed, as émigrés and refugees on these desks sought to present the news from a Polish or Hungarian point of view rather than an American perspective. Some of the VOA desks were also engulfed in bitter infighting between various national groups. Through Representative Dan Flood (D–Pa.), Slovak nationalists in the United States found an advocate for their desire to detach VOA Slovak broadcasts from the Czech language desk. In October 1952 Flood told VOA officials that a separate Slovak desk, with new personnel, was needed. From the VOA's point of view, "[t]hose who are pushing for a separate Slovak desk are not so much concerned with the effectiveness of VOA broadcasts as they are with promoting an independent Slovakia," an independence issue that the U.S. government was currently avoiding. But when told that the VOA would not act on his suggestion, Flood brusquely indicated that he would use all means possible to create a Slovak desk.[44] Like the Ukrainians critical of the VOA, Flood and his Slovak constituents did not give full thought to the serious problems that the VOA, as an officially recognized agency of the U.S. government, could cause by fomenting revolt in nations with which the United States maintained diplomatic relations. On the other hand, these critics were simply carrying America's commitment to spreading democracy to a logical, if risky, conclusion. As Barrett had pointed out, the setting of policy was not the VOA's responsibility, but as the VOA continually realized, the critics of the message often went after the messenger.

The early broadcasts of RFE showed just how intent its directors were on accomplishing what the VOA had yet to do: tangibly undermine the communist governments in Eastern Europe and openly promote liberation. Robert E. Lang, RFE's first director, recruited young, recent refugees, and while few had any radio experience, American broadcasters were hired to teach them at the Munich headquarters. Frank Altschul initially expected the CIA, through the Office of Policy Coordination, to provide policy guidance and raw material to use in broadcasts, but the OPC usually only sent

---

44. Barrett to Smith, June 12, 1951, box 76, folder "Smith," RG 59, RIIA. For the disputes on language desks, see USIA Alumni Association Oral History Project, Interview with Barry Zorthian by Cliff Groce, October 20 and 26, 1988, USIA Historical Collection, 8–9. For the debate on the Slovak desk, see Sargeant to Compton, October 7, 1952; Compton to Sargeant, October 8, 1952; Compton to Flood, October 15, 1952; Flood to Compton, October 28, 1952, box 5, folder "Congressional Relations," RG 306, Office of Administration Files, 1952-1955.

translations of outdated newspaper articles. With airtime to fill and scant relevant background material available, RFE's eager new broadcasters attacked the Soviet-supported governments in their homelands in ways the VOA did not: diatribes against communism, ad hominem attacks on individual government officials, even identification of collaborators. A policy handbook, drafted in 1950 and 1951, captured the RFE's strident, emotional, and somewhat unrealistic sense of purpose: "sowing dissension in each regime through exposing of the ineptitude of its officials, and sowing fear among the officials by denouncing confirmed acts of oppression and cruelty, and threatening retribution."[45] Threatening retribution? Such a bold statement could hardly be found in VOA policy papers. By 1951 RFE had eased the aggressive, charged tone of its broadcasts, but the basic goal of promoting the liberation of Eastern Europe remained, and this was still an issue that the VOA had to treat carefully and obliquely.

Aware of the constraints on their own output and the use of exiles, VOA officials worked with RFE, though the collaboration was, of course, kept secret. In August 1949, just one month after planning for RFE broadcasts began, the director of the Office of International Information, which oversaw the VOA, stated that cooperation between RFE and VOA was to be conducted in the most discreet manner possible, without leaving any signs that the VOA was involved. As plans to implement the Campaign of Truth unfolded in June 1950 the State Department's Office of Public Affairs indicated that it supported RFE's plan to build megawatt transmitters in Germany: both the NCFE and RFE were useful as unofficial promoters of U.S. policy, and the department was ready to work with RFE to broadcast "gray propaganda," which the VOA could not transmit. (Gray propaganda is material in which the source might or might not be accurately identified, and in which the validity of the claims offered are not clear.) As RFE expanded during its first year on the air, it asked the State Department for additional help in procuring high-frequency radio facilities. Accordingly, a member of the department's Program and Evaluation staff indicated that he would set up a working group that included department members as well as representatives from the Joint Chiefs of Staff and the CIA.[46] In a

45. Mickelson, *America's Other Voice*, 31, 37–42; Hixson, *Parting the Curtain*, 60–62; Nelson, *War of the Black Heavens*, 51; "Radio Free Europe Handbook," cited in Holt, *Radio Free Europe*, 22.

46. International Broadcasting Division Policy Paper 2, March 16, 1950, box 110, folder "OII Policy Action Papers"; W. K. Scott to Edward Barrett, June 26, 1950, box 14,

January 1951 paper Assistant Secretary of State for Public Affairs Edward Barrett provided an overview of the relationship between the State Department and RFE. The department supported both the NCFE and RFE, and had publicly expressed its approval. However, the number of people who knew "the full background of the Committee" needed to be minimized so that RFE's appearance as independently produced propaganda was maintained. Barrett also reiterated the need to conceal all contact between the department and RFE: "such cooperation as is necessary and desirable should be carried on in the most discreet manner possible."[47] This secrecy did not simply serve RFE's interests; it also protected the VOA from charges that it was ineffective, restrained, even unnecessary.

The image of State Department officials skulking about to help RFE produce broadcasts that the VOA could not air depicts vividly the paradoxical nature of the Campaign of Truth. After a long struggle the VOA and its supporters had triumphed over opponents in Congress, and were, by 1950 and 1951, seeking in excess of $100 million to add dozens of new languages and to build a worldwide ring of transmitters to overcome Soviet jamming. Yet the ability of the VOA to take advantage of this massive expansion remained limited. Frugal members of Congress scrutinized line items in budget requests; conservatives pored over scripts looking for a liberal bias and searched employee ranks for suspected communists and/or liberals; State Department policy makers rebuffed VOA efforts to procure cutting-edge guidance. It is no surprise, then, that the VOA welcomed rather than resisted the creation of the RFE, and worked behind the scenes to help it.

The origins, operations, and purposes of Radio Liberation (renamed Radio Liberty in 1964), resembled closely that of RFE and fulfilled a similar role vis-à-vis the VOA. Like RFE, Radio Liberation (RL) was set up under the auspices of a private foundation, the American Committee for the Liberation of the Peoples of Russia (AmComLib), which was incorporated in January 1951. (The original name was the American Committee for Freedom for the Peoples of the USSR, Inc.; in May 1951 it was changed to the American Committee for the Liberation of the Peoples of Russia,

folder "Free Nations (Europe)"; Fred Trimmer to William Stone, November 3, 1950, box 4, folder "Radio," RG 59, RIIA. For a definition of gray propaganda, see Jowett and O'Donnell, *Propaganda and Persuasion*, 17.

47. Edward Barrett, "Radio Free Europe," January 24, 1951, box 5, folder "G-Deputy Undersecretary, 1951," RG 59, Barrett Files.

Inc.) Impetus for the committee's creation came from the State Department and the CIA, again working through Frank Wisner and the OPC. Wisner's aide Franklin Lindsay, who had served under Wisner in the OSS during World War II, began putting together the committee and overseeing its incorporation in 1950. As it did for RFE, the CIA secretly provided financial support for years to come, as well as, to a lesser extent, operational oversight. Copying the pattern established by RFE, AmComLib sought to broadcast to the Soviet Union using émigrés and refugees from the various republics that now constituted the Soviet Union. This was no easy task. The refugees were a diverse, fractious group, and AmComLib's directors were continually frustrated in their efforts to draft goals acceptable to the refugees and the separate organizations that they had already founded for themselves. Russian émigrés alone had five separate groups; several other organizations represented non-Russian nationalities and ethnic groups. The fact that refugees from the Soviet Union were scattered throughout Western Europe and the United States made the work of unification even more difficult. Plans to begin radio broadcasts to the Soviet Union thus went forward before common ideological ground was found. Indeed, Radio Liberation never fully integrated the various refugee groups. In 1952 a New York office was set up so that a broadcast production team could begin work, and AmComLib purchased the RFE base at Lampertheim and installed transmitters.[48]

Radio Liberation debuted on March 1, 1953, broadcasting to the Soviet Union. The death of Stalin just days later, as well as workers' riots in East Berlin in June, provided RL with dramatic events to cover. Compared to RFE, though, RL was a much smaller operation. During its first year on the air it had just over three hundred employees, far fewer than RFE's seventeen hundred. RL's foreign-born employees tended to regard the operation as their own, one in which Americans were present to provide financial support and occasional advice. As an American employed at RL commented in his memoir, "[t]here were two worlds at Radio Liberty, American and émigré. For the most part, the inhabitants of those worlds lived separately from, and in ignorance of, one another."[49] Still, both the Americans and émigrés had a common purpose, to liberate the republics of the Soviet Union from communism, and like RFE, RL enjoyed more flexibility than did the VOA.

48. Mickelson, *America's Other Voice*, 59–69; Nelson, *War of the Black Heavens*, 56–68.
49. Hixson, *Parting the Curtain*, 63; James Critchlow, *Radio Hole-in-the-Head/Radio Liberty: An Insider's Story*, 6, 31.

RFE and RL were made possible in part by the VOA's hard-fought battle to secure permanent standing, a struggle won when Congress passed the Smith-Mundt Act in January 1948. Propaganda became an established component of the United States' fight against communism after 1948, and the crisis atmosphere accompanying the Korean War increased the importance of propaganda. While the VOA's Campaign of Truth predated the outbreak of conflict on the Korean peninsula, the hostilities there helped smooth the way for the campaign's implementation and seemed to confirm the need for more stations like RFE and RL. In this sense the VOA's ambitious expansion and the creation of RFE and RL represented a resounding victory over opponents in Congress, who had almost orchestrated the VOA's demise in 1946 and 1947. However, the VOA's position was far from firm even by 1950 and 1951, as demonstrated by the congressional backlash against the Campaign of Truth budget, the search for liberal bias in its scripts, and the State Department's own neglect of the VOA. In light of these difficulties, the attraction that RFE and RL held for propaganda supporters within the executive branch are readily apparent. With the brunt of their funds coming from the CIA, neither RFE nor RL had to answer to tough questions about its spending. As supposedly private outfits, RFE and RL also did not have to explain discrepancies between their broadcasts and U.S. policy, thus allowing them to promote openly liberation and rankle the officials of communist regimes in Eastern Europe and the Soviet Union. Both stations could hire freely, while the VOA chafed under the Smith-Mundt's employment restrictions. In short, RFE and RL could do what the VOA could not—why? The facade provided by private corporations made all the difference, because it detached RFE and RL from the sticky problems that the VOA suffered: lingering discomfort among many members of Congress concerning government-operated media; suspicions about partisan bias in programming; use of the VOA and its broadcasts to serve political, even personal aims; and the State Department's concern that the VOA might misrepresent U.S. policy and cause both domestic and international political problems. Congressional investigations in 1952 and 1953 drove home these points.

Chapter 7

"A Very, Very Tough Period"
The 1952–1953 Congressional Investigations

In 1952 and 1953 the VOA's domestic difficulties converged and intensified as a result of two Senate investigations, the first led by a Foreign Relations subcommittee chaired by Bourke B. Hickenlooper, and the second directed by the Committee on Government Operation's Permanent Subcommittee on Investigations, headed by Joe McCarthy. The Hickenlooper subcommittee had its origins in a 1951 effort by former Assistant Secretary of State William Benton, now a Democratic senator from Connecticut, to detach the VOA and other media units from the State Department. In an attempt to block this move and shore up its crumbling credibility with members of Congress, the VOA's parent office was reorganized in early 1952 as the International Information Administration. But the change mattered little. Ostensibly, both the Hickenlooper and McCarthy subcommittees sought to demonstrate the VOA's limited effectiveness and propose recommendations for improvement, but their purposes hardly ended there. The 1952 election brought Dwight D. Eisenhower to the White House, the first Republican president since 1928. Republicans also obtained a majority in both houses of Congress. Foreign policy was a major campaign issue as Republican candidates and incumbents characterized containment as morally bankrupt and a policy of defeatism, themes that resonated with a public frustrated with the stalemated war in Korea. To replace containment, Eisenhower and congressional Republicans offered rollback, positive and vigorous action aimed at eradicating communism in addition to halting its expansion. Rollback placed the VOA in a precarious situation. By simple inference the VOA itself was morally bankrupt and defeatist, for it had touted containment and its applications to the world for seven years. By targeting the VOA, the Senate investigations pointed to deficiencies in the Truman administration's conduct of foreign affairs and highlighted Republicans' resolve to change the basic goal of American anticommunism. As Senator Charles Potter (R–Mich.) commented after McCarthy's hearings revealed problems with the VOA's operations, "I think it probably should be made clear . . . that we are referring to the old team; I mean, the administration that has been in power."[1]

Finger-pointing was not without cause, however, for the VOA did have serious problems. Between 1951 and 1952, cost overruns, misuse of funds, and poor planning afflicted the VOA's ambitious counter-jamming initiative proposed in the 1950 Campaign of Truth. As part of its wide-ranging investigation the Hickenlooper subcommittee sought to uncover the sources of these problems, but before it could finish its investigation, McCarthy's hearings quickly eclipsed its work. McCarthy's motives for investigating the VOA included much more than the desire to discredit the Truman administration; the Wisconsin Republican also sought to reaffirm his reputation as the country's premiere anticommunist. When McCarthy began his hearings in February 1953, three years had passed since he received national attention for his charges against the State Department. A lawsuit and an attempted resolution at censure targeted McCarthy in Wheeling's wake, but the 1952 election showed that he was far from finished. Wisconsin voters returned McCarthy to the Senate by nearly 140,000 votes, and the Committee on Committees gave him the chairmanship of the Committee on Government Operations and its Permanent Subcommittee on Investigations. The manner in which he conducted his probe of the VOA during the first months of 1953 made it quickly apparent that McCarthy was far less interested in improving the VOA than he was in showing Congress and the public that the already beleaguered agency was riddled with communist saboteurs, sexual deviants, and an atheist, and that he was responsible for identifying these subversives.

Eisenhower's reaction to McCarthy's investigation was guarded and conspicuously quiet; he and Secretary of State John Foster Dulles did not attempt to rein in McCarthy even as the investigation disrupted the VOA's operations. Yet neither Dulles nor Eisenhower wanted to give the appearance that they were doing nothing to fix the VOA's problems. Accordingly, Eisenhower appointed two independent commissions, the President's Committee on International Information Activities and the

---

1. Senate Committee on Government Operations, *Hearings before the Permanent Subcommittee on Investigations of the Committee on Government Operations,* 83d Cong., 1st sess., February 1953, pt. 1, 209 (hereafter cited as McCarthy Hearings).

Rockefeller committee, to also examine the VOA's and other media's operations and provide recommendations. The creation of these two commissions, which are the subject of chapter eight, meant that in 1953 four separate entities were investigating the VOA and the International Information Administration. In 1950 President Truman and Dean Acheson had unveiled the Campaign of Truth in part to reassert their dedication to anticommunism. In a similar fashion, these four investigations sought to show that their Republican sponsors were actively trying to fix a supposedly vital part of the nation's anticommunist program at the same time they served varying domestic political needs.

I. Retrenchment Fails

In 1951 William Benton publicized the VOA's troubles within the State Department by leading an unsuccessful initiative to remove the VOA and other media units from the department. Benton was now the junior senator from Connecticut, and in November 1950 he informed Edward Barrett that colleagues in Congress had asked him to introduce a bill setting up an independent executive agency to operate the VOA. As former assistant secretary of state for Public Affairs, Benton knew firsthand the guidance problems and lack of support suffered by the information programs. In a January 1951 letter to Secretary of State Acheson, released publicly, Benton criticized the programs' effectiveness, proposed that they be removed from the State Department, and advocated a quadruple increase in their annual budget. Acheson politely disagreed with Benton, claiming that the Campaign of Truth was successfully rebuilding the programs in the ways Benton had envisioned when he still served as assistant secretary of state. While Acheson did not believe in general that the State Department should have operational responsibilities, he did think that the information programs belonged in the department because there was nowhere else to place them in the executive branch. (In other words, the information program was easier to monitor inside the department rather than outside). Acheson had the letter to Benton written in an informal style because, as one of his aides commented, "Senator Benton, although familiar with Department procedures, still likes to cling to the illusion that the Secretary writes to him personally." This sly attempt to mollify Benton had little effect. In his reply to Acheson's letter Benton reiterated his claims about the program's inadequacies and called for a congressional study of his proposals. To a reporter Benton later stated, "[T]he State Department under Secretary of State Acheson's leadership has been inadequate in its requests for funds and in its leadership in the newly emerging psychological warfare."[2]

While Acheson prepared a public position for the State Department regarding Benton's proposal, Edward Barrett handled the actual planning. His personal response was more direct than Acheson's (and written by himself), opening with, "Dear Bill: You are not going to like this. In fact, you will probably want to shoot me." Barrett promised to fight to keep the information program within State and to prevent expansion from occurring quickly, reminding Benton that "all the Taber-like snipers will continue at work" if too much money was requested. Publicly, though, Barrett did not react so strongly to Benton's proposal. A Department of State press release welcomed Benton's interest and a possible congressional investigation of the information programs' operations within the department. Public Affairs officials were not sanguine about the outcome of such a probe, however. They feared Congress would recommend detaching the information programs from the State Department, a move that they did not want. In early February, Deputy Assistant Secretary of State for Public Affairs Howland Sargeant predicted to Barrett that the "chances that a Congressional inquiry would support leaving the operations in the Department of State seem mighty slim." Sargeant suggested several ways to act on Benton's proposals without actually separating the information programs from the State Department, including asking President Truman to appoint an independent commission to carry out the investigation. Sargeant also advised that Benton should be consulted directly in the planning process. A more direct effort to co-opt Benton's call for separation was the proposed "Foreign Information Administration" (FIA), intended to operate as a semi-autonomous agency within the State Department without breaking policy connections. Planning for the FIA began in earnest after Benton brought his proposals to the Senate floor. On February 19, 1951, Benton and Alexander Wiley (R–Wisc.) introduced S.R. 74, which was essentially a revision of Benton's Marshall Plan of Ideas bill (see chapter 4). Hearings on the Marshall Plan of Ideas had been held in July 1950 but the Senate Foreign Relations Committee never reported the bill out. S.R. 74 pro-

2. Benton to Barrett, November 28, 1950, 511.00/11–2850, RG 59, CDF; Acheson to Benton, January 24, 1951, box 68, folder "Benton," RG 59, RIIA; Secretary's office to Patterson, January 9, 1951, 511.00/12–1450, RG 59, CDF; Benton to Acheson, January 31, 1951, box 4, folder "Correspondence, Deputy Assistant Secretary of State for Public Affairs," Howland H. Sargeant Papers, Harry S. Truman Presidential Library, Independence, Mo.; Joan David, "Senator William Benton."

posed the formation of a subcommittee to investigate the information and cultural programs with the aim of determining needed reorganization or rebuilding. Outlines of the Foreign Information Administration drafted in April indicated that one of the primary goals was to "avoid the separation of the program from the Department entirely."[3]

Why? Considering the persistent problems that the VOA experienced in the State Department, resistance to Benton's separation plan seems misplaced. In fact, officials feared that detachment would increase the State Department's neglect of the information program. Regardless of the program's ultimate placement, the State Department would still provide guidance on U.S. foreign policy, and the program stood a better chance of fixing its persistent guidance problems as an in-house agency rather than as an independent agency. As Barrett wrote to Undersecretary of State James Webb, a key supporter of the VOA, a top official from the information program needed to be in regular contact with the secretary of state, especially since "some of the top policy-making officials are not naturally public-relations-minded [sic]." Barrett proposed that he be allowed to attend the secretary's morning meetings on Mondays and Fridays. If the assistant secretary of state for Public Affairs had to seek permission to attend regular high-level meetings, what chance did the administrator of an independent agency stand of being included? Concern over further exclusion extended to field operations as well. Plans stressed the importance of integrating the Foreign Information Administration with both the department's Regional Bureaus and the missions abroad.[4]

Barrett also regarded the FIA as a way of collapsing the Economic Cooperation Administration's (ECA) information activities into the State Department. When it passed the Marshall Plan in March 1948, Congress had authorized the ECA to operate its own information program. As a result the ECA and State Department conflicted continually over areas of operation, overlapping efforts, and resource usage and sharing. As far as

---

3. Barrett to Benton, January 1951, box 68, folder "Benton," RG 59, RIIA; Barrett to Benton, February 3, 1951, box 4, folder "Correspondence, Deputy Assistant Secretary of State for Public Affairs," Sargeant Papers; Sargeant to Barrett, February 5, 1951, drawer 24, 1–3; Carlisle Humelsine to Undersecretary James Webb, February 8, 1951, drawer 21; "Principles for Reorganization of the USIE Program," April 6, 1951, drawer 21, Lawson File, 1. For the text of the "Marshall Plan of Ideas," see S.R. 74, *Congressional Record*, 82d Cong., 1st sess., February 19, 1951, vol. 97, 1400–1402.

4. Barrett to James Webb, February 1, 1951, box 5, folder "U-Under Secretary 1951," RG 59, Barrett Files; "Principles for Reorganization of the USIE Program," 3; Under Secretary's Meetings Notes, April 9, 1951, drawer 21, Lawson File, 3.

Barrett was concerned the ECA's information program had fulfilled its raison d'etre by 1951—most of Europe knew about the Marshall Plan. Yet ECA information personnel were now trying to keep their operation alive by explaining all of U.S. foreign policy and its aims, which was the State Department's responsibility. Some ECA staff were even taking criticisms of the State Department to members of Congress in hopes of improving their own standing. To prevent further tension, integration seemed appropriate, and it strengthened the chances of keeping the information program within the State Department.[5]

Delayed action on Benton's bill gave Barrett the opportunity to put together the Foreign Information Administration before Congress acted. S.R. 74 languished in the Senate Foreign Relations Committee for more than a year while one of its members, Karl Mundt, arranged to enact a bill he was sponsoring. Since June 1950 Mundt had been urging the State Department to begin worldwide television broadcasts, which Mundt called "The Vision of America." In September 1950 Mundt had secured the help of Representative Mike Mansfield in bringing his "Vision of America" proposal to the House floor, but they were unsuccessful. In June 1951 Mundt wrote to Barrett that it was imperative that the House pass the bill before the Senate took action on Benton's Resolution.[6] While Mundt worked in vain to secure House support for his Vision of America plan, the State Department went forward with planning for the new, semi-autonomous agency. The amount of control that the State Department was to have over the agency's operations caused much debate. Although an ostensible purpose of creating the Foreign Information Administration was to give the VOA and other media independence while maintaining policy ties, several department officials were reluctant to give up control over hiring, field operations, and administrative matters.[7]

When the agency was unveiled in January 1952 with the new name of the International Information Administration (IIA), the advocates of preponderate State Department control had prevailed. On the surface the IIA seemed new, but structurally it closely resembled its predecessor, the Office

5. Barrett to James Webb, January 5, 1951, drawer 23, Lawson File; Barrett to Webb, January 12, 1951, box 5, folder "U-Under Secretary 1951," RG 59, Barrett Files.

6. Mundt to Barrett, June 1, 1951, box 6, folder "TV: Correspondence 1951," Henry F. Holthusen Papers, Herbert Hoover Presidential Library, West Branch, Iowa.

7. Minutes of the Undersecretaries of State meeting, October 23, 1951, box 6, folder "FIA," RG 59, Records of the Bureau of Public Affairs, Records Relating to World-Wide Program Objectives.

of International Information (OII).[8] The position of administrator was created and placed in charge of all international information and cultural
activities, while the assistant secretary of state for Public Affairs assumed
responsibility for domestic public relations. The individual media and cultural units (radio, press, movies, libraries, and exchange) were reorganized
and placed under the supervision of assistant administrators. Unit reorganization and the division of international and domestic public affairs were
the greatest changes; other areas of the operations were left untouched. The
drafting of policy still remained the responsibility of the State Department's
regional desks; the department also continued to handle administrative,
hiring, and personnel matters.[9] Finally, the IIA maintained the VOA's dual
offices in New York and Washington, a separation that accounted for many
of the VOA's problems in obtaining guidance.

With the new agency came change at the top; Barrett resigned as assistant secretary of state for Public Affairs in December 1951. While Barrett's
public resignation letter avoided reference to the numerous frustrations he
experienced during his two-year tenure, he did mention one in a private
letter to Dean Acheson: "[i]t's all but impossible to run such an international information program with a board of directors of 531 members of
Congress." Howland Sargeant replaced Barrett while Dr. Wilson
Compton, the president of Washington State College, was appointed the
first IIA administrator. Compton's government experience was limited to
a pre-WWI stint as a staff economist for the Federal Trade Commission,
and he had no background in either media operations or foreign relations.
However, Compton was an ideal candidate in one aspect—he was a
Republican. During a December 1951 meeting with Undersecretary of
State James Webb, Sargeant noted Compton's lack of applicable experience, dubbing him "a calculated risk." But Compton was a Republican,
Sargeant continued, and there seemed to be no alternative. Webb reported
that Barrett had said as much about Compton. Influential Republicans
were tipped off to Compton's political leanings in a letter Barrett wrote to
the Senate Appropriations Committee in February. After thanking William
Knowland, Styles Bridges, Homer Ferguson, and Alexander Wiley for
their help while he was assistant secretary, Barrett expressed his hope that

8. The creation of the IIA superseded a December 1, 1951, State Department order
that had created the Office of International Broadcasting (OIB) within the Office of
International Information.
9. "Establishment of the United States International Information Administration,"
Departmental Announcement no. 4, January 16, 1952, *FRUS* 1952–54, vol. 2, pt. 2, 1591–95.

they would also support Compton, who "bears a Republican label, by the way." (This aside was omitted from the letter sent to Appropriations Committee Democrats).[10]

But efforts to please Republicans did not go far in 1952, an election year. Familiar complaints resurfaced as Republicans used attacks on the VOA to discredit the Democratic administration. In February 1952 an IIA liaison officer met with Republican National Committee (RNC) officials in Washington to discuss ways to improve the information program. According to the liaison officer's record of the meeting, the director of the RNC's Ethnic Origins Division "sought to indicate a veritable flood of complaints against the VOA," and said "one suggestion we might convey was that his party desired a change in national administrations. (Broad smile on his part.)" The official concluded that Republicans were going to encourage attacks on the VOA and other media units solely for partisan reasons without actually seeking response or action on the IIA's part. His predictions seemed to come true that summer. In June Representative Daniel Reed (R–N.Y.) attacked the VOA in a press release, claiming that the radio agency was offending South Koreans by criticizing Syngman Rhee. "There should be a clean-out from top to bottom in the Voice agency," Reed stated. In July Republican members of Congress coordinated a public assault on the VOA in an apparent attempt to discredit and oust Dean Acheson. The Republican Policy Committee attached an amendment to the State Department appropriations bill that prohibited the use of department funds to pay the salaries of officials who had previous connections to law firms doing business with foreign governments. Under this provision, Acheson could not receive his salary. House Republicans then led a floor attack on the VOA, reading from photocopied statements. Democrats charged the RNC with planning and carrying out the demonstration.[11]

Coverage of the election-year activities also drew attention. In March Senator Ferguson called Deputy IIA Administrator Reed Harris to ask if the VOA was covering the New Hampshire primaries. Harris told him that the VOA was using material picked up from CBS and NBC, and the IIA's

10. Barrett to Acheson, December 5, 1951, drawer 21, Lawson File. For discussion of Compton's political leanings, see handwritten notes of meeting, December 17, 1951, box 2, folder "Undersecretary-U," RG 59, Records of the Office of the Assistant Secretary for Public Affairs, 1949–53. Barrett memorandum, February 1, 1952, box 86, folder "Senate Appropriations Committee," RG 59, RIIA.

11. Harry B. Lyford to Charles P. Arnot, February 29, 1952, 511.004/2–2952, RG 59, CDF; "Statement by Representative Daniel A. Reed, of New York," June 14, 1952, Lawson File; "House GOP Moves to 'Get Acheson,'" *New York Times*, July 24, 1952.

International Press Service had assigned a writer to cover the event. In June a Scripps-Howard correspondent reported that the State Department's Wireless Bulletin, which provided news roundups for use by American diplomats abroad, was forwarding partisan commentary on the upcoming presidential race. The column singled out by the correspondent had reported that Truman believed Robert Taft would be easier for the Democrats to beat in November than Dwight Eisenhower. After the story broke, Compton and Acheson ordered the weekly column dropped from the Wireless Bulletin. To guard against charges that the VOA favored Democrats, in May the China desk began tallying the number of lines devoted to both Democrats and Republicans in its daily news broadcasts. Tallies were kept through mid-November 1952. Although the other language desks did not make notations on their respective daily schedules, such counting was common according to former VOA employee Barry Zorthian. "[W]e even did it in the Central News Room to make sure because we knew that kind of charge [slanting] was going to come up," Zorthian said in an interview.

Special election guidance, issued in July, attempted to strike a balance between the VOA's and affiliate media's de facto need to satisfy members of Congress who might be monitoring output and the de jure mandate to inform foreign audiences about U.S. foreign policy. The guidance even referred to this point within the 1948 Smith-Mundt Act, indicating that "coverage of the presidential campaign has basis only to the extent that it serves this broad criterion." As a general rule, the guidance suggested that media write news relying on patterns of foreign rather than domestic audience interest. In using outside commentaries, equal space or time was to be given to each party and their various candidates. With regard to editorials originating within the IIA, the guidance forbade writers from making predictions about the election's outcome, drawing conclusions, or commenting on the personalities of the candidates. However, detachment of the campaign's domestic and partisan aspects from the conduct of American foreign affairs was easier to state than practice. As the guidance itself noted, "U.S. foreign policy is a central campaign issue."[12]

---

12. Memorandum of Conversation between Harris and Ferguson, March 7, 1952, box 5, folder "Congressional Relations," RG 306, Office of Administration Files, 1952–1955. For the VOA's coverage of the presidential race, see "Acheson Bans Political News," *Washington Daily News*, June 20, 1952; daily broadcast schedules for China, May to November 1952, boxes 41–56, RG 306, VOA Reports; Barry Zorthian, interview by the author, tape recording, Arlington, Va., November 7, 1995; "1952 U.S. Presidential

Capitalizing on the protracted war in Korea, Republicans were denouncing containment and its creator, the Truman administration. Containment remained official U.S. guiding policy, yet by continuing to report it as such the VOA gave the impression that it was giving short shrift to the Republican position. Moreover, just as it had during the 1948 and 1950 elections, the VOA was trying to balance conflicting audience needs. Its unofficial listeners, conservative members of Congress, were interested in what foreign listeners were not (or so policy officers believed): the domestic aspects of the campaign.

Just as the creation of the IIA did not end the VOA's troubles with congressional Republicans, it did not end the long-standing guidance and support problems with the State Department. In January 1952 a member of the Psychological Strategy Board visited the VOA's New York studios and reported that the VOA needed clearer statements of national policy. As Howland Sargeant prepared for Senate hearings on his nomination as assistant secretary of state for Public Affairs, Senator Tom Connally criticized the IIA as "remote control" for the State Department. Between February and June 1952 an IIA official surveyed the information program's operations at U.S. embassies worldwide. His report showed that the formation of the IIA had done little to improve the relationship between the media units and the diplomatic missions. Policy guidance was still weak, slow to arrive, and inadequate. In its sixth semiannual report the U.S. Advisory Commission on Information, set up by the Smith-Mundt Act of 1948, reported that coordination between the Psychological Strategy Board and the IIA was still lacking. In September 1952 the VOA in New York reported persisting difficulty in obtaining information from the political desks in Washington.[13]

The IIA may have kept the VOA and other media units within the State Department, but as these incidents show, the victory was pyrrhic. The

Campaign," Special Instruction PO-53–1, July 8, 1952, box 35, folder "IIA," RG 59, Miscellaneous Records of the Bureau of Public Affairs, Records of the Assistant Director of the Office of Public Affairs, 2–5.

13. Charles R. Norberg, memorandum for the files, January 28, 1952, box 3, folder "040 VOA," PSB Files; Sargeant memorandum, February 5, 1952, box 4, folder "Correspondence Deputy Assistant Secretary of State for Public Affairs," Sargeant Papers; Thurman L. Barnard, "Highlights of Trip to Various Missions," box 5, folder "IIA Correspondence," RG 46, SEN 83A-F7, Subcommittee on Overseas Information Program SR 44 (and SR 74); U.S. Advisory Commission on Information, *6th Semi Annual Report*, July 1952, 14; Sydney Sulkin to Alfred Morton, September 18, 1952, 511.004/9–1852, RG 59, CDF.

usual domestic troubles afflicted the VOA and other media units. Even diehard supporters expressed dissatisfaction. In April 1952 the *New Haven Register* reported Karl Mundt as saying that the VOA was ineffective. When asked by IIA officials if the *Register* had quoted him accurately, Mundt said yes, that the VOA's message needed to be more aggressive and aim at influencing people. As IIA Administrator Wilson Compton penciled in the margin, "[t]o do what?"[14] This was the essential problem. What exactly did each of the following want the VOA to do and not to do: individual members of Congress, whether Republican or Democrat; State Department officials from the secretary down to rank-and-file Foreign Service officers; members of the National Security Council, Joint Chiefs of Staff, Central Intelligence Agency, and Psychological Strategy Board? Everyone seemed to have a differing opinion and normative plan.

II. The Ring Plan's Continuing Troubles

Difficulties attending the VOA's counter-jamming initiative compounded its problems with both congressional Republicans and the national security establishment. Since the VOA's efforts to overcome Soviet blockage of broadcasts figured prominently in both the Hickenlooper and McCarthy investigations, it is necessary to first explain the development of the VOA's counter-jamming initiative. After the Campaign of Truth was announced in April 1950 the VOA hired consultants from universities, industry, and government to devise a counter-jamming program. Led by MIT's Research Laboratory of Electronics, this team proposed the Ring Plan, which called for the construction abroad of fourteen one-megawatt medium-wave transmitters and six one-megawatt shortwave transmitters in the United States, all aimed at strengthening relay signals and overriding Soviet jamming of the VOA's signal. Congress approved more than $40 million for the Ring Plan in fall 1950 but slashed a second budget request from $97 million to $9.5 million in spring 1951. At the time, members of the House Appropriations Committee indicated that they did not believe the VOA was effectively using the funds already appropriated for the Ring Plan. In a summer 1951 report on programs for national security the NSC blamed Congress's refusal to grant more funds for causing "an indefinite postponement of the completion of the radio ring" and stated that the public and members of

14. *New Haven Register*, April 25, 1952; Joseph Sitrick to Wilson Compton, May 2, 1952, box 5, folder "Congressional Relations," RG 306, Office of Administration Files.

Congress did not realize the "significant role an adequate information program can and must play in the defense of the United States."[15]

The Ring Plan's troubles were not entirely the result of a parsimonious and unappreciative Congress, though. The Baker West transmitter was plagued from the start. Efforts by Senator William Knowland to influence the location and construction of this West Coast relay station had delayed the acquisition of needed land in spring 1951. Furthermore, the VOA's consultants and engineers disagreed on whether the transmitters should be built in Washington State or southern California. Those favoring the southern site claimed that an auroral belt in the atmosphere above Washington would disrupt broadcast waves, a concern dismissed by other engineers. As Chief VOA Engineer George Herrick admitted in October 1951 to Foy Kohler, the VOA's general manager, "dissention [sic] of opinion exists even in our own shop" over the desirability of the northern site, the leading choice. That same month an investigator for the U.S. Advisory Commission's Radio Advisory Committee began studying the sites and wanted to know why a northern rather than southern site was favored for Baker West. Despite these concerns, plans to construct Baker West in Washington went ahead. The project was already behind schedule, and pressure to complete the Ring Plan was mounting. In January 1952 the State Department officially announced that it had selected Dungeness near Port Angeles, Washington, as the Baker West site.[16]

Yet second-guessing of the site continued. On May 2, 1952, Wilson Compton wrote to Deputy IIA Administrator Reed Harris that from an engineering standpoint, the transmitter sites were poorly chosen. Less than two weeks later, however, VOA officials in New York called a meeting

15. Pirsein, "Voice of America," 175–77. Although the State Department had asked MIT to focus on counter-jamming, the consultants proposed expanding the scope of their work to include innovative ways to penetrate the so-called Iron Curtain. A contract for this research was signed in October 1950, after Congress appropriated funds for the Ring Plan. In February 1951 the MIT consultants delivered a report entitled Project TROY, which proposed using balloons to drop leaflets, worldwide distribution of small, easily concealed crystal radio receivers, and the increased use of defectors in propaganda activities. See "Project Troy," box 63, folder "MIT," RG 59, RIIA; Allan A. Needell, "'Truth Is Our Weapon': Project TROY, Political Warfare, and Government-Academic Relations in the National Security State." For NSC impatience with Congress, see NSC 114/1, "Status and Timing of Current U.S. Programs for National Security," August 8, 1951, box 214, folder "Meeting 99, August 8, 1951," NSC Files.

16. Herrick to Foy Kohler, October 15, 1951; Kohler to Barnard, October 23, 1951, box 5, folder "IIA Correspondence," RG 46, SEN 83A-F7; Department of State Press Release #65, January 24, 1952.

about the Ring Plan and concluded that it was technically sound. Neither Compton nor Harris attended this meeting.[17] To further complicate the matter, in May the Senate Appropriations Committee hired Murry Brophy of Phoenix, Arizona, to inspect VOA transmitters overseas. Brophy had a background in radio, but he did not come to his task as an independent consultant. In March 1952 Brophy had told Reed Harris that he wanted the bid to construct the Baker West transmitter. Selection of the bids was scheduled for summer 1952; thus Brophy was inspecting VOA installations while he competed for a lucrative VOA contract. Furthermore, Brophy was close to some of Congress's most conservative members, including John Taber, Styles Bridges, Karl Mundt, and Pat McCarran, chair of the Subcommittee on the State Department. Indeed, the IIA administrator's special assistant reported that McCarran had asked Brophy to look over the operations of the USIS and send him weekly reports. Once abroad, Brophy wrote to Reed Harris to check on the status of the Baker West bid and requested translations of VOA scripts about the Republican National Convention, which were promptly sent. As for the bid, in August 1952 Compton informed Brophy that the Baker West project was being delayed while an outside consultant conducted a survey of existing facilities and provided recommendations, which Compton hoped to have by September.[18]

Brophy's personal interest in Baker West and his ties to McCarran meant that knowledge about this delay was certain to reach McCarran. But Nevada's senior senator already knew. In June, State Department Communications Consultant Frank Stoner informed McCarran that the department had hired Booz-Hamilton to determine whether or not any of the contracts for the Ring Plan's domestic transmitters should be canceled or modified. Stoner indicated that the department wanted to make sure McCarran had no objections, which he apparently did not.[19] While Booz-Hamilton conducted its survey, Stoner went forward with his own investigation, which he completed in mid-July. His findings were not encouraging. In May 1951 consultants from MIT's Research Laboratory

17. Compton to Harris, May 2, 1952, 511.004/5–1352, RG 59, CDF.

18. Compton to Senator Kilgore, March 7, 1952, box 5, folder "Congressional Relations"; Compton to Harris, May 6, 1952; Anthony Miccoci to Foy Kohler, May 9, 1952; Brophy to Harris, May 24, 1952; Miccoci, July 31, 1952; Compton to Brophy, August 12, 1952, box 5, folder "Brophy file," RG 306, Office of Administration Files, 1952–1955. Brophy reported his friendships with conservatives in a letter to Scott McLeod, January 17, 1954, box 2, folder "Brophy, Murry," RG 59, Records of the Bureau of Security and Consular Affairs, Name Files, 1953-1960.

19. Stoner to McCarran, June 4, 1952, 511.004/6–452, RG 59, CDF.

of Electronics had recommended three different sites for Baker West's location: Seattle; Anchorage, Alaska; and southern California. After the MIT consultants made the Seattle area their top choice, construction of the transmitter was delayed when the precise site was moved from Copalis, Washington, to Dungeness, Washington. By summer 1952 the State Department had purchased more than one thousand acres of needed land from thirteen owners, removed buildings, and cleared undergrowth at a cost of $350,000. However, tests conducted in June by the MIT consultants, working with the Army Signal Corps and Federal Communications Commission, revealed that auroral absorption in the area resulting from magnetic storms could lower transmission reliability to less than 50 percent during some months. For this reason Dr. Jerome B. Wiesner of MIT, who headed the State Department's consulting team, recommended that Baker West be moved to southern California, even though he had originally recommended Seattle. As Stoner indicated to Compton, the choices facing the department were difficult. Moving Baker West south would likely result in a congressional investigation and hurt future requests for transmitter construction funds. Completion of the Baker West project in Washington, however, was "more than a calculated risk" because of reception problems. Nevertheless, Stoner recommended that the department finish Baker West in Washington as soon as possible.[20]

Compton agreed. At the same time, his efforts to affix responsibility for the problem-plagued transmitters intensified the friction between the VOA's New York and Washington offices. Foy Kohler, the VOA's general manager in New York, denied Compton's charge that ineptitude within his office had caused the Ring Plan's troubles. Calling this claim "grossly unjust," Kohler said that the Ring Plan's problems resulted from the VOA's difficulties working with the New York Administrative Office and complained that Compton was ignoring his suggestions for improvement.[21] Angry and frustrated, Kohler resigned in late July, a move that did not displease Compton. The pressures and expectations that had long

20. Stoner to Compton, "Should the Administrator Change the Site of Baker West?" July 14, 1952, box 3, folder "IBS-Investigations and Surveys," RG 306, International Information Administration Files, 1952–1953. For a detailed explanation of the debate over the viability of the northern site and the problem of the auroral absorption belt, see Pirsein, "Voice of America," 245–55.

21. Kohler to Undersecretary of State David Bruce, August 20, 1952, 511.004/8–2052, RG 59, CDF.

weighed upon Kohler were wryly noted by Howland Sargeant, who commented to Dean Acheson, "[t]he ideal head of the VOA would combine executive competence of the highest order, radio programming and engineering experience, thorough knowledge of U.S. foreign policy . . . and a high order of talent in the field of congressional and public relations. There is probably no such man alive."[22]

Less than a year into his job as IIA administrator, Compton thus confronted several serious problems. He had inherited an expensive construction project that was quickly turning into a boondoggle. Indeed, in August the Joint Chiefs of Staff recommended to the Psychological Strategy Board that the Ring Plan be canceled because the Soviets' efforts to block VOA broadcasts helped them perfect methods that they could use to jam U.S. military transmissions during an emergency. Meanwhile, a contractor seeking a VOA bid was investigating the VOA for Pat McCarran, and the gap between the New York and Washington offices was widening. Finally, the Hickenlooper subcommittee had begun its investigation.[23]

III. The Hickenlooper Subcommittee

In June 1952 the Senate had approved the formation of a special subcommittee of the Foreign Relations Committee to examine the IIA's operations. Senator William Benton (D–Conn.) had originally proposed such an investigation in February 1951, when he led efforts to detach the information programs from the State Department. Benton's bill had remained in committee, however, for more than a year without action. Even after its formation the subcommittee began its work slowly. Senator William Fulbright (D–Ark.) was appointed chair, and while staff investigators began work in August, the subcommittee never met formally until after the November 1952 elections. With the Democrats now the minority party, Fulbright wondered if his Republican colleagues still wanted to continue with the investigation. Karl Mundt told Fulbright he thought they should, and so Bourke B. Hickenlooper replaced Fulbright as chair. Other members included Guy Gillette (D–Iowa), Benton, Mundt, and Alexander Wiley (R–Wisc.). In February 1953 William Knowland, Lister

22. Sargeant to Acheson, July 28, 1952, box 1, folder "The Secretary," RG 59, Records of the Office of the Assistant Secretary of State for Public Affairs, 1949–1953.

23. Linder to David Bruce, August 21, 1952, 511.004/8–2152, RG 59, CDF; Staff Memorandum, November 3, 1952, box 3, folder "Committee Members Correspondence," RG 46, SEN 83A-F7.

Hill (D–Ala.), and Theodore Francis Green (D–R.I.) joined the committee after the Senate voted to extend the investigation through June 1953 upon the recommendation of the subcommittee (Benton was defeated in his reelection bid in November 1952). Only after Fulbright turned over the chairmanship to Hickenlooper did the subcommittee articulate its specific goals, which included determining whether or not the IIA should remain in the State Department; reducing overlap with the activities of the NSC, Psychological Strategy Board, Mutual Security Agency, and the Technical Cooperation Administration; tightening ties between Congress and the IIA; and increasing the VOA's effectiveness.[24] Subcommittee members also traveled to Southeast Asia, the Middle East, and Western Europe to review field operations.

Hickenlooper came to his subcommittee duties with nagging suspicions about VOA personnel and broadcast effectiveness. In fall 1947 he had traveled with the congressional junket that surveyed VOA and USIS operations in Europe in order to make recommendations about the Smith-Mundt bill. At the time Hickenlooper had supported passage of the Smith-Mundt bill, but by late 1951 he was expressing doubts about the VOA. In a letter to RFE administrator Lucius Clay, Hickenlooper reported that during a recent trip to Europe he had received numerous suggestions that the VOA and RFE "are still dominated, in some departments, at least, by left wingers of a very pinkish hue, indeed." Right after Wilson Compton was appointed the IIA administrator, Hickenlooper wrote him, "the so-called 'Voice of America' . . . [is] not accomplishing very much and, in fact, on many occasions and no doubt without intention, gave some aid and comfort to Communist propaganda." And in May 1952 Hickenlooper attributed the VOA's troubles to its personnel, who he believed were not properly familiar with American principles and ideals.[25]

Even before Hickenlooper became chair, the subcommittee's investigators began accumulating information about VOA personnel and policy procedures. During August 1952 lead investigator Carl Marcy interviewed several VOA and State Department employees about the policy

24. Minutes of the subcommittee, November 10, 1952, box 86, folder "Overseas Information Subcommittee, 1952," Hickenlooper Papers.

25. Hickenlooper to Clay, David Sarnoff, Harold Stassen, and William Donovan, December 27, 1951; Hickenlooper to Charles Wennerstrum, May 15, 1952, box 135, folder "European Affairs, US Propaganda, 1950–52"; Hickenlooper to Compton, February 2, 1952, box 116, folder "Voice of America, 1951—52," Hickenlooper Papers.

channels between New York and Washington, working relationships between information personnel and Foreign Service officers, and the experience of the VOA's New York employees. Policy writer W. Bradley Connors told Marcy that many New York employees lacked experience in the field (meaning work at embassies abroad), "making it difficult to provide truly American guidance for many programs." Describing the lack of contact between the Washington and New York offices, policy writer Lloyd Lehrbas recommended that all of the VOA's operations be moved to Washington. Assistant Secretary of State for Congressional Relations Jack McFall suggested that the subcommittee study recruitment, promotion, and dismissal procedures because "OWI 'holdovers' have handicapped the effectiveness of the program." McFall and others were frustrated that civil service ratings protected former OWI employees they believed were mediocre, even incompetent.[26]

The subcommittee uncovered additional problems with the VOA as it conducted the bulk of its work during November and December 1952. A survey of mission chiefs abroad led the subcommittee to conclude that the VOA was the least effective part of the information and cultural program, "indeed, it is utterly ineffective in a majority of the countries." Hickenlooper himself traveled to the Far East in December 1952; his report indicated that with the exception of China, few persons listened to shortwave radio, and that Radio Moscow and the BBC had better reception than the VOA.[27] Wiley and Fulbright also went overseas and separately visited posts throughout Western Europe, while Gillette surveyed IIA operations in the Middle East. Before leaving, each senator had access to the information collected by Carl Marcy and his team during their August interviews in New York and Washington. The reports filed by the subcommittee members, which they compiled into an interim report delivered January 30, 1953, helped confirm the problems concerning personnel and policy implementation that officials had described to Marcy. Indeed, the subcommittee considered these and

26. Memorandum of conversation, Carl Marcy and George L. Harris, August 19, 1952, 511.00/8–1952, RG 59, CDF; memorandum of conversation, Carl Marcy and Helen Kirkpatrick, August 20, 1952; memorandum of conversation, Carl Marcy and Bradley Connors, August 22, 1952; memorandum of conversation, Lloyd Lehrbas and Francis Wilcox, August 28, 1952; memorandum of conversation, Francis Wilcox and Jack McFall, August 28, 1952, box 5, folder "IIA Correspondence," Subcommittee on Overseas Information Program SR 44 (and SR 74), RG 46, SEN 83A-F7.

27. Staff Memorandum #2, November 14, 1952, box 115, folder "USIS 1949–1953"; Report to the Subcommittee, December 1952, box 86, folder "Overseas Information Subcommittee, 1952," Hickenlooper Papers.

other problems to be so great that it asked for a continuance of its investiga-tion. The interim report outlined the issues requiring further attention. "What steps can be taken to enlarge the pool of qualified media and area specialists . . . to man the information program of this Government?" the subcommittee asked. Rotating field and home officers was proposed, as was an examination of personnel security measures. The interim report also pointed out the gap between policy statements and information guidance, emphasizing the need for "the closest coordination between policy-making officials and information officers both in Washington and in the field, and a recognition on the part of our highest officials of the importance of our infor-mation program." With regard to one of the subcommittee's original goals, the report described the problem of overlap between the State Department's information programs and those of the Mutual Security Agency (MSA) and the Technical Cooperation Administration (TCA) and questioned whether information programs for the latter two were necessary.[28] On February 20, 1953, the Senate extended the subcommittee's investigation through June 1953 and granted additional funds.

The Hickenlooper subcommittee's preliminary findings and proposals hardly caught State Department and IIA officials by surprise. Since 1945, each of the three assistant secretaries of state for Public Affairs—Benton, Allen, and Barrett—had struggled to convince both their superiors and rank-and-file Foreign Service officers of the information program's importance. Likewise, the lack of coordination between policy makers and information officers was far from new; the IIA's formation in January 1952 had aimed in part at tightening this relationship. And the overlap with the MSA and TCA represented growth of a problem that began with the Economic Cooperation Administration in 1951. The sub-committee's report simply publicized problems that the men and women of the VOA and other information programs had long confronted.

Missing from the report, however, were the details of the unrest and dis-satisfaction that was steadily growing in the VOA's studios and offices. In their interviews with subcommittee lead investigator Carl Marcy, VOA and State Department officials had complained of incompetent employees, of OWI holdovers protected by civil service personnel regulations. Whether intended or not, such complaints invited the charge of subversion. W. Bradley Connors had revealed just how thin the line was between job qual-

28. Senate Committee on Foreign Relations, *Overseas Information Programs of the United States Interim Report*, 83d Cong., 1st sess., January 31, 1953, Senate Report #30.

ifications and subversion when he spoke of a lack of field experience pre-venting "truly American" guidance. Hickenlooper too had blurred this line when he suggested to IIA Administrator Wilson Compton that VOA inef-fectiveness had many times inadvertently helped communist propaganda. Were mistakes genuine or intentional? This became an easy question to ask, yet a difficult one to answer conclusively. An employee might be unquali-fied, but that raised the issue of who was responsible for hiring the person—might they be trying to sabotage the VOA? Another problem was the friction resulting from workaday disagreements over broadcast output and content, a common occurrence in any newsroom. Compton wrestled with these problems soon after he assumed his post. In May 1952 Compton wrote to Deputy Administrator Reed Harris that various sources told him the IIA was hiring "misfits" and mediocre people. A month later Compton indicated that the IIA needed to avoid hiring "problem" and "highly con-troversial persons." Likewise, the media units needed to avoid extreme views and controversial ideas. In the fall of 1952 Compton followed through on these stipulations by asking the IIA's Division of Security to col-lect allegations about New York VOA employees and conduct interviews. A "new era" will begin in the VOA effective October 1, Compton told a security officer, and while reckless accusations were not to be tolerated, an effective security operation was needed to get rid of the "rotten apples."[29]

But the individual most responsible for blurring the line between mediocre workplace performance and political subversion was Joe McCarthy, who chaired the Senate Committee on Government Operations and its Permanent Subcommittee on Investigations. Just four days before the Senate voted to extend the Hickenlooper investigation, McCarthy opened hearings in Washington on the VOA. The Hickenlooper subcommittee became nearly invisible as the McCarthy hearings seized national attention, helped in no small way by the presence of television cameras, intensive press coverage, and McCarthy's flamboyance. While both subcommittees essentially focused on the same subjects—administrative ineptitude, finan-cial waste, program ineffectiveness—McCarthy and head counsel Roy Cohn spiced their hearings with charges or insinuations of sexual promiscuity,

29. Compton to Harris, May 2, 1952; Compton to Harris, June 9, 1952, box 5, folder "Director (General) 1952–53," RG 306, Office of Administration Files, 1952–1955; Bush (IMA/U), memorandum for the records, September 19, 1952; Compton to Bush, September 24, 1952, box 3, folder "IBS-Investigations and Surveys," RG 306, International Information Administration Files, 1952–1953.

godlessness, and communist sabotage. Taking advantage of a rancorous working environment within the VOA, McCarthy also had the willing help of a group of New York VOA employees who called themselves "The Loyal Underground." Even the 1948 Know North America hearings, in which hostile members of Congress questioned VOA personnel about broadcasts on beer rinse shampoos and naked Indian girls, looked benign compared to the McCarthy hearings. As a veteran of the hearings simply put it years later, "We had a very, very tough period."[30]

IV. God, Monogamy, and the Newsroom? McCarthy's Investigation

Although few could have known it at the time, the origins of the McCarthy investigation were hinted at in a July 26, 1952, newspaper column written by Howard Rushmore of the *New York Journal American*: "A group of patriotic State Department employees have formed what they ironically term "an underground cell" in the Voice of America on 57th St." Rushmore claimed that these employees were prepared to tell the FBI and Congress about "left-wingers" and "pro-Reds" in the VOA and could provide dozens of examples of broadcasts being slanted to the favor of the Soviet Union. This "underground cell" came to be known as the Loyal Underground, and it began forwarding information about supposedly subversive VOA employees to Rushmore, McCarthy, and John Taber.[31]

McCarthy had had his eye on the VOA before. In a Senate floor speech delivered March 30, 1950, he had described the VOA and the State Department's Far Eastern desk as "interlocking areas of operations [that] are almost completely controlled and dominated by individuals who are more loyal to the ideals and designs of Communism than to those of the free, God-fearing half of the world."[32] After his party gained control of

30. Barry Zorthian, interview by Cliff Groce, October 20 and 26, 1988, United States Information Agency Alumni Association, Oral History Project, USIA Historical Collection, 17.

31. Howard Rushmore, "The Subversive Front: Pro-Reds Hold Voice Jobs," *New York Journal American*, July 26, 1952. Estimates on the number of "Loyalists" vary. Former VOA employees have stated there were between six and twelve. Zorthian, Groce interview, 17; Tibor Borgida, interview by Cliff Groce, August 20, 1987, United States Information Agency Alumni Oral History Project; see also David M. Oshinsky, *A Conspiracy So Immense: The World of Joe McCarthy*, 267. In a letter written to John Foster Dulles, John Taber reported that he was approached directly by VOA employee Alice T. Shephard in early December 1952. Shephard gave Taber a list of "completely trustworthy" and "very untrustworthy" VOA employees in New York. Taber to Dulles, December 5, 1952, 511.00/12–552, RG 59, CDF.

32. *Congressional Record*, 81st Cong., 2d sess., March 30, 1950, vol. 96, 4374.

the Senate in 1953, McCarthy assumed chairmanship of the Committee of Government Operations and its Permanent Subcommittee on Investigations, positions that provided him with the power to pursue both his existing suspicions about the VOA and the charges made by the Loyal Underground. Before beginning his investigation, McCarthy sought and received the approval of Alexander Wiley, the senior Wisconsin senator. As a member of the Hickenlooper subcommittee and the chair of the Foreign Relations Committee, Wiley helped protect McCarthy from charges that he was duplicating the subcommittee's work. At the end of January 1953 McCarthy asked Wiley if he was interested in the Committee on Government Operations' impending hearings. Wiley wrote back, "I feel that the sub-Committee [Hickenlooper] and the full Senate Foreign Relations Committee would welcome any contributions which your committee might feel itself in a position to render to us." Hickenlooper did not agree, especially since he had just asked the Senate to extend his subcommittee's work through June 1953 and to provide additional funds for that purpose. As Wiley pointed out to Hickenlooper, however, they were presented with a fait accompli—McCarthy was going ahead with his investigation with or without the subcommittee's cooperation.[33]

To prepare for McCarthy's hearings, Committee Counsel Roy Cohn and assistant David Schine took a suite at the New York Waldorf-Astoria Hotel where they collected accusations and stories from various members of the Loyal Underground. The motives of the underground were a mixture of the personal and political. One witness who cooperated with McCarthy reputedly did not get along well with the colleague he testified against. While testifying on the religious views of VOA Director of Religious Programming Roger Lyons, Alice P. Shephard mentioned that she had once dated Lyons, a reference that almost escaped the subcommittee's attention. "You would not have your testimony colored by the fact he did not go out with you any longer?" asked Stuart Symington (D–Mo.). "Oh, no," Shephard answered. Even before the hearings began, Shephard had reported that production engineer Howard Hotchner, a Loyal Underground member, was disgruntled that he did not receive a promotion. According to John Taber's record of a conversation with Shephard,

33. Wiley to McCarthy, February 2, 1953; Wiley to Hickenlooper, February 25, 1953, box 86, folder "Overseas Information Subcommittee, 1953, Jan.–Feb.," Hickenlooper Papers.

she had said that Hotchner "used to be in charge of all production and now is given a very small corner to work in and not much to do."[34]

Others in the Loyal Underground were frustrated that the VOA neither broadcast their normative views of American foreign policy nor was, in their opinions, sufficiently anticommunist. At the hearings Persian Desk Chief Gerard Dooher described four instances in which anticommunist programming was obstructed or cut and complained that Public Affairs officials in "country X" [Iran] told him to tone down the anticommunist content of broadcasts. Dooher wanted the VOA to portray Iranian leader Mohammed Mossadegh in an unfavorable light. In an interview, former information policy writer Wilson P. Dizard stated that Dooher tried to manipulate VOA programming in order to attack Mossadegh. Virgil Fulling, chief of the VOA's Latin American News Service, testified at the hearings that the phrase "anti-communists" had been replaced by "citizens" in a script about Guatemalans cheering Eisenhower's inauguration. When asked if this was an isolated case, Fulling indicated that it was not. Though such revisions in news text seem inconsequential, Fulling's complaint highlighted a common challenge in the VOA newsroom: maintaining journalistic standards of objectivity while trying to deliver a strong anticommunist message. As the former chief of news for the English section put it, objectivity for the VOA was often measured by how anti-Russian or anticommunist the programming was. For individuals such as Fulling, the McCarthy hearings offered an opportunity not only to make anticommunist language standard in the news but also to punish those who disagreed. For McCarthy, these personal grudges and dissatisfaction with the VOA's anticommunist tone offered the raw material with which to construct his charges of subversion.[35]

The first public session of the Permanent Subcommittee on Investigations convened on February 16, 1953, several days after executive sessions were held in which many of the witnesses had already been questioned. NBC broadcast the public hearings live on television for two hours each day from 2 to 4 P.M. The Republican members of the subcommittee were Karl Mundt, Everett Dirksen, and Charles Potter; representing the Democrats

34. Roger Lyons, interview by the author, tape recording, Silver Spring, Md., October 24, 1995; Philip Horton, "Voices within the Voice"; Raymond Swing, "V.O.A.—A Survey of the Wreckage"; Pirsein, "Voice of America," 241–42; McCarthy Hearings, pt. 4, 320–21, 324; Taber to Dulles, December 5, 1952, 511.00/12–552, RG 59, CDF.
35. McCarthy Hearings, pts. 3 and 9, 152–55, 158, 757; Wilson P. Dizard, interview by the author, tape recording, Washington D.C., November 3, 1995; Zorthian interview.

were Henry Jackson (Wash.), John McClellan (Ark.), and Stuart Symington. Given the Loyal Underground's cooperation with McCarthy and the friction among VOA employees, it is not surprising that witnesses at the hearings produced titillating, occasionally bizarre stories. Using leading questions, cooperative witnesses, and the troubled history of the Ring Plan, McCarthy first tried to show that saboteurs had disrupted construction of the VOA's transmitters. The first witness, former VOA engineer Lewis McKesson, testified at length that Baker West and Baker East (being built in Arcadia, North Carolina) were both being built in an auroral absorption belt that interfered with radio waves. After questioning McKesson about the site selection process, McCarthy asked him, "[n]ow, has it ever been suggested by those who worked with you in the Voice that this mislocation of stations, the waste in the construction program, has not been entirely as a result of incompetence, but that some of it may have been purposely planned that way?" McKesson said yes.[36] In raising this issue, McCarthy took advantage of the long-standing strife within the VOA over the Ring Plan, as described in the previous section. Because of Cohn's and Schine's interviews with Loyal Underground members, McCarthy was well aware of the internal disagreements and problems afflicting the transmitters, and he had also acquired correspondence concerning the site selection process, which he shared with Hickenlooper. In February an investigator for the Iowa senator's subcommittee received from McCarthy copies of memoranda written by a State Department official in July 1952 outlining the technical problems with the final sites.[37] By alluding to these troubles, McCarthy made it difficult for witnesses to refute the sabotage explanation.

He also tried to strengthen the case for sabotage by suggesting that some VOA officials had ties to communism, as seen in the questioning of W. Bradley Connors. A policy writer, Connors was not directly involved with the Ring Plan's development. Nevertheless, Cohn sought to first show that prominent academic John Fairbanks, who Cohn claimed was a communist, had sought a promotion for Connors. Then McCarthy charged Connors with promoting communism by issuing a February 3, 1953, directive that approved Howard Fast's novels for circulation at USIS libraries. After this line of questioning, McCarthy brought up the Ring Plan: did Connors think that the mistakes made in the transmitter

36. McCarthy Hearings, pt. 1, 3–4, 9.
37. McCarthy memorandum, February 18, 1953, box 86, folder "Overseas Information Subcommittee, 1953 Jan. to Feb.," Hickenlooper Papers.

site selections showed an intent to sabotage the VOA? Replied Connors, "So far as I know the locations were picked based on surveys by competent radio engineers and a study by MIT. This is outside of my sphere of responsibility, and I do not have all the facts."[38] Connors' careful response showed the precarious position in which witnesses found themselves— anyone who denied the possibility of sabotage exposed themselves to pointed questions about the Ring Plan's various problems. Furthermore, Connors' credibility was already suspect because of Cohn's and McCarthy's questions about Fairbanks and Fast. Finally, McCarthy was successfully exploiting themes long expounded by congressional critics of the VOA: suspicious personnel, fiscal waste, and mismanagement.

After testimony on the troubled Ring Plan, McCarthy focused on the VOA's French desk and religious programming. Here McCarthy took a novel approach. In questioning VOA engineers such as McKesson, McCarthy simply cast the shroud of sabotage over the entire Ring Plan and its developers. With regard to VOA broadcasts, the Wisconsin Republican targeted the lifestyles and religious beliefs of individual VOA employees in order to substantiate charges of communism influence. Along with chief counsel Roy Cohn, McCarthy used two unstated syllogisms to describe communist infiltration of the VOA. The first worked like this: communists believe in anti-family, collective living; the head of the VOA's French desk tried to recruit an employee for a collective (or so we are told); therefore, the head of the VOA's French desk must be a communist. McCarthy formed the second syllogism from atheism. Communists are atheists; the head of the VOA's religious programming does not believe in God (or so we are told); therefore, that VOA employee must be a communist. In the latter example, the final connection was left dangling, giving observers the opportunity to complete the syllogism themselves. By constructing accusations out of personal values and behavior, McCarthy increased greatly the burden of rebuttal for the accused. Instead of explaining memoranda written years ago or long-lapsed membership in political organizations, the accused were now forced to prove that they did, indeed, believe in God, or else deny trying to recruit an unmarried woman to bear children for a suburban New York Marxist collective.

Troup Mathews, chief of the VOA's French desk, found himself caught up in the first syllogism as a result of the testimony of Dr. Nancy

38. McCarthy Hearings, pt. 2, 118–36.

Lenkeith, a former writer of French-language VOA broadcasts. Though a cooperative witness, Lenkeith gave rambling, sometimes incoherent answers, prompting McCarthy to turn questioning over to Cohn. Lenkeith managed to state that when she worked for the French desk, damaging programming was aired. Lenkeith, who had been fired, also claimed that Mathews maintained lax supervision of broadcasts. And in the charge that drew the most attention, she said that when Mathews had interviewed her, he tried to get her to join a collective and begin having children as a member, even though she was unmarried. At this point McCarthy interrupted her, stating that because children might be watching the televised hearings, she should not continue.[39] McCarthy made sure to mention that he had already heard Lenkeith's full story during the subcommittee's executive sessions, and he released excerpts to the press. According to Lenkeith's account, Mathews had said he was thinking of forming "in an old Dutch house a group dedicated to collective living, which would embody the good aspects of Marxism." Lenkeith also claimed that Mathews had also said he wanted people "who have no dogmatic religious beliefs."[40]

The Marxist, free-love collective was actually a cooperative housing venture in suburban New York; Mathews had simply asked Lenkeith if she was interested in buying into the cooperative.[41] However, the distinction between collective and housing cooperative was a long time coming. Lenkeith had repeated her accusations during the public hearings, but McCarthy did not allow Mathews to take the stand to rebut the charges. Mathews, a veteran who had lost his left leg during World War II, was heard only in closed executive session. To reporters he said, "[Communism] embodies all the aspects of nazism, against which I fought." He also said, "I'm a firm believer in monogamy, and I've got a wife and four kids to prove it." However, Mathews' rebuttal was printed nearly a week after McCarthy released Lenkeith's executive session testimony and was buried at the bottom of page 12 of the *New York Times*.[42]

Like Troup Mathews, Religious Programming Director Roger Lyons was also the target of ad hominem attacks. Dr. John Cocutz, a writer for

39. Ibid., pt. 3, 164–66; Oshinsky, *Conspiracy So Immense*, 271–72.

40. "State Department Heeds McCarthy," *New York Times*, February 21, 1953, 1.

41. Wilson P. Dizard, *The Strategy of Truth: The Story of the U.S. Information Service*, 42; Dizard interview.

42. *New York Times*, February 27, 1953, 12; Reeves, *Life and Times of Joe McCarthy*, 482.

the Rumanian desk, testified on March 2 that he heard New York Policy Officer Edwin Kretzmann say that Lyons was an atheist. When called to the witness stand, Kretzmann explained that what he had actually said was that he was not aware of Lyons' specific religious beliefs and that for all he knew, Lyons might be an atheist.[43] Kretzmann's clarification of his humorous aside did little, however, to correct the immediate impression of the subcommittee that the head of religious programming for the VOA did not believe in God. Lyons was not present when Cocutz gave his testimony; he was at work in the VOA's New York studios. At first Lyons and his coworkers laughed when a VOA writer returning from Washington brought the news. Then Lyons was shown a wire from Washington reporting Cocutz's claim. Lyons was preparing a rebuttal statement when Roy Cohn called, asking Lyons if he wanted to testify before the committee. In his rush to the airport, Lyons did not even have time to call his wife and tell her what was happening.[44]

Why did the subcommittee give Lyons the chance to confront the charges made against him after denying the same opportunity to Mathews? Just that morning, subcommittee Democrats Stuart Symington and Henry Jackson had observed that the subjects of negative charges did not have the chance to defend themselves before the newspapers went to press, prompting Cohn's call to Lyons.[45] Symington and Jackson were not the only subcommittee members concerned about the fairness of questioning. The week before Karl Mundt, a friend of McCarthy's, had asked Cohn to call witnesses supportive of the VOA and State Department in order to keep the hearings balanced. That a Republican made this request is revealing. According to a VOA announcer who was called by McCarthy to testify, Jackson had intimated privately that because of the Alger Hiss case, the Democrats on the subcommittee were reluctant to denounce McCarthy's and Cohn's tactics.[46]

When he arrived in Washington, Lyons had finished his statement. "I do believe in God, and I would have never accepted the position as Director of Religious Programming if I did not realize the religious and moral factors in Voice of America broadcasts."[47] Though given the

43. McCarthy Hearings, pt. 4, 235–38, 307–8.
44. Roger Lyons, "McCarthy Revisited: 40 Years After," 3.
45. Ibid., 1–4.
46. Mundt to Cohn, February 21, 1953, box 206, folder 6, Mundt Papers; Robert Bauer, interview by the author, tape recording, Washington, D.C., October 24, 1995.
47. "Statement by Roger Lyons," press release, March 2, 1953.

chance to clear his name, it quickly became apparent that the subcommittee was not going to make it easy for Lyons. McCarthy, Jackson, and John McClellan brusquely questioned him at length about his religious beliefs and the conversation that Cocutz overheard. McClellan asked that Lyons provide proof of his belief in God, while McCarthy wanted to know if Lyons had stated whether or not he believed in a "Divine Being" in his graduate thesis. Lyons emphasized that he was a deeply religious man, that Cocutz was mistaken. Asserting that he was neither an atheist nor an agnostic, Lyons even offered that he had attended a church service in New Jersey and put ten dollars in the collection plate. After Lyons finished testifying, however, Alice Shephard appeared before the subcommittee and stated that when she first knew him, he seemed confused and in the midst of a personal crisis. She also said that Lyons did not believe in God when they were dating in 1944.[48] Both the subcommittee and observers were left with sworn testimony that Lyons had not believed in God.

A distinct pattern emerges from the questioning of Mathews and Lyons. First, Cohn and Schine drew accusations from stories or statements given by friendly witnesses, in these two cases, Nancy Lenkeith and Alice Shephard. Second, the line of questioning taken by Cohn and McCarthy led directly to the revelations of free-love advocacy and atheism. Third, the stories were crafted carefully so that the syllogisms supposedly proving the communist leanings of Mathews and Lyons did not have to be spelled out for observers. In the case of Mathews, Lenkeith used the words "collective" and "Marxism" to prompt observers to the necessary connections of logic. In the case of Lyons, the charge of atheism sufficed. With these syllogisms, McCarthy did not have to accuse Mathews and Lyons of being card-carrying communists. The burden lay on Mathews and Lyons to prove that they were not communists by proving that they were not anti-family or anti-God. McCarthy, it seems, had learned well the lessons of Wheeling and its unexpected wake. For Lyons, the burden of rebuttal was particularly high. How does one definitively prove one's belief in God? Finally, and most important, in hearings devoted to showing the existence of political subversion within the VOA, McCarthy had skirted the issue of Mathews's and Lyons's political beliefs. Yet the charges made against the two men, based on their supposed lifestyle choices or lack of religious beliefs, created instant and lasting impressions about their politics—they were subversive.

48. McCarthy Hearings, pt. 4, 298–324.

Evidence suggests that witnesses such as Lenkeith, Cocutz, and Shephard were coached prior to their testimony in order to ensure the appearance of subversion on the part of the accused. In turning the questioning of Nancy Lenkeith over to Cohn, McCarthy pointed out that Cohn had interviewed her several times. McCarthy's use of television cameras also shows a conscious effort to shape witnesses' testimony. As mentioned, McCarthy held several days of closed session hearings before the subcommittee's public hearings were held, giving him the opportunity to rehearse witnesses' testimony.[49] Once the television cameras were present, McCarthy was able to bring out statements and stories calculated to draw maximum attention, as he did with Lenkeith's claims about the free-love collective. By cutting short her description, McCarthy left viewers wondering exactly what Mathews had asked Lenkeith to do. Other evidence of coaching comes from Barry Zorthian, who was chief of news for the English section. Dismayed at the battering the VOA was taking and the treatment his coworkers were receiving during the hearings, Zorthian asked to meet with Cohn and Schine at the Waldorf. To his surprise, VOA production engineer Howard Hotchner ushered him into the hotel suite. Zorthian tried to convince Cohn and Schine that the VOA was doing the best job possible. But that's not what the two McCarthy aides wanted to hear, as Zorthian said in an interview:

> I really came out feeling both scared and evil. Their pitch was that look, it's not our job to say what's good, could you testify to us that 100% of the time the news room hasn't made a mistake, and I said of course not. Any news operation particularly with the volume we're running is going to make mistakes. "That's what we want you to testify on, who made those mistakes, what was the cause of them. If you want to come down to Washington and testify on that we'd be happy to have you. We don't want you to come down and say the news room is doing a good job."[50]

According to Dr. Jerome Wiesner, the head of the MIT consulting team that selected the Baker West site, Cohn made a similar request of him. In a conversation about the site, Cohn "tried hard to get me to agree that the Seattle site was inferior. I refused. He misrepresented my position." Finally, Cohn told Wiesner that he would not be subpoenaed; then at the

---

49. Oshinsky, *Conspiracy So Immense*, 272; Edwin R. Bayley, *Joe McCarthy and the Press*, 182.

50. Zorthian interview; Zorthian's account of his meeting with Cohn and Schine also served as the basis for an article by Philip Horton, "Voices within the Voice."

hearings, Cohn attributed to Wiesner criticisms of the northern Baker West site.[51] In both meetings with Zorthian and Wiesner, Cohn and Schine were looking for statements and stories easily adapted to suggest evidence of subversion within the VOA.

McCarthy did not need Zorthian's or Wiesner's testimony, though. Throughout the hearings McCarthy continued to receive support from VOA and State Department employees who provided him with helpful leaks. According to the U.S. Embassy in France, Undersecretary of State Walter Bedell Smith complained that high-ranking State Department officials were being summoned before the McCarthy subcommittee in the afternoon to explain things they had said that morning during supposedly secret conferences. The embassy also reported that confidential information about the hearings had appeared in a French magazine article. Frances Knight, who worked as a special assistant in the IIA, acted as a liaison between McCarthy and conservative columnist Westbrook Pegler. Immediately after televised coverage of the hearings ended for the day on March 3, Knight called Pegler to say she would have Schine or Cohn send over the transcripts. And according to Wilson Dizard, a secretary attached to the information policy planning section of the Near East desk forwarded classified telegrams to McCarthy.[52]

The Loyal Underground's cooperation and McCarthy's investigation had immediate and dramatic effects even before the Washington hearings ended in April. The troubled Bakers East and West projects were canceled. Shaken by the grilling he received from McCarthy, Wilson Compton resigned as IIA administrator on February 18, just two days after the hearings had begun. Also on February 18, Information Bulletin #272 was issued: "no repeat no materials by any communists, fellow travellers, etc., will be used under any circumstances by any IIA media." The ban, which Secretary

51. Pirsein, "Voice of America," 254; Hixson, *Parting the Curtain*, 53. It should be noted that Wiesner had vacillated in recommending a site for Baker West. After proposing Seattle as the best choice in May 1951, Wiesner said in July 1952 that the Baker West transmitter should be relocated to California. In February 1953 he changed his mind again, writing to Compton that Washington State was the best site.

52. Paris to Washington, March 12, 1953, 511.5141/3–1253, RG 59, CDF. For Knight's liaison work, see unsigned memorandum to "Mr. P.," March 3, 1953, box 21, folder "McCarthy, Joseph, 1953," Westbrook Pegler Papers, Subject Files, Hoover Library. During his tenure as assistant secretary of state of Public Affairs, Edward Barrett believed Knight to be a spy for Karl Mundt, Styles Bridges, John Taber, and Karl Stefan. See Bob McCaughey to Mundt, October 18, 1951, box 1404, folder 9, Mundt Papers. Information about the secretary comes from the Dizard interview.

of State John Foster Dulles ordered, was prompted in part by the recent decision to allow Howard Fast's books into USIS libraries and coincided with the appearance of Fast before the subcommittee. Five times Fast was asked if he was a communist; in each instance he refused to answer, citing his rights under the Fifth Amendment.[53]

The ban on communist materials caused an uproar. VOA commentator Raymond Swing protested that the order forbade him to quote from the statements of communist officials when trying to rebut them. Gerard Dooher, who had testified about interference with anticommunist programming, complained that the order was "a reduction to absurdity of the sense of Congressional criticisms of previous policy guidances." The VOA's director, Alfred Morton, even refused to obey Information Bulletin #272, telling Connors that the VOA would "continue to use the works and words of Communists, fellow-travelers, etc., to expose them or to make them eat their own words or in the furtherance of the American national interest." He was suspended from his job.[54] Despite these protests, the order was upheld and extended on March 17 by Infoguide #303, which banned all works by communist authors from USIS centers. The revised guidance also prohibited the identification by name of any living communists unless absolutely necessary, proposing instead terms such as "international communist" or "Stalinist." Again, a storm of complaint ensued. John Begg, head of the IIA's unit for cooperation with private enterprise, asked how such an order could be carried out when the IIA organized art exhibitions that contained paintings or art made by artists who were communists. Another IIA official pointed out that background checks on all authors featured at the USIS libraries

53. Information Bulletin #272, February 18, 1953, Subject File Cabinet 10, folder "McCarthyism," USIA Historical Collection. On February 12 an unidentified phone caller informed Policy Officer Carl McCardle that the VOA had been instructed to use writers like Fast. The caller was apparently referring to IA Instruction PO-5, an outgoing airgram issued on January 30, 1953, by Assistant Administrator for Policy and Plans W. Bradley Connors stating that if controversial works such as Fast's were not used by the IIA, its credibility with foreign listeners was seriously impaired. On February 13 McCardle rescinded the instruction; Connors supported the move. Thus the impetus for Information Bulletin #272 began before Fast testified to the McCarthy Subcommittee. Untitled, undated summary, Subject File Cabinet 10, folder "McCarthyism," USIA Historical Collection. For Fast's appearance before the McCarthy subcommittee, see McCarthy Hearings, pt. 2, 98.

54. Swing to Edwin Kretzmann, February 24, 1953; Dooher to Edwin Kretzmann, February 24, 1953; Untitled summary of #272; Walter Bedell Smith to Morton, February 24, 1953, Subject File Cabinet 10, folder "McCarthyism," USIA Historical Collection.

would encompass eighty-five thousand persons; the current annual workload covered just twelve hundred persons.[55]

McCarthy's hearings also caused trouble for the VOA in France, where domestic media picked up McCarthy's statement that the VOA needed to attack French communism. In early March France's Minister of Information warned the U.S. Embassy that if the VOA acted on McCarthy's suggestion, he would recommend dropping the VOA from the French radio relay network. The French government carried out its threat; in April the director general of French radio informed the embassy that the VOA would be dropped after June 30, 1953. The embassy in Paris was told that an attempt to keep the VOA on the air in France would be made, but that staff reductions on the troubled French desk would diminish the quality of the broadcasts.[56]

Although McCarthy ended his Washington hearings during the first week of April, Roy Cohn and David Schine continued the investigation by visiting USIS libraries in Europe, where they led highly publicized shelf searches for books and materials written by communists. Their actions evoked a response from President Eisenhower, who told Dartmouth's graduating class in June 1953, "[d]on't think you are going to conceal faults by concealing evidence that they ever existed. Don't be afraid to go in your library and read every book as long as any document does not offend our own ideas of decency."[57] Eisenhower's statement was one of the few public comments that the president had made during the previous five months concerning McCarthy's investigation. Yet even after the Dartmouth speech, aides indicated that the president was not referring to anyone in particular. Why was Eisenhower, who was certainly no admirer of McCarthy's, reluctant to criticize the maverick senator? As the following chapter explains, the detachment of Eisenhower and Secretary of State Dulles from the McCarthy spectacle was calculated.

55. Infoguide #303, March 17, 1953, 511.00/3–1753; Begg to Connors, March 26, 1953, 511.00/3–2653; Humphrey to Connors, April 3, 1953, 511.00/4–353, RG 59, CDF.

56. Paris to Washington, March 6, 1953, 511.514/3–653; Paris to Washington, April 1, 1953, 511.514/4–153; Dulles to Paris, May 8, 1953, 511.514/5–853, RG 59, CDF.

57. Reeves, *Life and Times of Joe McCarthy,* 488–91, 495.

Chapter 8

Leaving State
The Formation of the USIA, 1953

In early December 1952 John Foster Dulles received a long letter from John Taber, who was preparing to assume the chairmanship of the House Appropriations Committee. Taber told Dulles that a VOA employee named Alice Shephard had come to see him "with a story of the Information Service of the State Department in their New York office." According to Taber's retelling, the VOA's New York office was a mess. IIA Administrator Wilson Compton had fired ten homosexuals, "but none of the commies." Loyal employees were shunted aside and threatened with dismissal, while communists and their sympathizers controlled broadcast output. Based on Shephard's information, Taber provided Dulles with a list of "completely trustworthy" and "very untrustworthy" employees. Because this information corroborated things he had already heard about the VOA, Taber concluded, "I do not see how I could avoid passing them on." This was not Taber's first memorandum to Dulles concerning the VOA. One day before posting the letter about Shephard, Taber told Dulles that the VOA needed a complete cleaning carried out by the FBI.[1] Taber's animosity toward the VOA was hardly new—he had long been one of the agency's fiercest critics, and his December complaints echoed those he had made in past years. The significance of Taber's letters lies in their timing and the recipient, Dulles. Two months before McCarthy opened his hearings the new secretary of state had the same information that McCarthy would use, the accusations and stories of the Loyal Underground. Dulles also knew how McCarthy planned to conduct his hearings. In a February 12, 1953, phone conversation, syndicated columnist George Sokolsky told Dulles that

1. Taber to Dulles, December 5, 1952, 511.00/12–552; Taber to Dulles, December 4, 1952, 511.00/12–452, RG 59, CDF.

McCarthy would characterize VOA broadcasts as pro-left. According to Dulles's memorandum of the conversation, Sokolsky "wanted Mr. Dulles to know these things and that he will be protected." Since he had taken office just a few weeks before, Dulles pointed out, he was not yet familiar with the VOA. Dulles also told Sokolsky that the president had appointed a committee to determine whether or not the VOA belonged in the State Department, and that he (Dulles) was reluctant to act until the committee finished its work. With regard to McCarthy's investigation, Dulles indicated that it might prove helpful if it did "not unfairly try to blame him for things he has nothing to do with."[2]

The committee to which Dulles was referring was the President's Committee on International Information Activities (known informally as the Jackson committee), which Eisenhower had formed on January 24, 1953. New York investment banker William H. Jackson served as chair. The committee's seven other members included prominent businessmen and government officials, though only two—Gordon Gray and Sigurd Larmon—were directly familiar with the State Department's international information program. Gray had chaired the Psychological Strategy Board, and Larmon was a member of the U.S. Advisory Committee on Information. Eisenhower instructed the committee "to make a survey and evaluation of the international information policies and activities of the Executive Branch of the Government."[3] Five days later Eisenhower created another committee, the President's Advisory Committee on Government Organization (known informally as the Rockefeller committee, after its chair, Nelson Rockefeller), which studied possible reorganization of the IIA as part of its duties. The IIA was now being simultaneously reviewed by two Senate subcommittees—Hickenlooper's and McCarthy's—and these two presidential committees.

I. Dulles and the VOA

In his conversation with Sokolsky, Dulles revealed several important things about his attitude toward the VOA. The new secretary of state seemed to approve of McCarthy's investigation, as long as the hearings identified the VOA's present problems as the previous administration's responsibility. Maintaining harmonious relations with Congress was

2. Memorandum of Telephone Conversation, John Foster Dulles and George Sokolsky, February 12, 1953, *FRUS* 1952–1954, vol. 2, pt. 2, 1670–71.

3. Eisenhower to James Lay, January 24, 1953, *FRUS* 1952–1954, vol. 2, pt. 2, 1867.

important to Dulles, and in a Republican-controlled Congress, denouncement of McCarthy was likely to alienate powerful Republicans such as Alexander Wiley, who chaired the Senate Foreign Relations Committee, or House Appropriations Chair John Taber.[4] By pointing out his lack of knowledge about the VOA, Dulles further distanced himself from the radio agency. And while giving Sokolsky the impression that the Jackson committee would determine the VOA's proper placement, Dulles had already made up his mind—the State Department was not the place for the VOA. Indeed, in the weeks to come, the secretary's failure to respond to McCarthy's roughshod treatment of the VOA would suggest that Dulles was using the investigation to smooth the way for the VOA's removal from the State Department.

In allowing the McCarthy investigation to run its course without protest, Dulles had the support of the president, who also remained detached from the McCarthy investigation. Eisenhower's unwillingness to confront or denounce McCarthy was evident during the 1952 campaign and continued after the senator opened hearings on the VOA. At a February 25, 1953, press conference a reporter asked the president whether or not McCarthy's investigation was aiding the anticommunist drive. Eisenhower replied that he was not sure what McCarthy was trying to accomplish. On March 5 the president warned obliquely that he might have to step in if the hearings threatened to damage American interests or to produce misunderstandings abroad. However, Eisenhower added that "it would be extremely dangerous to try to limit the power of the Congress to investigate." As *Newsweek* commented, the president was avoiding "any evaluation of the McCarthy committee's operations." Like Dulles, Eisenhower did not want to erode Republican support in the Senate by openly criticizing McCarthy or trying to impede his investigation. The president also believed that the more attention McCarthy received, the more durable his particular brand of anticommunism became. "I was convinced that his influence, such as it was, would be gone completely if he lost his headline value," Eisenhower wrote in his memoir. The president's noninvolvement not only allowed the McCarthy investigation to go forward unchecked but also gave Dulles the opportunity to plan for the VOA's removal from the State Department.[5]

4. Ronald W. Pruessen, "John Foster Dulles and the Predicaments of Power," 30.
5. *Congressional Quarterly Almanac* vol. 9, 337; Stephen E. Ambrose, *Eisenhower,* vol. 2, *The President,* 57, 62; "The Voice on TV," *Newsweek* 41:10 (March 9, 1953): 20; Dwight D. Eisenhower, *The White House Years: Waging Peace, 1956–1961,* 320.

On several occasions before becoming secretary of state, Dulles had indicated that the VOA was ineffective and did not belong in the State Department. While George V. Allen was still assistant secretary of state for Public Affairs, Dulles proposed the creation of an independent, cabinet-level agency to operate the VOA and oversee psychological warfare activities. In a May 1952 article published in *Life,* Dulles explained that the United States needed to make a positive commitment to freeing people abroad from the shackles of communism. Dulles pointed to the VOA and Radio Free Europe, suggesting that they should encourage citizens in communist nations to liberate themselves. In September a Public Affairs official recounted Dulles's recent criticisms of the government's approaches to psychological warfare activities. Before a group of reporters in New York City, Dulles said that the VOA "shoot[s] a lot of words into the air—a lot of blah—and it doesn't do any good . . ." For this reason, Dulles went on, a board of strategy, perhaps attached to the National Security Council, was needed to sharpen and direct the message being put out.[6]

Despite this expressed interest in relocating and improving the VOA, Dulles let the agency fend for itself during McCarthy's hearings. Shortly after the hearings began Wilson Compton explained at the secretary's staff meeting that McCarthy was describing a plot of communist sabotage in the VOA stretching back more than ten years. Such charges were based on slanted testimony and half-truths, Compton continued, but McCarthy did not allow IIA officials a fair opportunity to respond. Compton suggested that the secretary appoint a "top custodial officer in IIA if only on an interim basis," apparently to demonstrate the department's eagerness to make improvements in the IIA's operations. After Compton finished, however, Dulles simply told him to pass any suggestions along to Donald Lourie, the new undersecretary of state for Administration.[7] As the spectacle of the hearings grew, this willingness to let the IIA twist in the wind attracted attention. "For the present, at least, it appeared to be Administration policy to give McCarthy a free hand," reported *Newsweek. The New Republic*

6. Undated memorandum, Howland Sargeant to George Allen, box 125, folder "Misc. 1947–48," RG 59, RIIA; John Foster Dulles, "A Policy of Boldness," 146; Grant Manson to Howland Sargeant, September 18, 1952, box 9, folder "Pre-election statements on psy-war policy by Ike and Dulles," RG 59, Miscellaneous Records of the Bureau of Public Affairs, Records Relating to World-Wide Program Objectives.

7. Notes of Secretary's Staff Meeting, February 19, 1953, box 1, folder "Aug. 26, 1952–April 14, 1953, Meeting Notes 61–120," RG 59, Minutes and Notes of the Secretary's Staff Meetings, 1952–1961.

characterized this noninvolvement as "craven cowardice" and surmised that Dulles had a "Master Plan"—after McCarthy finished, the State Department "will trot out its champions." Meanwhile, McCarthy had control of the situation, conducting the hearings as he saw fit. *Newsweek* agreed: "[E]ager to get rid of many Democratic holdovers in the State Department, Dulles welcomed a certain amount of heat from Congress to force him to do what he wanted to do anyway."[8] Accordingly, Dulles agreed to provide summaries of confidential executive personnel files to McCarthy and other Republican committee chairmen after McCarthy requested the full files for his investigation.

The secretary's behind-the-scenes actions corroborated *Newsweek*'s and the *New Republic*'s reading of the situation. Within a week of Compton's resignation as IIA Administrator on February 18, Dulles asked Temple University President Robert Johnson to take over as acting administrator. Johnson indicated that he wanted to make a detailed survey of the information programs before becoming the permanent director. But Dulles had another purpose in mind for Johnson—preparing the information programs for removal from the State Department. In a letter to Eisenhower, Dulles wrote that Johnson "took office with the understanding that we planned as soon as practicable to take that Administration [IIA] out of the State Department and make it an independent agency." While carrying out his long-standing aim to detach the VOA and other media from the State Department, Dulles was in contact with McCarthy's subcommittee. At the March 12 secretary's staff meeting Dulles was told that someone from the McCarthy subcommittee had called to ask if it was now alright to prepare a line of questioning related to problems in Iran. (The week before, Walter Bedell Smith had told members of the McCarthy subcommittee not to bring up Iran.) Dulles said no, explaining that such questions might cause damaging foreign reactions. Dulles also corresponded with McCarthy himself. On April 7 the Wisconsin Republican wrote to update Dulles on his investigation and express his appreciation for the secretary's decision to remove from the State Department's libraries abroad all books written by communists. In his reply Dulles welcomed any further information McCarthy had about the information programs and agreed that "the present conditions

---

8. "McCarthy and the Voice," *Newsweek* 41:9 (March 2, 1953): 24; "Joseph McCarthy, Secretary of State," *New Republic* 128:9 (March 2, 1953): 6; "The Voice of America?" *New Republic* 128:10 (March 9, 1953): 7; "Battle Unjoined," *Newsweek* 41:12 (March 23, 1953): 28.

were created some time in the past under a previous Administration."[9] For Dulles, the advantages of McCarthy's hearings were twofold. The VOA and other media were weakened and discredited, justifying their removal from the State Department. At the same time, McCarthy's charges about subversives warranted the revamping of security procedures.

With the appointment of R. W. Scott McLeod in March 1953 as the State Department's security officer, Dulles followed through on his reported desire to rid the department of "holdovers." McLeod was a former administrative assistant to Senator Styles Bridges, who now chaired the Appropriations Subcommittee on the State Department. Consistent with the notion of subversion that McCarthy had used to attack Troup Mathews and Roger Lyons, McLeod included sexual orientation, promiscuity, and personal behavior in his understanding of what was politically subversive. The case of Marcelle Henry is illustrative. During McCarthy's hearings witnesses had testified that Henry, a writer for the VOA's French desk, did not like the United States and worked derogatory comments into scripts. Michael Horneffer, who processed French VOA audience mail, claimed that in a December 1952 review of Edna Ferber's book *Giant*, Henry included slurs against Texas. Nancy Lenkeith claimed that VOA official Alfred Puhan had told her that Henry was subversive. In an apparent attempt to boost Henry's patriotism, Troup Mathews had given her a book on Abraham Lincoln, prompting Karl Mundt to comment, "It would be much easier, it seems to me, to find an employee in the first instance who believes in America." Following McLeod's appointment as head of security, Henry discovered that her patriotism was not the primary concern—her sex life was. More than "twenty allegations were made concerning Miss Henry's morals," security officer John Ford wrote McLeod. During investigations of these charges, Ford continued, "she admitted having sexual relations with a number of men." She was fired in May 1953. Angry at the treatment she received at both the hands of McCarthy and the State Department, Henry took her story to the *New York Post*. After reviewing the flimsy nature of the charges against Henry, the *Post* observed that she was fired for "a disregard for the generally accepted standards of conventional behavior."[10]

9. Dulles to Eisenhower, June 27, 1953; McCarthy to Dulles, April 7, 1953; Dulles to McCarthy, April 10, 1953, *FRUS* 1952–1954, vol. 2, pt. 2, 1697–99, 1715–16; Notes of Secretary's Staff Meeting, March 12, 1953, box 1, folder "Aug. 26, 1952–April 14, 1953, Meeting Notes 61–120," RG 59, Minutes and Notes of the Secretary's Staff Meetings, 1952–1961.

10. McCarthy Hearings, pt. 3, 166, 174–79; Ford to McLeod, June 10, 1953, box 8,

In April McLeod appeared before Styles Bridges's subcommittee to testi-fy about his efforts to identify and remove unfit employees from the State Department. Since taking office McLeod said that he had rejected fifty-four applicants for security reasons, fired nineteen homosexuals, and let four-teen other employees go because of their personal habits, private lives, and for other reasons. McLeod also accepted resignations from four individuals facing such charges.[11] For many employees, especially those with years of service to the State Department, resignation seemed their only choice when confronted with accusations about their sexuality or personal habits that flaunted conventional norms. Former VOA Russia Chief Charles Thayer resigned his consul-general post in Munich on March 26, 1953, because of morals charges stemming from his affair with a Russian woman while he was stationed in Moscow. For several years Thayer had also been dogged by rumors that he was gay. Yet even Thayer's departure from the State Department caused controversy; McCarthy charged that Thayer, who was Charles Bohlen's brother-in-law, had been allowed to resign in order to avoid negative attention.[12]

In addition to hiring McLeod as security officer, the State Department moved Frances Knight from the IIA to the department's Bureau of Security. Knight, who had forwarded McCarthy subcommittee materials to conservative columnist Westbrook Pegler during the hearings, was a longtime friend of Karl Mundt and other prominent conservatives. Mundt often personally asked Knight and McLeod to conduct security investigations and purge State Department employees that he consid-ered subversive. In May 1953 Mundt sent to McLeod a list of writers and film directors being recruited by the State Department for work with the VOA and the IIA's motion pictures unit. Mundt suggested that McLeod keep the lengthy list for reference because "one of the places that the communists get in their most destructive work in the Voice of America set up is through the contractual arrangements they make for selling scripts and film strips to our information service." In July Mundt wrote

folder "Henry, Marcelle," RG 59, Records of the Bureau of Security and Consular Affairs, Name Files, 1953–60; Fern Marja, "Joe McCarthy and the Peephole Probe," *New York Post,* June 11, 1953.

11. "Senators Act to Oust State Undesirables," *Washington Times Herald,* April 21, 1953; "19 Lose US Posts on Morals Charge," *New York Times,* April 21, 1953.

12. Hixson, *Parting the Curtain,* 54; Thomas Corti, "Diplomat in the Caviar: Charles Wheeler Thayer, 1910–1969," 420; "19 Lose US Posts on Morals Charge," *New York Times,* April 21, 1953.

to Knight, "I am hopeful you will both [Knight and McLeod] 'make hay while the sun shines' and weed out as many unfit and undesirables as possible." Such security reviews, whether initiated by State Department security officers or by the requests of conservatives such as Mundt, resulted in the resignations or firings of hundreds of IIA and State Department employees.[13]

In the meantime, Dulles's intention to place the VOA in an independent agency received outside support. In its semiannual report the U.S. Advisory Commission on Information, which the 1948 Smith-Mundt Act had created to advise Congress, proposed that the IIA be removed from the State Department and placed in a new, cabinet-level agency. Previously, the commission had supported keeping the information programs in the State Department. To explain its changed position, the commission pointed to the IIA's inability to receive policy guidance from the State Department.[14] On April 7, 1953, the Rockefeller committee completed its study of the IIA and submitted its recommendations to the president. In order for the secretary of state to concentrate fully on his primary task of helping the president formulate and implement American foreign policy, the committee suggested that "foreign program operations," meaning the VOA and other information programs, be moved to a new executive branch agency. In addition to the State Department's programs, the new agency would also be responsible for the information activities currently carried out by the Mutual Security Agency and the Technical Cooperation Administration. The Rockefeller committee did not propose, however, that all ties with the State Department be broken. The fourth recommendation stated: "Hereafter the term "Voice of America" should be applied only to statements of the official United States' positions, including those on current developments, for use abroad." The State Department was to remain responsible for the drafting and deliverance of these statements. To execute the reorganization, the committee proposed that the president submit a plan for approval by the Congress rather than seek legislation.[15]

---

13. According to Mundt's former administrative assistant, "she [Knight] was one of his closet friends." Robert McCaughey, interview by the author, tape recording, Madison, S.D., June 19, 1995; Mundt to McLeod, May 22, 1953, box 206, folder 6; Mundt to Knight, July 15, 1953, box 206, folder 7, Mundt Papers. For resignations and firings, see Reeves, *Life and Times of Joe McCarthy*, 491; Pirsein, "Voice of America," 294–95.

14. U.S. Advisory Commission on Information, *7th Semi Annual Report*, February 1953, 1.

15. Memorandum for the President by the President's Advisory Committee on Government Organization, April 7, 1953, *FRUS* 1952–1954, vol. 2, pt. 2, 1691–97.

The Rockefeller committee's recommendations were given to Eisenhower without being made public, but two weeks later new IIA administrator Robert Johnson told the Hickenlooper subcommittee about the detachment plans. On February 20 the Senate had voted to continue the subcommittee's work through June, and hearings were held in March and April. Appearing for testimony on April 22, Johnson stated that he and Dulles believed that the IIA should be taken out of the State Department. This revelation prompted Hickenlooper to ask the president to defer a decision until the subcommittee completed its work. On May 8 the subcommittee adopted a resolution that the IIA not be removed from the State Department.[16] Although it had not yet finished its work, the Jackson committee on May 2 also recommended that the IIA remain with the State Department, though the committee did agree with the Rockefeller committee that the functions of the IIA, MSA, and TCA needed to be consolidated. By this time, however, the creation of an independent agency to operate the VOA and other media was practically a done deal. On April 16 Assistant Secretary of State for Public Affairs Howland Sargeant submitted to the Bureau of Budget drafts of a reorganization plan and a presidential transmittal message for Congress. Sargeant pointed out that this reorganization plan did not represent the State Department's official view, but rather had been drafted at the request of the Bureau of the Budget.[17]

Whatever Sargeant's misgivings, it was already clear that the separation of the information programs from the State Department represented Dulles's view, and planning for the detachment went forward. On May 7 Sargeant outlined task forces for the expected reorganization. Estimates were made on the cost and work involved in relocating the VOA studios to Washington.[18] On June 1 the consolidation and detachment of the information programs of the government was made public with Reorganization

16. *Congressional Quarterly*, vol. 9, 228; Hickenlooper to Eisenhower, April 22, 1953, box 86, folder "Overseas Information Subcommittee, 1953, March to April"; Subcommittee Resolution, May 8, 1953, box 86, folder "Overseas Information Subcommittee, 1953, May," Hickenlooper Papers, Foreign Relations Subseries.

17. The President's Committee on International Information Activities to the President, May 2, 1953; Sargeant to Ralph Burton, April 16, 1953, *FRUS* 1952–1954, vol. 2, pt. 2, 1697, 1868–71.

18. Sargeant to Radius, May 7, 1953, box 59, folder "Reorganization Plans," RG 59, Miscellaneous Records of the Bureau of Public Affairs, Subject Files of the Policy Plans and Guidance Staff; Early to Seymour, May 21, 1953, box 5, folder "IBS NY Move Funds and Costs," RG 306, Office of Administration Files, 1952–1955.

Plan No. 8, "Relating to the Establishment of the U.S. Information Agency," which Eisenhower submitted to the House of Representatives. Consistent with the recommendations of the Rockefeller committee, the plan stated that a new organization, the United States Information Agency (USIA), should assume responsibility for the activities of the IIA and the information programs of the MSA, TCA, and American armed forces in West Germany. However, the plan maintained the State Department's control of information policy: "[t]he Secretary of State shall direct the policy and control the content of a program, for use abroad, on official US positions."[19] According to the plan, the USIA's director and deputy director were to be appointed by the president with the Senate's approval.

While the House considered Reorganization Plan No. 8, the Jackson committee submitted its report after six months of work. A total of 250 witnesses had been interviewed; many others had sent written suggestions. More than fifty thousand words in length, the Jackson committee report included chapters on the conflict between the United States and the Soviet Union, the Soviet aim of world domination, and propaganda campaigns in the free world. With regard to the VOA, the committee made recommendations that included changing output to the Soviet Union back to factual, news-based reporting and ending broadcasts to certain free world nations if further study showed that propaganda objectives were not being met. However, the Jackson report shied away from a forceful recommendation concerning the most important problem of all: should the information programs, including the VOA, remain within the State Department? The committee did state that the State Department should maintain operational responsibilities, which reiterated the committee's May 2 memorandum to the president. But then the committee observed, "[i]nasmuch as the [State] Department itself is reluctant at this time to exercise the operating functions involved and a reorganization plan has been sent to Congress, the committee does not make any recommendation on this point."[20] The timing of the final report, June 30, 1953, made all the difference—any proposed action concerning detachment from the State Department was now moot since the president had already submitted the reorganization plan to Congress.

19. "Reorganization Plan No. 8 of 1953," Department of State Bulletin 28 (June 15, 1953): 854.

20. "The Report of the President's Committee on International Information Activities," June 30, 1953, FRUS 1952–1954, vol. 2, pt. 2, 1796, 1826, 1846, 1863.

Although the Jackson committee was not responsible for being pre-empted, the recommendations it did provide were still strikingly repeti-tive or contradictory. For example, in pointing out that the information programs needed the closest possible connection to the units responsible for the articulation of foreign policy, the Jackson committee simply echoed a point that had been made by, among others, proponents of the IIA's cre-ation, the U.S. Advisory Commission on Information, the Hickenlooper subcommittee, and various VOA officials.[21] With reference to personnel difficulties, the committee stated that "the need [is] to produce a clear understanding of the national policies and an individual determination to support them." If solid leadership was provided, this need would be met. As VOA policy writers knew all too well, this was much easier said than done. At times the report contradicted its own observations. Consider the committee's suggestion that in order to improve the effectiveness of VOA broadcasts, "information material should be presented abroad to meet local needs." In the preceding paragraph, however, the report said that guidance on local objectives should be limited to global or regional themes. Muddling the issue even further, the report observed that not all of the free world defined their problems within the context of the Soviet-American conflict.[22] How could these clashing points be synthesized, let alone used to begin rewriting VOA broadcasts?

In one sense, the repetitive import of the Jackson committee's recom-mendations did not negate their relevance. Procurement of timely and pertinent policy, enthusiastic leadership, clear objectives—these needs had long proven elusive to the VOA and its administrators. But the fact that the Jackson committee, for all its effort and elaboration, was joining

21. After the extension of its mandate in February 1953 the Hickenlooper Subcommittee called thirty-five witnesses for testimony on the overseas libraries, the motion pictures unit, student exchange, and reorganization. As these hearings were taking place, subcommittee investigators reviewed security files on Public Affairs offi-cers stationed in Germany and studied the VOA's evaluation unit. In both its hearings and behind-the-scenes work the Hickenlooper Subcommittee uncovered evidence of waste, mismanagement, program ineffectiveness, and employees it considered to be security risks. Despite these problems and his own suspicions about State Department personnel, Hickenlooper did not want the information program pulled out of the State Department. In mid-June the Hickenlooper Subcommittee issued its report, which called for greater autonomy for the IIA. Senate Committee on Foreign Relations, *Report of the Subcommittee on Overseas Information Programs of the United States*, 83d Cong., 1st sess., June 15, 1953, 22–23.

22. "The Report of the President's Committee on International Information Activities." 1841, 1864.

a familiar chorus simply pointed to a greater, persistent problem faced by the VOA. Who controlled the foreign policy of the United States? For the Rockefeller committee, the problem was simple: the secretary of state made foreign policy, in accordance with the president, and it needed to be delivered to the VOA. Yet as demonstrated by the VOA's constant run-ins with conservative members of Congress for the past eight years, this formulation overlooked the existence of dissent and conflict within the government over foreign policy. And what were the ultimate goals of American foreign policy? To contain communism, to liberate communist-controlled nations, to spread democracy—such generalities were of little use to writers and announcers with daily broadcast schedules. Perhaps the greatest oversight of the Jackson committee, as well as the Rockefeller committee and Reorganization Plan No. 8, was the collective failure to recognize the extent to which propaganda activities often served domestic purposes at the same time they tried to meet international purposes. Herein lay an irony. The Rockefeller and Jackson committees had been created in part to serve a domestic political need and a personal aim: to distance the president and the secretary of state from the debacle caused by the McCarthy investigation, and to pave the way for the removal of the VOA and other programs from the State Department.

II. The USIA in Action

After approval of Reorganization Plan No. 8 by the House of Representatives, the United States Information Agency came into official existence on August 1, 1953. The new agency was created to solve a host of problems. In accordance with Secretary of State John Foster Dulles's long-standing wish, the VOA and other information programs were now out of the State Department, although the educational exchange program remained. Consolidation of the information services of the International Information Administration, Mutual Security Agency, Technical Cooperation Administration, and American forces in West Germany addressed the persistent problem of overlap that the Hickenlooper subcommittee had criticized heavily during its investigation. The planned transfer of the VOA studios from New York to Washington aimed at ending the physical distance between the policy-making and the broadcast production centers of the VOA. In the wake of McCarthy's investigation, the USIA offered the VOA and other information programs a fresh start. Finally, the USIA seemed to give the creators and disseminators of American propaganda a much-needed measure of autonomy.

President Eisenhower appointed Theodore Streibert as the USIA's director. With a graduate degree in business and years of experience in the film and radio broadcast industries, including serving as president of radio station WOR in New York City, Streibert was qualified to handle the administrative and operational challenges posed by the consolidation of several different information programs. Streibert's decisive and forceful management style was also an asset, considering the battering the information programs had recently taken. While his aggressive manner sometimes upset subordinates who received upbraidings, Streibert immediately set out to make the USIA an effective and efficient operation. In order to provide clear guidance for all the media, Streibert created the Office of Policy and Programs, which was responsible for defining goals, policies, and content. In an effort to establish clear lines of authority, several assistant directors were appointed to oversee specific global regions and the more than two hundred United States Information Service libraries operating in seventy-six countries.[23]

In carrying out his tasks, Streibert found that he had support at the top. In contrast to his avoidance of the VOA during the McCarthy investigation, Eisenhower stepped in to help the USIA. To boost morale, the president made a personal appearance before the USIA's staff in Washington in November 1953, making a promise of support. During the upcoming years Eisenhower also lobbied on behalf of budget increases for the USIA. After learning that other executive branch agencies were ignoring the USIA, he told his cabinet members to make sure that they worked with the agency. Dulles, however, maintained distance between the State Department and the USIA at the same time he sought to ensure that the USIA's activities did not disrupt or encroach upon the State Department's. In order to keep tabs on USIA public statements, Dulles required Streibert to submit his speeches to the State Department for review prior to delivery. While Dulles did not resist Eisenhower's decision to let Streibert attend National Security Council meetings beginning in 1955, Streibert was present only as an observer. And in 1957 when several senators, including Majority Leader Lyndon B. Johnson (D–Texas), proposed that the USIA be placed back into the State Department, Dulles blocked the move, even though Eisenhower supported it.[24]

Despite the formation of the USIA, the appointment of Streibert as its first director, and the support of the president, the domestic troubles of

23. Thomas C. Sorensen, *The Word War: The Story of American Propaganda*, 47–49.
24. Hixson, *Parting the Curtain*, 124–25; Sorensen, *Word War*, 82.

the VOA and its new parent agency persisted. Reorganization Plan No. 8 left the State Department in charge of defining and giving policy guidance to the USIA. As explained in chapter 6, information policy writers had resisted the push in 1951 for the VOA's placement in an independent agency because they feared procurement of policy would be even more difficult outside of the State Department than within. They were right. In June 1953 a comprehensive study of the VOA's and other information programs' operations was commissioned in order to help the USIA make a smooth start. Leo Bogart, the study's author, found that policy neglect remained a pressing problem. As was the case prior to the USIA's creation, Foreign Service officers and State Department policy makers took a dim view of propaganda activities and worked around the agency.[25] At the same time, the State Department guarded against attempts by the USIA to expand its operations. In 1955 Streibert sketched out an ambitious new program for the USIA that sought to inundate communist nations with publications, exhibits, trade fairs, television programs, radio broadcasts, even visiting sports teams and delegations. To pay for this broad-based effort, a doubling of the USIA's budget was proposed. The State Department criticized Streibert's plan as wasteful and extravagant, also indicating that the plan showed "our own lack of leadership and policy direction over USIA."[26] In other words, the State Department wanted to rein in, rather than help run, the agency.

The VOA's and other information programs' unpredictable and strained relationship with Congress was also little changed by the USIA's creation. An imbroglio involving the USIA's second director, Arthur Larson, is illustrative. Between 1954 and 1957, when he replaced Streibert, Larson served as undersecretary of Labor. A Rhodes scholar and the former dean of the University of Pittsburgh Law School, Larson was also the author of the book *A Republican Looks at His Party*, published in 1956. One of Larson's first tasks as USIA director was to win congressional approval in spring 1957 of a proposed $144 million budget for the upcoming year. Representative John Rooney (D–N.Y.), who chaired the House Appropriations Subcommittee that handled the USIA's budget, reduced the amount to $105 million. Two weeks before the USIA tried to convince the Senate to restore the cut funds, Larson delivered a speech in Hawaii

25. Leo Bogart, *Premises for Propaganda: The United States Information Agency's Operating Assumptions in the Cold War*, 35–38; Sorensen, *Word War*, 56.
26. Hixson, *Parting the Curtain*, 104–5.

before a Republican gathering. Said Larson, "throughout the New and Fair Deals, this country was in the grip of a somewhat alien philosophy, imported from Europe." Unfortunately for Larson, this statement caught the attention of Lyndon Johnson, who chaired the Appropriations Subcommittee deciding whether or not to restore the USIA's budget. At the May hearings Johnson's questioning of the director mixed sarcasm and derision. Were USIA films screened for any "alien philosophy?" Johnson pointedly asked Larson, who did not help himself or the agency by becoming excited and failing to provide specific answers to senators' questions. Not surprisingly, the Senate made further cuts in the USIA's budget, approving just $90.2 million, which represented a total reduction of more than $50 million from the original request. In its report the Senate advised that the USIA focus on improving its personnel—a gibe at Larson—and proposed that the USIA's operations be moved back to the State Department.[27] That the incident resulted from Larson's partisan description of the New and Fair Deals is almost too apt. Between 1945 and 1952 VOA officials had continually defended the agency against Republican charges that VOA programs openly favored liberalism. In 1957 the VOA's parent agency found itself in a reverse situation. Larson made his remark about the New and Fair Deals in a forum unrelated to his tasks as USIA director, yet the repercussions of the critical comment directly affected the agency. The lesson was new for Larson; for the VOA's staff—whether past or present—it was not.

27. Sorensen, *Word War*, 94–97; Hixson, *Parting the Curtain*, 125.

Conclusion

The VOA's troubles between 1945 and 1953 reveal much about the early Cold War, particularly the effects of partisanship on the formulation of a cohesive, broadly accepted government propaganda program. For advocates of such a program, the first challenge was to convincingly establish a pressing need for the U.S. government to permanently maintain global media operations. As World War II drew to a close, the U.S. government was administering numerous agencies that disseminated propaganda abroad, most notably the Office of War Information (OWI) and the Office of Inter-American Affairs (OIAA). Their primary goal was to nurture worldwide support for U.S. war aims. In developing these agencies, the Roosevelt administration used both the World War I–era Committee on Public Information and its own New Deal publicity offices as models, precedents that might suggest that government international information and cultural operations had widespread approval as the United States entered the postwar years. That was not the case, however; opposition to such agencies was fierce, persistent, and most of all partisan. Throughout the war, Republicans and conservative Southern Democrats in Congress had accused the OWI of overtly promoting the New Deal and its liberal tenets. With Allied victory imminent in 1945, these legislators attempted to dismantle the OWI, an effort stymied by President Truman's executive order transferring the functions of the OWI, including the VOA, to the State Department. Underlying Truman's action was the liberal proposition that the federal government could promote peace and correct misunderstandings about the United States by disseminating "full and fair" information to foreign publics. By presenting government media as a facilitator of peaceful international relations, Truman's executive order challenged the argument that propaganda was required only during war. When World War II formally ended in September 1945 the VOA was still on the air.

The VOA's congressional critics were not persuaded. For most, their opposition extended from political differences with the Roosevelt and Truman administrations' *domestic aims*. From the conservative point of view, liberal Democrats had spread, at great financial cost, the powers and responsibilities of the federal government into areas in which it had no prerogative, and the VOA was just another example of this encroachment. Furthermore, the VOA acted only under the authority of an executive order, which rankled members of Congress who already worried that the executive branch was over-stepping its bounds. Enhancing this already strong resistance was the suspicion that the VOA's handlers would use the airwaves to promote a liberal agenda. Indeed, charges that the VOA harbored communists and other subversives masked the broader conservative initiative to discredit liberalism. Finally, conservatives argued that there was no need to tell other nations about America, that private news agencies already serviced much of the world. As a whole, this opposition exemplified a parochial mind-set—the evaluation of an international issue according to domestic political aims and concerns—but this did not necessarily mean its adherents were isolationists. As firm anticommunists these "parochialist" members of Congress were alarmed by the Soviet Union's expansion into Eastern Europe after World War II, and they believed that communists, both abroad and at home, were dedicated to destroying capitalism and democracy. Yet at the same time they continually questioned the Truman administration's ability, even its willingness, to stop the international and domestic spread of communism. It was here, teetering on the paradoxical fault-line between conservatives' ardent anticommunism and their equally strong criticism of the Truman administration, that the VOA and its handlers found themselves in early 1947.

As the Republican-controlled Eightieth Congress opened hearings on the upcoming year's federal budget, the State Department officials responsible for the VOA drafted strategies to win both appropriations and enabling legislation for the VOA. Already two attempts to introduce a bill providing permanent standing for the VOA had failed in Congress, then in April the House Appropriations Committee eliminated all operating funds for the VOA. Rescue for the troubled radio agency came thanks to the Truman Doctrine and the recognition by Assistant Secretary of State for Public Affairs William Benton that the burgeoning containment policy could provide a second chance for the VOA. A former advertising and public relations executive, Benton believed strongly in the power of the media to shape opinion, persuade, and educate listeners, whether they were potential consumers or foreign publics. Using Truman's declaration that the United States needed to support all peoples and nations resisting communism, Benton cast the VOA as a necessary corollary to containment. His presentation was simple but persuasive: if the United States' policies were misunderstood by the people they were supposed to help, they would likely fail, especially if Soviet denunciations about the United States went unanswered. With this argument Benton skillfully put together a potent justification for a permanent government information program. He not only established a pressing need for the VOA but also trapped conservatives with their own anticommunism—how could they loudly demand that the administration do more to halt communism without supporting the VOA? Furthermore, Benton blunted the conservative point that media channels were best left to private enterprise: was not telling the world about the United States' anticommunist policies a task too important to leave in the hands of news services that had other priorities? Finally, by juxtaposing the VOA with Soviet propaganda, Benton opened the door for the United States to practice aggressive propaganda and psychological warfare. Although the United States had engaged in both during World War II, especially through the Office of Strategic Services, many military and diplomatic officials believed such tactics were inappropriate in peacetime. As relations between the United States and the Soviet Union deteriorated during 1947, however, viewpoints quickly changed.

The belief that government-sponsored communication with foreign publics was an essential part of diplomacy, a proposition introduced by Woodrow Wilson during World War I and expanded by Franklin Roosevelt during World War II, was now folded into the postwar offensive against communism. This liberal internationalism, as adapted by Benton and his staff, began breaking down the parochial mind-set that had stirred so much opposition to the VOA. The developing power of the liberal internationalist position was seen in the introduction of the Smith-Mundt bill in May 1947. Karl Mundt, a fervent anticommunist with strong conservative convictions, proposed legislation to provide permanent standing for the VOA and the other media operated by the State Department. Although his political beliefs contrasted sharply with Benton's, Mundt also recognized that U.S. government propaganda would be essential in the struggle against communism. Mundt's realization thus overrode his anti–New Deal leanings and led him to pin his political fortunes to a program that his conservative colleagues were denouncing as New Deal excess. After long and bitter floor debate,

Mundt and supporters in the House won passage of the bill in June 1947. But opposition remained; the bill died in the Senate later that summer. Undeterred, Benton helped Mundt and his Senate cosponsor H. Alexander Smith organize a joint congressional junket that traveled across Europe in the fall of 1947. Alarmed by the negative and sometimes erroneous impressions that Europeans seemed to have of the United States, the Smith-Mundt subcommittee returned convinced that a great need for the VOA existed. The subcommittee had help in arriving at this decision; at each stop, U.S. embassy and information service personnel urged these legislators to push for immediate passage of the Marshall Plan, the proposed economic aid package for Western Europe, and a strengthened information program, which could then carefully explain U.S. intentions in extending a helping hand to Europeans. In January 1948 Truman signed the Smith-Mundt bill into law; two months later Congress passed the Marshall Plan.

The triumph of the liberal internationalists over parochially minded members of Congress was far from complete, though. Mundt and his conservative colleagues had written and amended the VOA's enabling legislation in ways that gave the legislative body a good measure of control over the VOA's operations and its broadcasts. With regard to the former, the Smith-Mundt Act set up an Advisory Commission on Information, and its members were required to deliver quarterly reports to Congress about the VOA and other media (libraries, films, publications, exchange of persons). Another provision gave members of Congress the right to request translations of any script they wanted, an option that conservative legislators would soon frequently exercise. As passed, the Smith-Mundt Act addressed two other prominent conservative concerns, employee screening and cooperation with private enterprise. FBI background checks were ordered for every employee, and the hiring of aliens was prohibited unless no qualified American citizen could be found. These stipulations aimed at more than ensuring security among staffs privy to classified information; they also revealed Mundt's and other conservatives' fear that persons with left-leaning political views might come to dominate the ranks of the VOA and other media. Finally, by requiring the VOA and the other agencies to rely on private news services or organizations to tell the world about America, the Smith-Mundt Act tried to ensure that the federal government would not harm private enterprise. Viewed as a whole, these points of the law also represented an attempt to protect legislative prerogative from executive branch encroachment. Alarmed that Congress's part in the foreign policy–making process was increasingly becoming reactive, conservatives wanted to ensure that they had control over what was, for them, a newly accepted international responsibility for the United States.

By 1948 the VOA was still caught between the expectations and aims of two groups, liberal internationalists in the executive branch and conservatives in Congress. Both camps agreed that the federal government needed to deliver an important message to the peoples of the world. But what, exactly, was that message supposed to be, and who ultimately was responsible for defining it? These two essential problems continually beset the VOA and its personnel in the years to come. During 1948 and 1949 the VOA found itself drawn into rancorous, strange battles over its broadcast content. VOA news about labor groups' support of the Marshall Plan drew the ire of Republicans on the House Committee on Expenditures in the Executive Departments. In 1947 a VOA review of a biography of the Wallace family had incurred conservative criticism because scion Henry Wallace opposed taking a hard line with the Soviet Union, so when Wallace ran for president in 1948 VOA policy makers and writers assiduously avoided further controversy by overlooking or discrediting the campaign in their news. (This editorial choice also reflected Truman and his reelection campaign's own efforts to marginalize Wallace within the United States.) Again and again, VOA administrators heard conservatives express their concern, privately and publicly, that the VOA was promoting liberalism and other left-leaning ideas. Such complaints and concerns seemed overwrought or ill-conceived—if these legislators wanted to discredit liberalism, why not attack it at the source? After all, the VOA did not make policy, it delivered news abroad about that policy. Yet the VOA stood as a prominent, unique symbol. Ostensibly, it spoke for America; it was the official voice. One way to discredit liberalism was to describe, then damn, the VOA for being partisan. The VOA's news may have carried to listeners abroad, but complaints about political slant, whether real or perceived, fell on domestic ears.

The VOA also stood as a marker of receding congressional prerogative in foreign policy, which further explains its domestic troubles. Republican legislators believed that they were increasingly being shut out of the policy-making process, a view enhanced by the often imperious manner and actions of Truman's longest-serving secretary of state, Dean Acheson. Throughout 1949 a gap widened between the State Department and Republicans in Congress over American policy in the Far East.

Monitoring the VOA's "voice" (and those who crafted it) was weak over-sight of a foreign policy that Republican members of Congress saw slip-ping from their hands. Thus members of Congress's China bloc took interest in the VOA's coverage of events in China, and VOA policy writ-ers drafted their news with this attention in mind. In January 1950 news that the VOA had reported that the United States would not defend Taiwan (Formosa) from a communist takeover set off a months-long con-troversy over Far East policy. Acheson had intentionally allowed the VOA to reveal the decision about Taiwan, knowing that domestic opponents of this decision would quickly learn about the VOA's report. In other words, Acheson had used the VOA to "leak" an unpopular decision. Telling the world about the United States and discrediting communism was the VOA's primary task, yet as its administrators discovered in late 1949 and early 1950, the VOA often found itself caught within partisanship.

The Campaign of Truth's development and much publicized unveiling in 1950 showed the VOA again put to domestic uses. The campaign was twofold: construction of new, powerful VOA transmitters and counter-jamming equipment, and the transition to an aggressive, hard-hitting tone in broadcasts. Problems with the Soviet Union were the impetus, but the Truman administration's domestic political difficulties also affected the campaign's planning. During 1949 the Soviet Union had intensified its jamming of the VOA's signal, leading to an initiative with-in the State Department's Office of Public Affairs in early 1950 to devel-op a counter-jamming program. During this same period the president, Acheson, and the Office of Public Affairs considered ways to rebut Senator Joe McCarthy's charges that communists had worked their way into the State Department. Truman and Acheson believed that Senate hearings on McCarthy's charges would expose them as false and histri-onic, but the perception grew that the administration was not doing enough to stop the spread of communism. Ironically, at this time Paul Nitze was finishing the first draft of NSC 68, the top secret blueprint for intensifying the U.S. national security program. In April 1950 the Campaign of Truth offered the president an opportunity to publicly assert the administration's dedication to fighting communism abroad and to rebut Republican criticism. Describing the campaign to an audi-ence of U.S. newspaper editors, the president tapped into the rich symbolism afforded by the VOA. The VOA was the voice of truth and freedom, pitted against communist lies and oppression, and the admin-istration was taking direct action to make sure the VOA continued its difficult but important task. The president then juxtaposed this picture with oblique criticisms of McCarthy and his supporters.

By 1950 the VOA was practically serving dual purposes. Enlisted into the Cold War, its primary task was to promote democracy and capitalism while denouncing communism, but it also often found itself unexpectedly serving the political aims of both Republicans and Democrats. Not surprisingly, the partisanship that flared during the Korean War created new problems for the VOA. In order not to complicate an already tense world situation, policy writers prohibited the VOA from attributing North Korea's attack of South Korea to the Soviet Union, even though high-level administration officials believed this was true. For congressional Republicans, the VOA's delay in blaming the Soviets symbolized the appeasement of the Roosevelt and Truman administrations that they believed had helped lead to the invasion. During the summer of 1950 Republicans' requests for VOA scripts nearly overwhelmed translators, and though he was a busy man, Assistant Secretary of State for Public Affairs Edward Barrett ordered that he see these scripts before their delivery. As with the VOA's coverage of China and Taiwan, the monitoring of VOA news had no direct effect on international and national events. Whatever the VOA said or did not say about the Soviet Union's culpability for the invasion, the U.S.-led UN forces and the South Korean army were steadily losing ground that summer. Indirectly, however, the VOA provided the means to cast doubts over the Truman administration's capabilities and to ask pointed questions about Far East policy. Such was the case in April 1951 when the president relieved General Douglas MacArthur of his command in Korea. Immediately after this highly unpopular decision, congressional Republicans requested VOA scripts about the recall to see if coverage was favorable to Truman. By this time, VOA policy writers had formulated a news writing style that sought to meet both their international obligations and conservatives' expectations. Throughout 1950 and 1951 VOA news repackaged dissent and criticism of the administration, presenting it as a sort of productive, democratic dialogue. As VOA guidance emphasized repeatedly, it was imperative that the United States look united in order to sustain international support for the nation and its goals in Korea. At the same time Republican interest in VOA scripts, as well as news writers' dedication to journalistic standards, meant that domestic partisanship could not be ignored completely. Transformation of dissent and attacks on the administration into a broad consensus fulfilled both these needs.

Despite these problems, the Korean War smoothed the way for the Campaign of Truth. Hearings on the supplemental appropriations for the campaign opened soon after the invasion of Korea, and State Department officials used the war to justify the needed funds. In September 1950 Congress's Appropriations Committees approved nearly $64 million for the Campaign of Truth, and a vigorous program of expansion for the VOA went forward. New languages were added, additional staff was hired, and construction of a ring of powerful transmitters began. Within a year, however, the developing campaign suffered numerous setbacks. In the spring of 1951 the VOA requested another $97.5 million for transmitter construction. Members of the House Appropriations Subcommittee on the State Department questioned whether or not the VOA had efficiently used the funds already granted and approved only $9.5 million. During this same period certain VOA personnel were singled out as communist sympathizers during hearings held by Senator Pat McCarran. This prompted interest in the political backgrounds of VOA employees, as conservatives charged that the VOA only awarded freelance contracts to liberal writers. In an attempt to restore congressional confidence in the VOA and to improve output and effectiveness, the VOA's parent office within the State Department was reorganized in early 1952 as a semi-autonomous entity, the International Information Agency (IIA). The IIA was not able, however, to provide the stability needed by the VOA in its congressional relations and program operations.

Given the VOA's uncertain situation, it is not surprising that McCarthy's 1953 Senate investigation left the VOA battered almost beyond repair. McCarthy sought to refurbish his fame as the nation's top hunter of communists within the federal government. Taking advantage of persistent difficulties with the VOA's transmitter construction projects, he used a variety of novel, eye-catching tactics to characterize certain VOA personnel as communists or communist sympathizers. As his investigation continued, the operations of the VOA and other media were disrupted and top IIA officials resigned, but Republican Secretary of State John Foster Dulles and President Dwight D. Eisenhower did little to stop the damage being done. Although Eisenhower loathed McCarthy, he reasoned that any action he took to stop the investigation would actually help the Wisconsin senator, and so he refrained from intervening. Dulles wanted two things: a good working relationship with congressional Republicans, and the removal of the VOA from the State Department. His studious neglect of the VOA during McCarthy's hearings served both these purposes. Even before McCarthy was finished in April 1953, plans were underway to remove the VOA and other media and place them in an independent executive agency.

Dulles's desire to rid the State Department of operational responsibility for the VOA reinforced the animus of other diplomatic personnel toward it and the other information and cultural programs. Continually buffeted by the winds of partisanship, the VOA found that the State Department provided insufficient shelter. The department had not wanted to take the VOA after World War II, and for the next eight years the men and women responsible for the VOA struggled to integrate the radio agency into the main apparatus of American diplomacy. Securing guidance from policy makers was a constant problem, often forcing VOA policy writers to guess what was official U.S. policy. Such internal troubles contrasted with the public support top State Department officials seemed to give the VOA. More than once, Dean Acheson spoke of the VOA's vital role in carrying out American foreign policy, yet privately he believed the VOA to be nonessential and a nuisance, a view shared by other State Department officials, from Foreign Service officers to undersecretaries. The State Department also shared this ambivalence with other agencies in the national security structure, including the CIA, NSC, Defense Department, Joint Chiefs of Staff, and the Psychological Strategy Board. None of these agencies or its members advocated taking the VOA off the air. As their treatment or neglect of the VOA showed, however, they never fully worked out a comprehensive mission for the VOA, and their respective attitudes toward propaganda often conflicted or changed. In 1947 the NSC chastised the VOA for not doing enough in the important field of propaganda, yet three years later the NSC failed to provided much needed support for the radio agency's efforts to overcome Soviet jamming. Also in 1950, the CIA suggested that Soviet jamming was actually beneficial because it demonstrated to Soviet citizens that their government was trying to hide something from them. In a similar fashion the Joint Chiefs of Staff proposed halting construction on new VOA transmitters because it would push the Soviets to perfect their jamming methods, which then might be used against U.S. military radio transmissions during emergencies.

Underlying all the VOA's troubles was a fixation with appearance and impressions, revealing an awareness that the political weight of the VOA's presentations, and what was said at home about them, could be considerable, depending on the situation. There is an irony here. In its basic form, propaganda seeks to convince an audience of the veracity of its presentation over others offered, hopefully prodding the audience to accept certain beliefs and act accordingly. This the VOA sought to do abroad—persuade listeners that the United States told the truth while the Soviet Union did not, and that the United States was committed to spreading democracy and ensuring freedom across the globe. At the same time, members of Congress, the president, and other government officials frequently refracted the VOA's propagandistic potential toward the home front. In effect, they spun propaganda about the propaganda, whether it was through complaints that the VOA used only liberal writers, through the unveiling of the Campaign of Truth before the American Society of Newspaper Editors, or through the use of the VOA to leak the unpopular decision to not defend Taiwan. Just as propaganda seeks to influence beliefs and guide actions, so too did these criticisms or uses of the VOA seek to influence attitudes and events at home.

APPENDIX:

SELECTED "PAROCHIALLY MINDED" MEMBERS OF CONGRESS

Senate:	Dates of Service:
Joseph Ball (R–Minn.)	1940–1942; 1943–1949
H. Styles Bridges (R–N.H.)	1937–1961
Homer Ferguson (R–Mich.)	1943–1955
Bourke Hickenlooper (R–Iowa)	1945–1969
William Knowland (R–Calif.)	1945–1959
Henry Cabot Lodge, Jr. (R–Mass.)	1937–1944; 1947–1953
George Malone (R–Nev.)	1947–1959
Pat McCarran (D–Nev.)	1933–1954
Joe McCarthy (R–Wisc.)	1947–1957
H. Alexander Smith (R–N.J.)	1944–1959
Robert Taft (R–Ohio)	1939–1953
Kenneth Wherry (R–Nebr.)	1943–1951
Wallace White (R–Maine)	1931–1949
Alexander Wiley (R–Wisc.)	1939–1963

House:	
George Bender (R–Ohio)	1939–1949; 1951–1954
Howard Buffett (R–Nebr.)	1943–1949; 1951–1953
Fred Busbey (R–Ill.)	1943–1945; 1947–1949; 1951–1955
J. Edgar Chenowith (R–Colo.)	1941–1949; 1951–1965
Eugene Cox (D–Ga.)	1925–1952
George Dondero (R–Mich.)	1933–1957
Leon Gavin (R–Pa.)	1943–1963
Clare Hoffman (R–Mich.)	1935–1963
Walt Horan (R–Wash.)	1943–1965

Bartel Jonkman (R–Mich.)	1940–1949
Walter Judd (R–Minn.)	1943–1963
John D. Lodge (R–Conn.)	1947–1951
Noah Mason (R–Ill.)	1937–1963
John Rankin (D–Miss.)	1921–1953
Paul Shafer (R–Mich.)	1937–1954
Lawrence Smith (R–Wisc.)	1941–1958
Karl Stefan (R–Nebr.)	1935–1951
John Taber (R–N.Y.)	1923–1963
John Vorys (R–Ohio)	1939–1959
Richard Wigglesworth (R–Mass.)	1928–1959

House and Senate:

Everett Dirksen (R–Ill.)	House, 1933–1949; Senate, 1951–1969
Karl Mundt (R–S.D.)	House, 1939–1948; Senate, 1948–1973
Richard Nixon (R–Calif.)	House, 1947–1950; Senate, 1950–1953

BIBLIOGRAPHY

MANUSCRIPTS

Archival Collections

NATIONAL ARCHIVES AND RECORDS ADMINISTRATION, WASHINGTON, D.C.

Records of the United States Senate (RG 46)
Carl Marcy Papers
Records of the Senate Foreign Relations Committee
Records of the Senate Internal Security Subcommittee

Records of the United States House of Representatives (RG 233)
Records of the Committee on Expenditures in the Executive
Department

NATIONAL ARCHIVES AND RECORDS ADMINISTRATION, COLLEGE PARK, MD.
(ARCHIVES II)

Records of the Department of State (RG 59)

Central Decimal File
Minutes and Notes of the Secretary's Staff Meetings, 1952–1961
Miscellaneous Records of the Bureau of Public Affairs
Office of the Secretary of State Committee and Subject Files,
1943–1953
Office of the Assistant Secretary of State for Public Affairs, Office
of Public Affairs
Records of the Assistant Secretary of State for Public Affairs,
Office Symbol Files
Records of the Assistant Secretary of State for Public Affairs,
Edward Barrett 1950–1951
Records of the Bureau of Security and Consular Affairs

Records of the Office of the Assistant Secretary of State for Public Affairs, 1949–1953

Records of the Officer of Congressional Relations

Records of the Policy Planning Staff

Records Relating to International Information Activities, 1938–1953

Records of the United States Information Agency (RG 306)

International Information Administration Files, 1952–1953

Office of Administration Files, 1952–1955

Voice of America Daily Broadcast Content Reports and Script Translations, 1950–1955

United States Information Agency Historical Collection, Washington, D.C.

Murray G. Lawson History Card File

Subject File Cabinets

Other Collections

Dean Acheson Papers, Harry S. Truman Presidential Library, Independence, Mo.

William Benton Papers, Regenstein Library, University of Chicago, Chicago, Ill.

Everett McKinley Dirksen Papers, Everett McKinley Dirksen Congressional Center, Pekin, Ill.

George M. Elsey Papers, Harry S. Truman Presidential Library, Independence, Mo.

Bourke B. Hickenlooper Papers, Hoover Presidential Library, West Branch, Iowa

Henry F. Holthusen Papers, Hoover Presidential Library, West Branch, Iowa

Charles M. Hulten Papers, Harry S. Truman Presidential Library, Independence, Mo.

Karl E. Mundt Papers, Karl E. Mundt Archives, Madison, S.D.

J. Anthony Panuch Papers, Harry S. Truman Presidential Library, Independence, Mo.

Westbrook Pegler Papers, Hoover Presidential Library, West Branch, Iowa

Howland H. Sargeant Papers, Harry S. Truman Presidential Library, Independence, Mo.

Karl Stefan Papers, Nebraska State Historical Society, Lincoln, Nebr.
Charles W. Thayer Papers, Harry S. Truman Presidential Library, Independence, Mo.
Harry S. Truman Papers, Harry S. Truman Presidential Library, Independence, Mo.
President's Secretary's Files
Psychological Strategy Board Files
White House Central File
White House Official File
Kenneth S. Wherry Papers, Nebraska State Historical Society, Lincoln, Nebr.

ORAL HISTORIES

Edward W. Barrett. July 9, 1974. Harry S. Truman Presidential Library, Independence, Mo.
Tibor Borgida. August 20, 1987. United States Information Agency Historical Collection, Washington, D.C. USIA Alumni Association Oral History Project.
Mark Etheridge. June 4, 1974. Harry S. Truman Presidential Library, Independence, Mo.
Barry Zorthian. October 20 and 26, 1988. United States Information Agency Historical Collection, Washington, D.C. USIA Alumni Association Oral History Project.

PERSONAL INTERVIEWS WITH AUTHOR (IN AUTHOR'S FILES)

Robert Bauer. October 24, 1995. Washington, D.C.
Wilson Dizard. November 3, 1995. Washington, D.C.
Roger Lyons. October 24, 1995. Silver Spring, Md.
Robert McCaughey. June 19, 1995. Madison, S.D.
Barry Zorthian. November 7, 1995. Arlington, Va.

PUBLISHED COLLECTIONS, HEARINGS, AND SERIES

Bulletin of the American Society of Newspaper Editors
Congressional Quarterly Almanac
Congressional Record
Department of State Bulletin
Department of State. *United States Relations with China, with Special Reference to the Period 1944–1949*. Washington, D.C.: Government Printing Office, 1949.
Foreign Relations of the United States

MacMahon, Arthur. *Memorandum on the Postwar International Information Program of the United States.* Washington, D.C.: Government Printing Office, 1945.

Proceedings of the 23rd Annual Convention of the American Society of Newspaper Editors. Washington, D.C., 1946.

Roosevelt, Franklin D. *The Public Papers and Addresses of Franklin D. Roosevelt.* Vol. 11, *Humanity on the Defensive: 1942.* New York: Russell and Russell.

Sarnoff, David. *Looking Ahead: The Papers of David Sarnoff.* New York: McGraw-Hill, 1968.

Truman, Harry S. *Public Papers of the Presidents of the United States: Harry S. Truman, 1947.* Washington, D.C.: Government Printing Office, 1961–1963.

———. *Public Papers of the Presidents of the United States: Harry S. Truman, 1951.* Washington, D.C.: Government Printing Office, 1965.

U.S. Advisory Commission on Information. *6th Semi Annual Report.* July 1952.

———. *7th Semi Annual Report.* February 1953.

U.S. Congress. House. Subcommittee of the Committee on Appropriations. *Department of State Appropriation Bill, Hearings before the Subcommittee of the Committee on Appropriations.* For the following years:

    1946 (79th Cong., 1st sess., 1945)
    1947 (79th Cong., 2d sess., 1946)
    1948 (80th Cong., 1st sess., 1947)
    1949 (80th Cong., 2d sess., 1948)
    1950 (81st Cong., 1st sess., 1949)
    1952 (82d Cong., 1st sess., 1951)

———. *Hearings on the National War Agencies Appropriations Bill.* For the following years:

    1945 (78th Cong., 2d sess., 1944)
    1946 (79th Cong., 1st sess., 1945)

———. *Hearings on the Supplemental Appropriation Bill for 1951.* 81st Cong., 2d sess., 1950

———. *State, Justice, Commerce, and the Judiciary Appropriation Bill.* For the following years:

    1947 (79th Cong., 2d sess., 1946)
    1948 (80th Cong., 1st sess., 1947)
    1949 (80th Cong., 2d sess., 1948)
    1951 (81st Cong., 2d sess., 1950)
    1952 (82d Cong., 1st sess., 1951)

———. *Third Supplemental Appropriation Bill, 1951.* 82d Cong., 1st sess., 1951.

U.S. Congress. House. Committee on Expenditures in the Executive Departments. *Investigation of the State Department Voice of America Broadcasts.* 80th Cong., 2d sess., June 15, 1948.

U.S. Congress. House. Committee on Foreign Affairs. *Assistance to Greece and Turkey, Hearings before the Committee on Foreign Affairs on H.R. 2616.* 80th Cong., 1st sess., March–April 1947.

———. *Interchange of Knowledge and Skills between the People of the United States and Peoples of Other Countries, Hearing before the House Committee on Foreign Affairs on H.R. 4368 and H.R. 4982.* 79th Cong., 1st and 2d sess., 1945 and 1946.

———. *Hearings on H.R. 3342.* 80th Cong., 1st sess., May 1947.

U.S. Congress. Senate. Subcommittee of the Committee on Appropriations. *Departments of State, Justice, Commerce, and the Judiciary, Hearings before the Subcommittee of the Committee on Appropriations.* For the following years:

    1947 (79th Cong., 2d sess., 1946)
    1948 (80th Cong., 1st sess., 1947)
    1949 (80th Cong., 2d sess., 1948)
    1950 (81st Cong., 1st sess., 1949)
    1951 (81st Cong., 2d sess., 1950)
    1952 (82d Cong., 1st sess., 1951)
    1953 (82d Cong., 2d sess., 1952)

———. *Departments of State, Justice, Commerce, and the Judiciary for 1947, Hearings Part 2, State Department—Informational and Cultural Program, World Wide Broadcasting Foundation,* 79th Cong., 2d sess., June 17, 1946.

———. *Departments of State, Justice, Commerce, and the Judiciary Appropriation Bill.* For the following years:

    1947 (79th Cong., 2d sess., 1946)
    1948 (80th Cong., 1st sess., 1947)
    1952 (82d Cong., 1st sess., 1951)

———. *Hearings on the National War Agencies Appropriations Bill.* For the following years:

    1944 (78th Cong., 1st sess., 1943)
    1945 (78th Cong., 2d sess., 1944)

———. *Hearings on the Second Deficiency Appropriation Bill for 1946.* 79th Cong., 2d sess., April 17, 1946.

U.S. Congress. Senate. Committee on Armed Services and Committee on Foreign Relations. *Military Situation in the Far East, Hearings before the*

Committee on Armed Services and Committee on Foreign Relations. 82d Cong., 1st sess., pt. 1, May 1951.

U.S. Congress. Senate. Committee on Foreign Relations. *Assistance to Greece and Turkey, Hearings before the Committee on Foreign Relations,* 80th Cong., 1st sess., March 1947.

———. *Executive Sessions of the Senate Foreign Relations Committee,* vol. 1. 80th Cong., 1st and 2d sess., 1947–1948. Washington, D.C.: Government Printing Office, 1976.

———. *Hearings on H.R. 3342.* 80th Cong., 1st sess., July 1947.

———. *Hearings on S.R. 243, Expanded International Information Program,* 81st Cong., 2d sess., July 5–7, 1950.

———. *The Legislative Origins of the Truman Doctrine, Hearings Held in Executive Session before the Committee on Foreign Relations.* 80th Cong., 1st sess., 1947. Washington, D.C.: Government Printing Office, 1973.

———. *Overseas Information Programs of the United States Interim Report.* 83d Cong., 1st sess., January 1953.

———. *Report of the Subcommittee on Overseas Information Programs of the United States.* 83d Cong., 1st sess., June 1953.

———. *The United States Information Service in Europe.* 80th Cong., 2d sess., January 30, 1948.

U.S. Congress. Senate. Committee on Government Operations. *Hearings before the Permanent Subcommittee on Investigations of the Committee on Government Operations.* 83d Cong., 1st sess., February–March 1953.

———. *Report of the Committee on Government Operations Made by Its Senate Permanent Subcommittee on Investigations.* 83d Cong., 2d sess., January 1954.

U.S. Public Law 402. 80th Cong., 2d sess., January 27, 1948. *United States Information and Educational Exchange Act of 1948.*

Vandenberg, Arthur, Jr., ed. *The Private Papers of Senator Arthur Vandenberg.* Boston: Houghton Mifflin, 1952.

NEWSPAPERS AND MAGAZINES

Los Angeles Examiner
Pathfinder
Newsweek
New Haven Register (Conn.)
New Republic
New York Herald Tribune
New York Journal-American
New York Post
New York Sun

New York Times
New York World-Telegram
Washington Daily News
Washington Post
Washington Star
Washington Times-Herald
U.S. News and World Report

BOOKS AND ARTICLES

Acheson, Dean. *Present at the Creation: My Years in the State Department.*
   New York: W. W. Norton, 1969.
Adler, Selig. *The Isolationist Impulse: Its Twentieth-Century Reaction.*
   London and New York: Abelard-Schuman, Ltd., 1957. Reprt.,
   Westport, Conn.: Greenwood Press, 1974.
Agar, Herbert. "They Want to Know." *Saturday Review of Literature,*
   February 9, 1946.
Allen, Frederick Lewis. "Must We Tell the World." *Harper's Magazine* 191
   (December 1945): 553–59.
Ambrose, Stephen E. *Eisenhower.* Vol. 2, *The President.* New York: Simon
   and Schuster, 1984.
Ambrosius, Lloyd E. *Wilsonian Statecraft: Theory and Practice of Liberal
   Internationalism during World War I.* Wilmington, Del.: Scholarly
   Resources, 1991.
"America—As Others See Us." Radio broadcast, January 3, 1946.
   Department of State Bulletin 14 (January 6–13, 1946): 11–16.
Ausfeld, Margaret Lynne, and Virginia M. Mecklenburg. *Advancing
   American Art: Policy and Aesthetics in the State Department Exhibition,
   1946–1948.* Montgomery, Ala.: Montgomery Museum of Fine Arts, 1984.
Barnes, William, and John Heath Morgan. *The Foreign Service of the United
   States: Origins, Development, and Functions.* Washington, D.C.: Department
   of State Historical Office, 1961.
Barrett, Edward W. *Truth Is Our Weapon.* New York: Funk and Wagnalls, 1953.
Bayley, Edwin R. *Joe McCarthy and the Press.* Madison: University of Wisconsin
   Press, 1981.
Beisner, Robert L. *From the Old Diplomacy to the New, 1865–1900.* 2d ed.
   Arlington Heights, Ill.: Harlan Davidson, Inc., 1986.
Belmonte, Laura A. "Defining Democracy: Images of Politics in U.S. Propaganda,
   1945–1959." Paper presented at the annual meeting of the Society for
   Historians of American Foreign Relations, Georgetown University,
   Washington, D.C., June 1997.

Benton, William. "A New Instrument of U.S. Foreign Policy." *Department of State Bulletin* 14 (October 1, 1946): 4.

———. "Our International Information Service." *Democratic Digest* 23, no. 11 (November 1946): 8.

———. "Self Portrait—By Uncle Sam." *New York Times Magazine,* December 2, 1945.

———. "The Voice of America." *Department of State Bulletin* 13 (November 4, 1945): 712–14.

Bernhard, Nancy E. "Clearer than Truth: Public Affairs Television and the State Department's Domestic Information Campaigns, 1947–1952." *Diplomatic History* 21, no. 4 (fall 1997): 561 ff.

———. *US Television News and Cold War Propaganda, 1947–1960.* Cambridge: Cambridge University Press, 1999.

Blum, Robert M. *Drawing the Line: The Origin of the American Containment Policy in East Asia.* New York: W. W. Norton, 1982.

Bogart, Leo. *Premises for Propaganda: The United States Information Agency's Operating Assumptions in the Cold War.* New York: Free Press, 1976.

Boylan, James. *The New Deal Coalition and the Election of 1946.* New York: Garland, 1981.

Brewer, Susan A. *To Win the Peace: British Propaganda in the United States during World War II.* Ithaca, N.Y.: Cornell University Press, 1997.

Browne, Donald R. *The Voice of America: Policies and Problems.* Journalism Monographs, no. 43. Lexington, Ky.: Association for Education in Journalism, 1976.

Buitenhuis, Peter. "Prelude to War: The Interventionist Propaganda of Archibald MacLeish, Robert E. Sherwood, and John Steinbeck." *Canadian Review of American Studies* 26, no. 1 (winter 1996): 1–30.

Caridi, Ronald J. *The Korean War and American Politics: The Republican Party as a Case Study.* Philadelphia: University of Pennsylvania Press, 1968.

Caute, David. *The Great Fear: The Anti-Communist Purge under Truman and Eisenhower.* New York: Simon and Schuster, 1978.

Cohen, Warren I. "Acheson, His Advisers, and China, 1949–1950." In *Uncertain Years: Chinese-American Relations, 1947–1950,* edited by Dorothy Borg and Waldo Heinrichs. New York: Columbia University Press, 1980.

———. *Empire without Tears: America's Foreign Relations, 1921–1933.* New York: Knopf, 1987.

Cole, Robert. *Propaganda in Twentieth Century War and Politics: An Annotated Bibliography.* Lanham, Md.: Scarecrow Press, 1996.

Cone, Stacey. "Presuming a Right to Deceive: Radio Free Europe, Radio Liberty, the CIA, and the News Media." *Journalism History* 24, no. 4 (winter 1998–1999): 148–56.

Cooper, John Milton. *The Vanity of Power: American Isolationism and the First World War, 1914–1917.* Westport, Conn.: Greenwood Press, 1969.

Costigliola, Frank. *Awkward Dominion: American Political, Economic, and Cultural Relations with Europe, 1919–1933.* Ithaca, N.Y.: Cornell University Press, 1984.

Cowan Shulman, Holly. *The Voice of America: Propaganda and Democracy, 1941–1945.* Madison: University of Wisconsin Press, 1990.

Creel, George. *How We Advertised America.* New York: Harper and Brothers, 1920. Reprt., New York: Arno Press, 1972.

Critchlow, James. *Radio Hole-in-the-Head/Radio Liberty: An Insider's Story.* Washington, D.C.: American University Press; Lanham, Md.: University Publishing Associates, 1995.

Cull, Nicholas. *Selling War: The British Propaganda Campaign against American "Neutrality" in World War II.* New York: Oxford University Press, 1995.

Cummings, Richard H. "Covert Broadcasting during the Cold War." *The Intelligencer* (December 1999): 15–17.

David, Joan. "Senator William Benton." *American Foreign Service Journal* 28, no. 4 (April 1951): 28–29.

Dizard, Wilson P. *The Strategy of Truth: The Story of the U.S. Information Service.* Washington, D.C.: Public Affairs Press, 1961.

Doenecke, Justus. *Not to the Swift: The Old Isolationists in the Cold War Era.* Lewisburg, Ky.: Bucknell University Press, 1979.

Dulles, John Foster. "A Policy of Boldness." *Life,* May 19, 1952.

Edwards, Jerome E. *Pat McCarran: Political Boss of Nevada.* Reno: University of Nevada Press, 1982.

Eisenhower, Dwight D. *The White House Years: Waging Peace, 1956–1961.* Garden City, N.Y.: Doubleday, 1965.

Ferrell, Robert H. *Harry S. Truman: A Life.* Columbia: University of Missouri Press, 1994.

Freeland, Richard M. *The Truman Doctrine and the Origins of McCarthyism: Foreign Policy, Domestic Politics, and Internal Security, 1946–1948.* New York: Alfred Knopf, 1972.

Gaddis, John Lewis. "Drawing Lines: The Defensive Perimeter Strategy in East Asia, 1947–1951." In *The Long Peace: Inquiries into the History of the Cold War.* New York: Oxford University Press, 1987.

———. *Strategies of Containment: A Critical Appraisal of Postwar American National Security Policy.* New York: Oxford University Press, 1982.

———. *The United States and the Origins of the Cold War, 1941–1947*. New York: Columbia University Press, 1972.

———. "Was the Truman Doctrine a Real Turning Point?" *Foreign Affairs* 52 (1974): 386–402.

Goodman, Walter. *The Committee: The Extraordinary Career of the House Committee on Un-American Activities*. New York: Farrar, Strauss and Giroux, 1968.

Guinsburg, Thomas N. *The Pursuit of Isolationism in the United States Senate from Versailles to Pearl Harbor*. New York: Garland Publishing, 1982.

Harper, Alan D. *The Politics of Loyalty: The White House and the Communist Issue, 1946–1952*. Westport, Conn.: Greenwood Press, 1969.

Hartmann, Susan. *Truman and the 80th Congress*. Columbia: University of Missouri Press, 1971.

Henderson, John W. *The United States Information Agency*. New York: Praeger, 1969.

Hinds, Lynn B., and Theodore O. Windt, Jr. *The Cold War as Rhetoric: The Beginnings, 1945–1950*. New York: Praeger, 1991.

Hixson, Walter L. *Parting the Curtain: Propaganda, Culture, and the Cold War, 1945–1961*. New York: St. Martin's Press, 1997.

Hogan, Michael J. *A Cross of Iron: Harry S. Truman and the Origins of the National Security State, 1945–1954*. Cambridge: Cambridge University Press, 1998.

———. *Informal Entente: The Private Structure of Cooperation in Anglo-American Economic Diplomacy, 1918–1928*. Columbia: University of Missouri Press, 1977.

———. *The Marshall Plan: America, Britain, and the Reconstruction of Western Europe, 1947–1952*. Cambridge: Cambridge University Press, 1987.

Holt, Robert. *Radio Free Europe*. Minneapolis: University of Minnesota Press, 1958.

Horton, Philip. "Voices within the Voice." *The Reporter* 9 (July 1953): 25–29.

Hyman, Sydney. *The Lives of William Benton*. Chicago: University of Chicago Press, 1969.

Inkeles, Alex. "The Soviet Attack on the Voice of America: A Case Study in Propaganda Warfare." *American Slavic and East European Review* 12 (1953): 319–42.

———. "The Soviet Characterization of the Voice of America." *Columbia Journal of International Affairs* 5 (1951): 44–55.

Jonas, Manfred. *Isolationism in America, 1935–1941*. Ithaca, N.Y.: Cornell University Press, 1966.

Jowett, Garth S., and Victoria O'Donnell. *Propaganda and Persuasion*. Newbury Park, Calif.: Sage Publications, 1986.

Kepley, David R. *The Collapse of the Middle Way: Senate Republicans and the Bipartisan Foreign Policy, 1948–1952.* New York: Greenwood Press, 1988.

Klehr, Harvey, John E. Haynes, and Fridrikh Igorevich Firsov. *The Secret World of American Communism.* New Haven, Conn.: Yale University Press, 1995.

Klehr, Harvey, and Ronald Radosh. *The Amerasia Spy Case: Prelude to McCarthyism.* Chapel Hill: University of North Carolina Press, 1996.

Laurie, Clayton D. *The Propaganda Warriors: America's Crusade against Nazi Germany.* Lawrence: University Press of Kansas, 1996.

Lee, Alfred McLung, and Elizabeth Briant Lee. *The Fine Art of Propaganda, Prepared for the Institute of Propaganda Analysis.* 1939. Reprt., New York: Octagon Books, 1972.

Leffler, Melvyn P. "The Interpretive Wars over the Cold War, 1945–60." In *American Foreign Relations Reconsidered, 1890–1993,* edited by Gordon Martel. New York: Routledge, 1994.

———. *Preponderance of Power: National Security, the Truman Administration, and the Cold War.* Stanford, Calif.: Stanford University Press, 1992.

———. *The Specter of Communism: The United States and the Origins of the Cold War, 1917–953.* New York: Hill and Wang, 1994.

———. "Was 1947 a Turning Point in American Foreign Policy?" In *Centerstage: American Diplomacy since World War II,* edited by L. Carl Brown. New York: Holmes and Meier, 1990.

Lucas, Scott. "Campaigns of Truth: The Psychological Strategy Board and American Ideology, 1951–1953." *International History Review* 18 (1996): 288 ff.

———. *Freedom's War: The American Crusade against the Soviet Union.* New York: New York University Press, 1999.

Lyons, Roger. "McCarthy Revisited: 40 Years After." Unpublished manuscript in possession of the author.

Manchester, William. *American Caesar: Douglas MacArthur 1880–1964.* Boston: Little, Brown, 1978.

May, Ernest R., ed. *American Cold War Strategy: Interpreting NSC 68.* Boston: St. Martin's Press, 1993.

———. *The Truman Administration and China, 1945–1949.* Philadelphia: J. B. Lippincott Co., 1975.

McCormick, Thomas J. *America's Half-Century: United States Foreign Policy in the Cold War, 1945–984.* Baltimore, Md.: Johns Hopkins University Press, 1989.

McCullough, David. *Truman.* New York: Simon and Schuster, 1992.

Meyerhoff, Arthur. *Strategies of Persuasion.* New York: Coward McCann, 1965.

Michie, Allan A. *Voices through the Iron Curtain, the Radio Free Europe Story.* New York: Dodd, Mead, 1963.

Mickelson, Sig. *America's Other Voice: The Story of Radio Free Europe and Radio Liberty.* New York: Praeger, 1983.

Mock, James R., and Cedric Larson. *Words That Won the War: The Story of the Committee on Public Information, 1917–1919.* Princeton, N.J.: Princeton University Press, 1939. Reprt., New York: Russell and Russell, 1968.

Moser, John E. *Twisting the Lion's Tail: American Anglophobia between the World Wars.* New York: New York University Press, 1999.

Needell, Allan A. "'Truth Is Our Weapon': Project TROY, Political Warfare, and Government-Academic Relations in the National Security State." *Diplomatic History* 17, no. 3 (summer 1993): 399–420.

Nelson, Garrison, et al. *Committees in the U.S. Congress, 1947–1992.* 2 vols. Washington, D.C.: Congressional Quarterly, Inc., 1994.

Nelson, Michael. *War of the Black Heavens: The Battles of Western Broadcasting in the Cold War.* Syracuse, N.Y.: Syracuse University Press, 1997.

Ninkovich, Frank A. *The Diplomacy of Ideas: U.S. Foreign Policy and Cultural Relations, 1938–1950.* Cambridge: Cambridge University Press, 1981.

O'Reilly, Kenneth. *Hoover and the Un-Americans: The FBI, HUAC, and the Red Menace.* Philadelphia: Temple University Press, 1983.

Oshinsky, David M. *A Conspiracy So Immense: The World of Joe McCarthy.* New York: Free Press, 1983.

Paterson, Thomas G. *On Every Front: The Making of the Cold War.* New York: W. W. Norton and Company, 1979.

Pells, Richard. *Not Like Us: How Europeans Have Loved, Hated, and Transformed American Culture since World War II.* New York: Basic Books, 1997.

Powers, Richard Gid. *Not without Honor: The History of American Anti-Communism.* New York: Free Press, 1995.

Pruessen, Ronald W. "John Foster Dulles and the Predicaments of Power." In *John Foster Dulles and the Diplomacy of the Cold War,* edited by Richard H. Immerman. Princeton, N.J.: Princeton University Press, 1990.

Puddington, Arch. *Broadcasting Freedom: the Cold War Triumph of Radio Free Europe and Radio Liberty.* Lexington: University Press of Kentucky, 2000.

Rawnsley, Gary D., ed. *Cold War Propaganda in the 1950s.* New York: St. Martin's Press, 1999.

———. *Radio Diplomacy and Propaganda: The BBC and VOA in International Politics, 1956–64.* New York: St. Martin's Press, 1996.

Reeves, Thomas C. *The Life and Times of Joe McCarthy: A Biography.* New York: Stein and Day, 1982.

Rosenberg, Emily Smith. *Spreading the American Dream: American Economic and Cultural Expansion, 1890–1945.* New York: Hill and Wang, 1982.

Ross, Stewart Halsey. *Propaganda for War: How the United States Was Conditioned to Fight the Great War of 1914–1918.* Jefferson, N.C.: McFarland, 1996.

Rydell, Robert W. *All the World's a Fair: Visions of Empire at American International Expositions, 1876–1916.* Chicago: University of Chicago Press, 1984.

Savage, Barbara Dianne. *Broadcasting Freedom: Radio, War, and the Politics of Race, 1938–1948.* Chapel Hill: University of North Carolina Press, 1999.

Soley, Lawrence C. *Radio Warfare: OSS and CIA Subversive Propaganda.* New York: Praeger, 1989.

Sorensen, Thomas C. *The Word War: The Story of American Propaganda.* New York: Harper and Row, 1968.

Steele, Richard W. *Propaganda in an Open Society: The Roosevelt Administration and the Media, 1933–1941.* Westport, Conn.: Greenwood Press, 1985.

Stromer, Marvin E. *The Making of a Political Leader: Kenneth S. Wherry and the U.S. Senate.* Lincoln: University of Nebraska Press, 1969.

Stueck, William W. *The Road to Confrontation: American Policy toward China and Korea, 1947–1950.* Chapel Hill: University of North Carolina Press, 1981.

Swing, Raymond. "V.O.A.—A Survey of the Wreckage." *The Reporter* 9 (July 1953): 20–33.

Thayer, Charles W. *Diplomat.* New York: Harper, 1959.

Theoharis, Athan G. *Seeds of Repression: Harry S. Truman and the Origins of McCarthyism.* Chicago: Quadrangle Books, 1971.

———. *The Yalta Myths: An Issue in U.S. Politics, 1945–1955.* Columbia: University of Missouri Press, 1970.

Thompson, Francis H. *The Frustration of Politics: Truman, Congress, and the Loyalty Issue, 1945–1953.* Rutherford, N.J.: Fairleigh Dickinson University Press, 1979.

Thomson, Charles A. H. *Overseas Information Service of the United States Government.* Washington, D.C.: Brookings Institute, 1948.

Truman, Harry S. "Going Forward with a Campaign of Truth." *Department of State Bulletin* 22 (May 1, 1950): 669 ff.

———. "Termination of O.W.I and Disposition of Certain Functions of O.I.A.A." *Department of State Bulletin* 13 (September 2, 1945): 306 ff.

Tucker, Nancy Bernkopf. *Patterns in the Dust: Chinese-American Relations and the Recognition Controversy, 1949–1950.* New York: Columbia University Press, 1983.

Tuveson, Ernest Lee. *Redeemer Nation: The Idea of America's Millennial Role.* Chicago: University of Chicago Press, 1968.

Ulam, Adam. *The Communists: The Story of Power and Lost Illusions, 1948–1991.* New York: Scribner's, 1992.

Urban, George R. *Radio Free Europe and the Pursuit of Democracy: My War within the Cold War.* New Haven, Conn.: Yale University Press, 1997.

Vaughn, Stephen. *Holding Fast the Inner Lines: Democracy, Nationalism, and the Committee on Public Information.* Chapel Hill: University of North Carolina Press, 1980.

Wagnleitner, Reinhold. *Coca-Colonization and the Cold War: The Cultural Mission of the United States in Austria after the Second World War.* Translated by Diana M. Wolf. Chapel Hill: University of North Carolina Press, 1994.

Walton, Richard J. *Henry Wallace, Harry Truman, and the Cold War.* New York: Viking Press, 1976.

Wasburn, Philo C. *Broadcasting Propaganda: International Radio Broadcasting and the Construction of Political Reality.* Westport, Conn.: Praeger, 1992.

Weathersby, Kathryn. "New Findings on the Korean War." *Cold War International History Project Bulletin* 3 (fall 1991): 1 ff.

Westerfield, H. Bradford. *Foreign Policy and Party Politics, Pearl Harbor to Korea.* New Haven, Conn.: Yale University Press, 1955.

White, Llewellyn, and Robert D. Leigh. *Peoples Speaking to Peoples: A Report on International Mass Communication from the Commission on Freedom of the Press.* Chicago: University of Chicago Press, 1946.

Winkler, Allan M. *The Politics of Propaganda: The Office of War Information, 1942–1945.* New Haven, Conn.: Yale University Press, 1978.

Young, Roland A. *Congressional Politics in the Second World War.* New York: Columbia University Press, 1956.

DISSERTATIONS AND THESES

Belmonte, Laura A. "Defending a Way of Life: American Propaganda and the Cold War, 1954–1959." Ph.D. diss., University of Virginia, 1996.

Corti, Thomas. "Diplomat in the Caviar: Charles Wheeler Thayer, 1910–1969." Ph.D. diss., St. Louis University, 1988.

Haap, Arvo Edwin. "The Organization and Operation of the Office of International Information and Cultural Affairs." Master's thesis, University of Minnesota, 1947.

Krugler, David F. "The Voice of America and the Republican Cold War, 1945 to 1953." Ph.D. diss., University of Illinois at Urbana-Champaign, 1997.

Parry-Giles, Shawn J. "Exporting America's Cold War Message: The Debate over America's First Peace-Time Propaganda Program, 1947–1953." Ph.D. diss., Indiana University, 1992.

Pirsein, Robert W. "The Voice of America: An History of the International
    Broadcasting Activities of the United States Government, 1940–1962." Ph.D.
    diss., Northwestern University, 1970. Reprt., New York: Arno Press, 1979.
Wolper, Gregg. "The Origins of Public Diplomacy: Woodrow Wilson, George
    Creel, and the Committee on Public Information." Ph.D. diss., University
    of Chicago, 1991.

Index